# SANCTIFIED

"And these words which I command thee this day, shall be in thy heart: And thou shalt tell them to thy children, and thou shalt meditate upon them, sitting in thy house, and walking on thy journey, sleeping and rising."            —Deuteronomy 6:6-7

*Absolutely Remember This.*

# THE SOUL SANCTIFIED

## CATHOLIC WISDOM ON
## THE WAY OF SALVATION

Meditations and Spiritual Readings For Daily Use,
Selected and Arranged From the Works of Saints
And Approved Writers of the Catholic Church

> *"Blessed is the man who hath not walked in the counsel of the ungodly, nor stood in the way of sinners, nor sat in the chair of pestilence. But his will is in the law of the Lord, and on his law he shall meditate day and night."* —Psalm 1:1-2

TAN BOOKS AND PUBLISHERS, INC.
Rockford, Illinois 61105

Previously published by Burns and Oates, London, in 1873, under the title *The Day Sanctified*.

Library of Congress Catalog Card No: 95-62379

ISBN: 0-89555-538-7

Cover illustration: Painting by Rembrandt van Rijn: "Titus, zoon van Rembrandt," in a monk's habit, by permission of the Rijksmuseum Foundation, Amsterdam. Cover design by Peter Massari, Rockford, Illinois.

Printed and bound in the United States of America.

TAN BOOKS AND PUBLISHERS, INC.
P.O. Box 424
Rockford, Illinois 61105
1996

This edition of *The Soul Sanctified* is fondly dedicated to the Blessed Virgin Mary, under her title of Our Lady of Good Counsel, humbly imploring her to direct most graciously the hearts and minds and thoughts of its readers in the way of salvation.

—The Publishers

# ORIGINAL PREFACE

THE present volume consists of a series of meditations founded on Holy Scripture and selected from the works of Saints and spiritual writers of the Catholic Church: St. Francis de Sales, St. Alphonsus Liguori, Rodriguez, Crasset, etc., etc. The extracts chosen are of such a length as to fit them either for private use or for spiritual reading in families and communities. And as there is no special arrangement for particular days, the subjects may be selected according to each one's devotions or the occasions on which they are used.

The meditations in the present series relate, as will be seen, to the principal doctrines and duties of our Holy Faith. Another series is intended to comprise the ecclesiastical seasons and the feasts of the Blessed Virgin and the Saints.[1]

The meditations may be preceded or followed by an Our Father and Hail Mary. In many cases, too, the full passage of Scripture to which the meditation refers may be read.

---

1. We do not know if this second series of meditations was ever published. —*Publisher,* 1996.

# CONTENTS

# Contents

# THE SOUL
# SANCTIFIED

*"Let not the book of this law depart from thy mouth: but thou shalt meditate on it day and night, that thou mayst observe and do all things that are written in it: then shalt thou direct thy way, and understand it."*
—Josue 1:8

# 1

## THE THOUGHT OF ETERNITY

*"So run that you may obtain."* —1 Corinthians 9:24

WE are not created for this earth: the end for which God has placed us in the world is this, that we should win a happy eternity and escape a miserable one. "The object for which we struggle is eternity." If assured of this end, we are forever blessed; if we fail of it, we are forever miserable.

Happy is he who always lives with eternity in view, with a lively faith that he must speedily die and enter upon eternity. "The just man lives by faith." (*Gal.* 3:11). It is faith that makes the just to live in the sight of God and which gives life to their souls, by withdrawing them from earthly affections and placing before their thoughts the eternal blessings which God promises to them that love Him.

It is the saying of St. Augustine that a man who believes in eternity, and yet is not converted to God, has either lost his senses or his faith. "O eternity," these are his words, "he that meditates upon thee and repents not either has not faith or has no heart!" In reference to this, St. John Chrysostom relates that the Gentiles, when they saw Christians sinning, thought them either liars or fools. They said, "If you believe not what you say you believe, you are liars;

if you believe in eternity and sin, you are fools."
"Woe to sinners who enter upon eternity without
having known it because they would not think upon
it!" exclaims St. Caesarius, and then he adds, "But
oh, double woe! They enter upon it, and they never
come forth."

St. Teresa said constantly to her disciples, "My
children, there is one soul, one eternity," by which
she meant to say, "My children, we have one soul,
and when that is lost, all is lost; and once lost, it is
lost forever."

St. Gregory wrote that they who meditate on eternity are neither puffed up by prosperity nor cast
down by adversity, for they desire nothing and they
fear nothing in this world. When it happens to us
to suffer any infirmities or persecutions, let us think
upon the Hell which we have deserved through our
sins. When we do this, every cross will seem light,
and we shall thank the Lord and say, "It is the mercy
of the Lord that we are not consumed." (*Lam.* 3:22).
We shall say with David, "Unless the Lord had been
my helper, my soul had almost dwelt in hell." (*Ps.*
93:17). Through myself I was already lost; Thou hast
done this, O God of mercy; Thou hast stretched
forth Thy hand and drawn me forth from Hell.
"Thou hast delivered my soul, that it should not perish." (*Is.* 38:17).

O my God, Thou knowest how often I have
deserved Hell; but notwithstanding, Thou biddest
me hope, and I desire to hope. My sins terrify
me, but Thy death giveth me courage and Thy
promise of pardon to him that repenteth. A con-

trite and humbled heart, O God, Thou wilt not despise.

---

## 2

## LIFE IS A PILGRIMAGE

*"I am a stranger upon earth."* —Psalm 118:19

WHILE we live in this life, we are so many pilgrims who wander up and down upon the earth, far from our country, which is Heaven, where the Lord awaits us, that we may rejoice forever in His glorious countenance. "While we are in the body," writes the Apostle, "we are absent from the Lord." If then we love God, we ought to have a continual desire to leave this place of exile by being separated from the body, that we may go and see Him. It was for this that St. Paul ever sighed as he said, "We are willing to be absent from the body, and to be present with the Lord." (*2 Cor.* 5:8.)

Before the common redemption of us miserable sons of Adam, the way of approach to God was closed up, but Jesus Christ, by His death, has obtained for us the grace of having it in our power to become the sons of God and thus has opened to us the gates by which we can have access, as children, to our Father, Almighty God.

On this account, St. Paul says, "Now, therefore, you are no more strangers and foreigners, but fellow-citizens with the saints." (*Eph.* 2:19). Thus, so long as we are in the grace of God, we enjoy the citizenship of Paradise and belong to the family of God. St. Augustine says, "Nature, corrupted with sin, produces citizens of an earthly city; but grace, which frees our nature from sin, makes us citizens of a heavenly country and vessels of mercy."

This fact coerced David to say, "I am a stranger on earth; hide not Thy commandments from me." (*Ps.* 118:119). O Lord, I am a pilgrim upon this earth; teach me to keep Thy precepts, which are the road by which I may reach my country in Heaven. It is not wonderful that the wicked should wish to live forever in this world, for they justly fear that they shall pass from the pains of this life to the eternal and infinitely more terrible pains of Hell. But how can he who loves God and has a moral certainty that he is in the state of grace, desire to go on living in this vale of tears, in continual bitterness, in straits of conscience, in peril of perishing? How can he help sighing to depart at once to unite himself with God in a blessed eternity, where there is no danger of his destroying himself? Souls which love God cry out with David, "Woe is me, for my banishment is prolonged." (*Ps.* 119:5). Therefore it is that the Saints have continually had this prayer upon their lips: "Thy kingdom come; quickly, O Lord, quickly carry us to Thy kingdom!" Let us make speed, then, as the Apostle exhorts us, to enter that kingdom where we shall find perfect peace and contentment: "Let us hasten to enter into that rest." (*Heb.* 4:11). Let us hasten, I say, with desire and not cease to walk onwards till we come to that blessed country which God prepares for them that love Him.

"He that runs," says St. John Chrysostom, "pays not heed to the spectators, but to the crown of victory; he stands not, but hastens on his course." Therefore, the Saint argues, the longer our life has been, the more we should hasten with good works to win the palm. Thus, our one constant prayer for relief from the troubles and trials which we endure in this life ought to be this: "Thy kingdom come," Lord; may Thy kingdom speedily come, where united eternally to Thee and loving Thee face-to-face with all our powers, we shall no longer know fear or danger of falling away. And when we find ourselves afflicted with the labors or dishonors of the world, let us comfort ourselves with the thought of the great reward which God prepares for those who suffer for the love of Him. "Rejoice in that day, and be glad; for behold, your reward is great in heaven." (*Luke* 6:23).

---

## 3

## GOD DESERVES TO BE SUPREMELY LOVED

*"Let us therefore love God because He first hath loved us."* —1 John 4:19

S T. TERESA said that it was a great favor that God should call a soul to love Him. Let us then love Him, since we are called to this love, and let us love Him as He desires to be loved. "Thou shalt love the Lord thy God with all thy heart." The venerable De Ponte felt ashamed at saying to God, "O Lord, I love Thee more than all creatures, than all riches, than all honors, than all earthly pleasures," for it seemed to him that it was equivalent to saying, "My God, I love Thee more than straw and smoke and dust."

But God is satisfied that we should love Him above all things. Therefore, at least let us say, "Yea, O Lord, I love Thee more than all the honors of the world, more than all its riches, more than all my kindred and friends. I love Thee more than health, more than my good name, more than knowledge, more than all my comforts. I love Thee more than everything I possess, more than myself."

And further still, let us say "O Lord, I value Thy graces and Thy gifts, but more than all Thy gifts, I love Thee Thyself, who alone art infinite goodness and a Good worthy of infinite love, which exceeds every other good thing. And, therefore, O my God, whatever Thou mayest give me short of Thyself, which is not Thyself, is not sufficient for me. If Thou givest me Thyself, Thou alone art sufficient for me. Let others seek what they will; I will seek nothing but Thee alone, my Love, my All! In Thee alone I receive all that I can find or desire."

O Jesus, my Saviour, when will it be that, stripped of any other affection, I may ask and seek for none but Thee! I would gladly detach myself from everything, but some importunate affections are ever entering my heart, to draw me away from Thee. Keep me, then, with Thy powerful hand, and make Thyself the one object of all my affections and all my thoughts.

St. Augustine said that he who has God has everything, and he who has not God has nothing. What does it profit a rich man that he possesses many treasures of gold and jewels, if he lives apart from God? What does it profit a monarch to extend his dominions, if he has not the grace of God? What does it profit a man of letters to understand many sciences and languages, if he knows not how to love his God? What does it profit a general to command an army, if he lives the slave of the devil and far from God? While David was yet king, but in the state of sin, he walked in his gardens, he went to his sports and all other pleasures, but these creatures seemed to say, "Where is thy God? Wouldst thou seek in us thy happiness? Go seek God, whom thou hast left, for He alone can give thee rest." And thus David confessed that in the midst of all his delights he found not peace and mourned night and day, considering that he was without God. "Tears were my bread, night and day, while they daily said to me, Where is now thy God?" (*Ps.* 41:4).

In the midst of the miseries and toils of this world, who can console us better than Jesus Christ? He alone says, "Come to me, all ye that labour and are heavy laden, and I will refresh you." (*Matt.* 11:28). Oh, folly of the worldly! One single tear shed for our sins, one cry, "My God!" uttered with love by a soul in the state of grace, is worth more to it than a thousand festivals, a thousand banquets, in giving contentment to a heart that is in love with the world. I say again, "Oh, folly!" And a folly, too, which none can remedy when there comes that death, when it is night, as the Gospel says, "The night cometh, in which no man can work." (*John* 9:4). Wherefore our Lord warns us to walk while we have the light, for the night will come when no man can walk. Let God alone, then, be all our treasure, all our love, and let all our desire be to please God, who will not suffer us to outdo Him in love. He rewards a hundredfold everything that we do to please Him.

———————

## 4

## THE CERTAINTY OF DEATH

*"Set thy house in order for thou shalt die."*
—Isaias 38:1

IT is a most useful thought for our salvation to say often to ourselves, "I must one day die." The Church every year on Ash Wednesday brings this to our remembrance: "O man, remember that thou art dust, and unto dust shalt thou return." And this certainty of death is brought to our recollection many times in the year, sometimes by the burial grounds, which we pass upon the road, sometimes by the graves which we behold in churches, sometimes by the dead who are carried to burial.

"The end is at hand." In this life, one man lives a longer, another a shorter time, but for every one, sooner or later, the end comes. And when that end is here, nothing will comfort us at the point of death but that we have loved Jesus Christ and have endured with patience the labors of this life for the love of Him. Then, neither the riches we have gained, nor the honors we have obtained, nor the pleasures we have enjoyed, will console us. All the greatness of the world cannot comfort a dying man; it rather adds to his pains, and the more he has gained of it, the more does he suffer.

Oh how many worldly persons are there to whom, at the very moment when they are busied in seeking for gain, power and office, the word of death comes: "Set thy house in order, for thou shalt die and not live." Why, O man, hast thou neglected to make thy will till the hour when thou art in sickness? O my God, what pain is suffered by him who is on the point of gaining some lawsuit or of taking possession of some palace or property who hears it said by the priest who has come to pray for his soul, "Depart, O Christian soul, from this world. Depart from this world and render thy account to Jesus Christ." "But now," he cries, "I am not well prepared." What matters that? Thou must now depart!

To every one the end comes, and with the end comes that decisive moment on which depends a happy or a wretched eternity. Oh what a moment, on which eternity depends! Oh that they were wise and would understand and would consider their latter end! Truly they would not then devote themselves to amassing riches, or labor to become great in this perishing world; they would think how to become Saints and to be great in that life which never ends.

If then we have faith, let us believe that there is

a death, a judgment, an eternity, and let us labor for the rest of our lives to live only for God. And therefore, let us take care to live as pilgrims on this earth, remembering that we must speedily leave it. Let us live ever with death before our eyes, and in all the affairs of life, let us take care to act precisely as we should act at the point of death. All things upon earth either leave us or we leave them. Let us hear Our Lord, who says, "Lay up for yourselves treasures in heaven, where neither moth nor rust destroy." (*Matt.* 6:20). Let us despise the treasures of earth, which cannot content us and which speedily end, and let us gain those heavenly treasures which will make us happy and which are everlasting.

---

# 5

## THE MERCY OF GOD

*"Through the tender mercies of our God."*
—Luke 1:78

SO GREAT is the desire which God has to give us His graces, that, as St. Augustine says, He has more desire to give them to us than we have to receive them from Him. And the reason is that goodness, as the philosophers say, is of its own nature *diffusive;* it is compelled by itself to pour itself forth in benefits to others. God, therefore, being infinite goodness, possesses an infinite desire to communicate Himself to us, His creatures, and to make us share His gifts.

Hence flows the boundless pity which the Lord has for our miseries. David said that the earth is full of the Divine mercy. It is not full of the Divine justice, inasmuch as God does not exercise His justice in punishing evil-doers, except when it is necessary and when He is, as it were, compelled to call it into operation. On the other hand, He is bounteous and liberal in showing forth His mercy to all, and at all times; whence Holy Scripture says, "Mercy is exalted over justice." (*James* 2:13). Mercy herself frequently stays the strokes which are prepared for sinners by the hand of justice and obtains their pardon. Therefore the Prophet calls God by the very name of Mercy: "My God, my mercy!" (*Ps.* 58:18). And for the same reason, he says, "For Thy name's sake, O Lord, be merciful to my sin." Lord, pardon me for Thy name's sake, for it is mercy itself.

Isaias said that chastisement is a work which is not dear to the heart of God, but alien and foreign to it, as if he would say that it was far from His inclinations: "The Lord shall be angry, as in the valley which is in Gabaon; that He may do His work, His strange work." (*Is.* 28:21). His mercy it was that brought Him to send His own Son on earth to be made man and to die upon a cross to deliver us from eternal death. Therefore Zacharias exclaimed, "Through the tender mercies of our God, when the Day Star visited us from on high." (*Luke* 1:78).

In order to see how great is the goodness of God towards us and the desire He has to give us His blessings, it is enough to read these few words of the

Gospel, "Seek, and it shall be given you." Who could say more to a friend to show him his affection? Yet this is what God says to every one of us. Seeing our misery, He invites us to come to Him and promises to relieve us: "Come unto me, all ye that labour and are heavy laden, and I will refresh you." (*Matt.* 11:28). On one occasion, the Jews complained of God and said they would no longer go and seek His graces; wherefore He said to the prophet, "Why will not My people come to Me? Am I become a desert, or a land slow of produce, which yields no fruit, or yields it out of season?" At the same time, the Lord was willing to explain the wrong which the Jews did to Him, while He is ever ready to comfort everyone who comes to Him, as He said, "Then shalt thou call, and the Lord shall hear." (*Is.* 58:9).

Art thou a sinner, and wilt thou have pardon? "Doubt not," said St. John Chrysostom, "that God has more desire to pardon thee than thou hast to be pardoned." If then God sees anyone obstinate in his sin, He waits in order to show mercy upon him. And therefore He points out the torment that awaits him, in order that he may learn wisdom. Now He stands and knocks at the door of our hearts, that we may open to Him: "Behold, I stand at the door, and knock." (*Apoc.* 3:20). And again He urges His people, saying, "Why will you die, O house of Israel?" (*Ezech.* 18:31). St. Dionysius writes: "As a lover, God even entreats those who turn from Him and entreats them not to perish." And this very thing was written before by the Apostle, when he entreated sinners, on the part of Jesus Christ, to be reconciled with God; on which St. Chrysostom remarks, "Christ Himself is beseeching you, and what is it that He prays of you, that ye would be reconciled to God?" (*2 Cor.* 5:20).

If then anyone determine to continue to be obstinate, what more can God do? He makes all understand that whosoever He sees come to Him in penitence He will not cast away: "Him that cometh to Me, I will not cast out." (*John* 6:37). He says that He is ready to embrace everyone who turns to Him: "Turn unto Me, and I will turn unto you." He promises to every ungodly man that, if he repents, He will pardon him and forget his sins. He even says, "Come and accept Me, saith the Lord; if your sins be as scarlet, they shall be made as white as snow." (*Is.* 1:18). As though He would say, "Come, penitent, unto Me, and if I embrace you not, rebuke Me as one who had failed in his word."

---

# 6

## CHRIST WAS MADE SIN FOR US

*"The joy being set before Him, He endured the cross."*
—Hebrews 12:2

WHEN the Divine Word offered Himself to redeem mankind, there were before Him two ways of redemption—the one of joy and glory, the other of pains and insults. It was His will, not only by His coming to deliver man from eternal death, but also to call forth the love of all the hearts of men, and therefore He rejected the way of joy and glory and chose that of pains and insults. In order that He might satisfy the Divine justice for us and at the same time inflame us with His holy love, He was willing to endure this burden of all our sins, that, dying upon a cross, He might obtain for us grace and the life of the blessed. This is what Isaias intended to express when he said, "He Himself hath borne our pains and carried our sorrows."

Of this there were two express figures in the Old Testament: the first was the annual ceremony of the scapegoat, which the high priest represented as bearing all the sins of the people; and therefore, all, loading it with curses, drove it into the desert, to be the object of the wrath of God. This goat was a figure of our Redeemer, who was willing to load Himself with all the curses deserved by us for our sins, being made a curse for us in order that He might obtain for us the Divine blessing. Therefore, the Apostle wrote in another place, "He made Him to be sin for us, who knew not sin, that we might be made the justice of God in Him." (*2 Cor.* 5:21). That is, as St. Ambrose and St. Anselm explain it, He made Him to be sin who was Innocence itself—that is, He presented Himself to God as if He had been sin itself. In a word, He took upon Himself the character of a sinner and endured the pains due to us sinners, in order to render us just before God.

The second type of the sacrifice which Jesus Christ offered to the eternal Father for us upon the Cross was that brazen serpent of the Old Law which was fixed to a tree, by looking upon which the Jews who were bitten by fiery serpents were healed. Accordingly, St. John writes: "As Moses lifted up the serpent in the wilderness, so must the Son of man be lifted up, that every one who believeth in Him should not perish, but have eternal life." (*John* 4:14).

We may here notice that in the *Book of Wisdom* the shameful death of Jesus Christ is clearly foretold. Although the words of the passage referred to may apply to the death of every just man, yet, say Tertullian, St. Cyprian, St. Jerome and many other holy Fathers, they principally refer to the death of Christ. It is said: "If He is the true Son of God, He will defend Him, and will deliver Him from the hands of his enemies." (*Wisd.* 2:18). These words exactly correspond with what the Jews said when Jesus was upon the Cross: "He trusted in God; let Him deliver Him, if He will have Him; for He said, I am the Son of God." (*Matt.* 27:43). The Wise Man goes on to say, "Let us try Him with insults and torments," that is, those of the cross, "and let us prove His patience; let us condemn Him to the most shameful death." The Jews chose the death of the cross for Jesus Christ because it is shameful, in order that His name might be forever infamous and no more held in remembrance, according to the other text of Jeremias: "Let us put wood on His bread, and cut Him off from the land of the living, and let His name be remembered no more." (*Jer.* 11:19). How, then, can the Jews of the present day say that it is false that Christ was the promised Messias because His life was ended by a most shameful death, when the prophets themselves foretold that He should die with a most dishonorable death?

And Jesus accepted such a death. He died to pay the price of our sins: And therefore, as in the case of sinners, He desired to be circumcised, to be redeemed with a price when He was presented in the temple, to receive the baptism of repentance from the Baptist and lastly, in His Passion, to be nailed upon the Cross to atone for our guilty wanderings, to atone for our avarice by being stripped of His garments, for our pride by the insults He endured, for our desires of power by submitting Himself to the executioner, for our evil thoughts by His crown of thorns, for our intemperance by the gall He tasted, and by the pangs of His Body for our sensual delights. Therefore, we ought continually, with tears of tenderness, to thank the eternal Father for having given His innocent Son to death, to deliver us from eternal death: "He spared not His own Son, but delivered Him up for us all; and how shall He not also with Him give us all things?" (*Rom.* 8:32). Thus said St. Paul, and thus Jesus Himself said in the Gospel of St. John: "God so loved the world, that He gave His only begotten Son." (*John* 3:16). On this account, Holy Church exclaims on Holy Saturday, "Oh, wonderful is it which Thy love has done for us! O Inestimable Gift of Love, that to redeem a servant, Thou shouldest give Thy Son." O infinite mercy, O infinite love of our God! O Holy Faith! How can he who believes and confesses this live without burning with holy love for God, who is so loving and so worthy of love?

# 7

# THE LOVE OF JESUS IN HIS PASSION

*"Jesus Christ hath been set forth, crucified among you."*
—Galatians 3:1

LET US give thanks to the Father, and let us give equal thanks to the Son, that He has been willing to take upon Himself our flesh and, together with it, our sins, to offer to God by His Passion a worthy satisfaction. It is on this account that the Apostle says that Jesus Christ has become our Mediator, that is, that He has bound Himself to pay our debts: "Jesus is made the mediator of a better testament." (*Heb.* 8:6). As the mediator between God and man, He has established a covenant with God by which He has bound Himself to satisfy the Divine justice for us, and on the other hand, has promised to us eternal life on the part of God. Therefore, in anticipation of this, the preacher warns us not to forget the grace of this Divine Surety, who to obtain salvation for us, has been willing to sacrifice His life. "Forget not the grace of the surety, for He hath given His soul for thee." It is to give us the better assurance of pardon, says St. Paul, that Jesus Christ with His Blood has blotted out the decree of our condemnation, in which the sentence of eternal death stands written against us, and has nailed it to the Cross on which He died to satisfy the Divine justice for us.

In a word, whatever blessing, whatever salvation, whatever hope we have, we have it all in Jesus Christ and in His merits. As St. Peter says, "There is salvation in none other; for there is no other name under heaven given to men whereby we must be saved." (*Acts* 4:12). Thus, there is no hope of salvation for us except through the merits of Jesus Christ, from which St. Thomas and all theologians conclude that, since the promulgation of the Gospel, we are bound to believe explicitly, of necessity, not only by precept, but by the necessity of the truth, that it is only through the means of our Redeemer that we can be saved.

The whole foundation, then, of our salvation consists in the Redemption of man wrought out by the divine Word upon earth. We must, therefore, reflect that, although the actions of Jesus Christ upon earth being the acts of a Divine person were of an infinite merit, so that the least of them was enough to satisfy the Divine justice for all the sins of men, yet nevertheless, the death of Jesus Christ is the great sacrifice by which our Redemption was completed, so that, in the Holy Scriptures, the Redemption of man is attributed chiefly to the death suffered by Him upon the Cross: "He humbled Himself, and was made obedient to death, even the death of the cross." (*Phil.* 2:8). Wherefore, the Apostle writes that, in receiving the Holy Eucharist, we ought to remember the Lord's death: "As often as ye shall eat this bread and drink this chalice, ye shall show the death of the Lord until He come." (*1 Cor.* 11:26). But why does he mention the death of the Lord and not His Incarnation, birth or Resurrection? He speaks of His death because this was the suffering of greatest pain and greatest shame, which Jesus Christ endured and which completed our Redemption.

Hence, St. Paul says, "I determined that I would know nothing but Jesus Christ, and Him crucified." (*1 Cor.* 2:2). The Apostle well knew that Jesus Christ was born in a cave, that for thirty years He inhabited a carpenter's shop, that He had risen from the dead and was ascended into Heaven; why, then, did he say that he would know nothing but Jesus crucified? Because the death suffered by Jesus Christ on the Cross was that which most moved him to love Him and induced him to exercise obedience toward God and love toward his neighbor, which were the virtues most specially inculcated by Jesus Christ from the chair of His Cross. St. Thomas, the Angelic Doctor, writes: "In whatever temptation we fall, in the Cross is our protection; there is obedience to God, love to our neighbor, patience in adversity." Whence St. Augustine says, "The cross was not only the instrument of death to the Sufferer, but His chair of teaching."

O Devout Souls, let us labor to imitate the spouse of the *Canticles*, who said, "I have sat under His shadow whom I desired." (*Cant.* 2:3). Let us place often before our eyes, especially on Fridays, Jesus dying on the Cross, and let us rest there for a while and contemplate with tender affection His sufferings and the love which He bore to us while He continued in agony upon that bed of pain. Let us also say,

"I have sat under His shadow whom I desired." Oh, how sweet is the repose that is found by souls who love God in the midst of the tumult of this world, in the temptations of Hell and even in fear of the Divine Justice, when they contemplate in solitude and silence our loving Redeemer as He hangs in agony upon the Cross. Oh, how the desires of worldly honors, of earthly riches, of sensual pleasures depart from our minds at the sight of Jesus crucified!

Then does there breathe from that Cross a heavenly breeze which sweetly detaches us from earthly things and lights up in us a holy love for Him who has been willing to suffer and die for love of us.

The devil would have us believe that it is impossible that we should be saved, by bringing our sins to our remembrance; but the sight of Jesus crucified assures us, O Lord, that Thou wilt not drive us from Thy face if we repent of having offended Thee and desire to love Thee. Yea, we repent and desire to love Thee with all our heart, and the memory of our sins shall serve to inflame us more and more with this love.

---

# 8

## THE KNOWLEDGE OF THE SAINTS

*"Oh, that they would be wise and understand, and know their latter end."* —Deuteronomy 32:29

THERE are two kinds of knowledge, one heavenly, the other worldly. The heavenly is that which leads us to please God and makes us great in Heaven. The worldly is that which moves us to please ourselves and to become great in the world. But this worldly knowledge is folly in the sight of God. "The wisdom of the world is foolishness with God." (*1 Cor.* 3:19). It is folly, for it makes fools of those who cultivate it; it makes them fools and like the brutes, for it teaches them to gratify their sensual appetites, like the beasts. St. John Chrysostom wrote, "We call him a man who preserves complete the image of a man; and what is the image of a man? To be rational." Hence it is that if a brute were ever to act according to reason, we should say that such a brute acted like a man; so also we say that a man who acts upon sensual appetites and contrary to reason acts like a brute.

Oh, if men would act by reason and the divine law and thus learn to provide, not so much for a temporal existence, which speedily ends, as for eternity, they would assuredly occupy themselves first and foremost in the attainment of that knowledge which will aid them in obtaining eternal happiness and avoiding eternal misery.

St. John Chrysostom advises us to walk among the tombs of the dead in order to learn the knowledge of salvation. Oh, what a school of truth are the sepulchers for learning the vanity of the world! "Let us go to the tombs; there," said the Saint, "there I see nothing but corruption, bones and worms." From all these skeletons which I see, I cannot tell which belonged to the ignorant and which to the learned. I only see that with death all the glories of the world were finished for them. What remained to a Cicero or a Demosthenes? "They have slept their sleep and have found nothing in their hands."

Blessed is he who has received from God the knowledge of the Saints. The knowledge of the Saints is to know the love of God. How many in the world are well versed in literature, in mathematics, in foreign and ancient languages! But what will all this profit them if they know not the love of God? Blessed is he, said St. Augustine, who knows God, even if he knows nothing else. He that knows God and loves Him, though he be ignorant of what others know, is more learned than the learned who know not how to love God.

"Thou hast hidden these things from the wise and prudent, and hast revealed them to babes." By the "wise," we are to understand the "worldly wise," who labor for the possessions and glories of the world and think little of eternal joys. And by "babes" we are to understand simple souls (like those of children) who know little of worldly wisdom, but devote their chief care to pleasing God.

Let us, then, not envy those who know many things; let us only envy those who know how to love Jesus Christ; and let us imitate St. Paul, who said that he desired to know nothing but Jesus Christ, and Him crucified. (*1 Cor.* 2:2). Happy are we if we attain to the knowledge of the love which Jesus crucified had for us and from this book of love attain to the love of Him. O Thou, who art my true and perfect lover, where shall I find one who has so loved me as Thou hast! I perceive that Thou callest me to Thy holy love; behold, from this day forth, my one thought shall be to please Thee, my Highest Good.

---

# 9

## THE JUDGMENT

*"We must all be manifested before the judgment seat of Christ."* —2 Corinthians 5:10

LET US consider the soul's appearance before God—the accusation, the examination, and the sentence. And first, with regard to the appearance of the soul before the Judge: it is a common opinion among theologians that the Particular Judgment takes place at the very moment in which a man expires, and that in the very place where the soul is separated from the body, he is judged by Jesus Christ, who will not send for him, but will Himself come to judge his cause: "At what hour you think not the Son of man will come." (*Luke* 12:40). "For the just, He will come in love," says St. Augustine, "for the wicked, in terror." Oh, what terror will he feel who beholds his Redeemer for the first time and beholds Him in His wrath? "Who shall stand before the face of His indignation?" (*Nahum* 1:6). The sight of the wrath of the Judge will be the forerunner of condemnation: "The wrath of a king is as messengers of death." (*Prov.* 16:14). St. Bernard says that the soul will then suffer more in seeing the indignation

of Jesus than in being in Hell itself: "She would
rather be in Hell." Criminals have been known
sometimes to fall into a cold sweat when brought
into the presence of an earthly judge. What a grief
is it to a child or to a subject to behold a parent or
a prince seriously offended! But oh, how much
greater a pain will it be to that soul to behold Jesus
Christ, whom she despised during life! "They shall
look on Him whom they pierced." (*John* 19:37). That
Lamb who in life had so much patience, the soul
will then behold Him enraged, without any hope of
appeasing Him; she will then call upon the mountains to fall upon her and thus hide her from the
fury of the wrathful Lamb: "Fall upon us, and hide
us from the wrath of the Lamb." (*Apoc.* 6:16). St.
Luke, speaking of the Judgment, says: "Then they
shall see the Son of man." (*Luke* 21:27). Oh, what
torment will it be to the sinner to behold the Judge
in the form of man, because the sight of Him who
as man died for his salvation will upbraid him the
more forcibly with his ingratitude! When the Saviour ascended into Heaven, the Angels said to the
disciples: "This Jesus, who is taken up from you into
heaven, shall so come as you have seen Him going
into heaven." (*Acts* 1:2). The Judge will then come
with the same wounds with which He left the earth:
"Great joy to the beholders, great terror to those who
are in expectation," says the Abbot Rupert. Those
wounds shall console the just and terrify the wicked.
When Joseph said to his brothers, "I am Joseph,
whom you sold," the Scriptures say that through fear
they were silent and unable to speak: "His brethren

could not answer him, being struck with exceeding great fear." (*Gen.* 45:3). How, then, will the sinner answer Jesus Christ? Will he dare ask for mercy, when he must first render an account of his abuse of past mercies? "With what face," says Eusebius Emissenus, "wilt thou ask for mercy, when thou must first be judged for the contempt of mercy?" What, then, will he do, says St. Augustine? Whither will he fly when he beholds his angry Judge above, Hell open below, on one side his sins accusing him, on the other devils prepared to execute the sentence and within him a remorseful conscience?

O God, exclaims St. Thomas of Villanova, with what indifference do we hear the Judgment spoken of, as if the sentence of condemnation could not touch us, or as if we were not to be judged! "Alas, with what security we speak and hear of these things, as if this sentence did not affect us, or as if that day would never arrive!" And what folly, adds the same Saint, to rest secure in so perilous a matter! Say not, my brother, St. Augustine admonishes thee, "Ah, God will not surely send me to Hell! Say it not," exclaims the Saint, "for the Jews also could not persuade themselves that they would be exterminated; just so, many of the damned would not believe that they would be sent to Hell; but still the punishment came at last." "The end is come, the end is come . . . now I will accomplish my anger in thee, and will judge thee." (*Ezech.* 7:6). And thus also, says St. Augustine, shall it happen to thee: "The day of judgment will come, and thou shalt find what God has threatened to be true." Now it rests with us to choose our own sentence. "Now it is in our own power what sentence we will have," says St. Eligius. What, then, must we do? Settle our accounts before the judgment! "Before judgment prepare thee justice." (*Ecclus.* 18:19). St. Bonaventure says that, to avoid failure, prudent merchants constantly look over and settle their accounts. "The judge may be appeased before judgment, but not during judgment," says St. Augustine. Let us, then, with St. Bernard, say to the Lord: "I desire to present myself before Thee already judged and not to be judged." My Judge, I desire to be judged, now that it is the time for mercy and that Thou canst pardon me, for after death it will be the time for justice.

---

# 10

## GRATITUDE TO JESUS CHRIST

*"That they who live may not now live to themselves, but unto Him who died for them, and rose again."*
—2 Corinthians 5:15

ST. AUGUSTINE says that Jesus Christ, having first given His life for us, has bound us to give our life for Him, and further, that when we go to the Eucharistic table to communicate, as we go to feed there upon the Body and Blood of Jesus Christ, we ought also, in gratitude, to prepare for Him the offering of our blood and of our life, if there is need for us to give either of them for His glory. Full of tenderness are the words of St. Francis of Sales on this text of St. Paul: "The charity of Christ presseth us." (*2 Cor.* 5:14). To what does it press us? To love Him. But let us hear what St. Francis says: "When we know that Jesus has loved us even to death, and that the death of the Cross, is not this to feel our hearts constrained by a violence as great as it is full of delight?" And then he adds, "My Jesus gives Himself wholly to me, and I give myself wholly to Him; I will live and die upon His breast, and neither death nor life shall ever separate me from Him."

St. Peter, in order that we might remember to be ever grateful to our Saviour, reminds us that we were not redeemed from the slavery of Hell with gold or silver, but with the Precious Blood of Jesus Christ, which He sacrificed for us as an innocent lamb upon the altar of the Cross. Great, therefore, will be the punishment of those who are thankless for such a blessing if they do not correspond to it. It is true that Jesus came to save all men who were lost, but it is also true what was said by the venerable Simeon when Mary presented the child Jesus in the temple: "Behold, this child is set for the fall and the rising again of many in Israel, and for a sign which shall be contradicted." (*Luke* 2:34). By the words, "for the rising again," he expresses the salvation which all believers should receive from Jesus Christ, who by faith should rise from death to the life of grace. But first, by the words, "he is set for the fall," he foretells that many shall fall into a greater ruin by their ingratitude to the Son of God, who came into the world to become a contradiction to His enemies, as the foregoing words imply, for Jesus Christ was set up as a sign, against which were hurled all the calumnies, the injuries and the insults which the Jews devised against Him. And this sign is contradicted or spoken against not only by the Jews of the present day, who deny him to be the Messias, but by those Christians who ungratefully return His love with offenses and by neglecting His commands.

Our Redeemer, says St. Paul, went so far as to give His life for us in order to make Himself the Lord of all our hearts, by displaying to us His love in dying for us. "For to this end Christ died and rose again, that He might be Lord both of the dead and of the living." (*Rom.* 14:9). No, writes the Apostle, we are no longer our own, since we have been redeemed by the Blood of Jesus Christ. "Whether we live, therefore, or die, we are the Lord's." (*Rom.* 14:8). Wherefore, if we do not love Him and obey His precepts, of which the first is that we should love Him, we are not only ungrateful, but unjust and deserve a double punishment. The obligation of a slave rescued by Jesus Christ from the hands of the devil is to devote himself wholly to love and serve Him, whether he live or die. St. John Chrysostom makes an excellent reflection upon the above-quoted text of St. Paul, saying that God has more care for us than we have for ourselves and therefore regards our life as His own riches and our death as His own loss, so that if we die, we die not to ourselves, but also to God. Oh how great is our glory while we live in this valley of tears, in the midst of so many dangers of perishing, that we should be able to say, "We are the Lord's; we are His possession; He will take care to preserve us in His grace in this life and to keep us with Himself throughout eternity in the life that is to come!"

Jesus Christ, then, died for every one of us, in order that every one of us might live only to his Redeemer, who died for love of him. "Christ died for all, that they who live should live no longer to themselves, but to Him who died for them and rose again." (*2 Cor.* 5:15). He that lives for himself directs all his desires, fears and pains to and places all his happiness in himself. But he that lives to Jesus Christ places all his desires in loving and pleasing Him, all his joys in gratifying Him; all his fears are that he should displease Him. He is only afflicted when he sees Jesus despised, and he only rejoices in seeing Him loved by others. This it is to live to Jesus Christ, and this He justly claims from us all. To gain this allegiance, He has bestowed all the pains which He suffered for love of us.

Does He ask too much in this? No, says St. Gregory, He cannot ask too much, when He has given such tokens of His love to us that He seems to have become a fool for our sakes. Without reserve, He has given Himself wholly for us; He has, therefore, a right to require that we should give ourselves wholly to Him and should fix all our love upon Him. And if we take from Him any portion of it by loving anything either apart from Him or not for His sake, He has reason to complain of us.

## 11

# ALL OUR HOPE IS IN THE MERITS OF JESUS CHRIST

*"Neither is there salvation in any other."*
—Acts 4:12

S T. PETER here says that all our salvation is in Jesus Christ, who by means of the Cross, where He sacrificed His life for us, opened for us a way to hope for every blessing from God. "There is no other name given among men whereby we must be saved." Let us hear what St. John Chrysostom says of the Cross: "The Cross is the hope of Christians, the staff of the lame, the comfort of the poor, the destruction of the proud, the victory over the devils, the guide of youth, the rudder of sailors, the refuge of those who are in danger, the counsellor of the just, the rest of the afflicted, the physician of the sick, the glory of martyrs." The Cross, i.e., Jesus crucified, is the "hope" of the faithful, because if we had not Jesus Christ, we should have no hope of salvation. It is the "staff" of the lame, because we are all lame in our present state of corruption; we should have no strength to walk in the way of salvation, except that which is communicated to us by the grace of Jesus Christ. It is the "comfort" of the poor, which we all are, for all we have we have from Jesus Christ. It is the "destruction" of the proud, for the followers of the Crucified cannot be proud, seeing Him dead as a malefactor upon the Cross. It is the "victory" over the devils, for the very Sign of the Cross is sufficient to drive them from us. It is the "instructor" of the young, for admirable is the teaching which they who are beginning to walk in the ways of God learn from the Cross. It is the "rudder" of mariners and guides us through the storms of this present life. It is the "refuge" of those in danger, for they who are in peril of perishing through temptations or strong passions find a secure harbor by flying to the Cross. It is the "counselor" of the just, for how many Saints learn wisdom from the Cross, i.e., from the troubles of this life. It is the "rest" of the afflicted, for where can they find greater relief than in contemplating the Cross on which God Himself suffers for love of them? It is the "physician" of the sick, for when they embrace it, they are healed of the wounds of the soul. It is the "glory" of martyrs, for to be made like Jesus Christ, the King of martyrs, is the greatest glory they can possess.

In a word, all our hopes are placed in the merits of Jesus Christ. The Apostle says, "I know how to be brought low, and I know how to abound; both to be full, and to be hungry; both to abound, and to suffer need. I can do all things in Him who strengtheneth me." (*Philip.* 4:12). Thus St. Paul, instructed by the Lord, says, I know how I ought to conduct myself; when God humbles me, I resign myself to His will; when He exalts me, to Him I give all the honor; when He gives me abundance, I thank Him; when He makes me endure poverty, still I bless Him; and I do all this, not by my own strength, but by the strength of the grace which God gives me. For he that trusts in Jesus Christ is strengthened with invincible power. The Lord, says St. Bernard, makes those who hope in Him all-powerful. The Saint also adds that a soul which does not presume upon its own strength, but is strengthened by the Word, can govern itself, so that no evil shall have power over it and that no force, no fraud, no snare can cast it down.

The Apostle prayed thrice to God that the impure temptation which troubled him might be driven away, and he was answered, "My grace is sufficient for thee, for My strength is made perfect in infirmity." (*2 Cor.* 12:9). How is this that the virtue of perfection consists in weakness? St. Thomas, with St. Chrysostom, explains it that the greater is our weakness and inclination to evil, the greater is the strength given us by God. Therefore, St. Paul himself says, "Gladly therefore will I glory in my infirmities, that the power of Christ may dwell in me. For which cause I take pleasure in my infirmities, in reproaches, in necessities, in persecutions, in distresses for Christ's sake; for when I am weak, then I am powerful." (*2 Cor.* 12:9).

"For the word of the cross to them that perish is foolishness, but to them that are saved it is the power of God." (*1 Cor.* 1:18). Thus St. Paul warns us not to follow after worldly men, who place their trust in riches, in their relations and friends in the world and who account the Saints fools for despising those earthly helps. Yet men ought to place all their hopes in the love of the Cross, i.e., of Jesus crucified, who gives every blessing to those who trust in Him. We must further remark that the power and strength of the world is altogether different from that of God; it is exercised in worldly riches and honors, but the latter in humility and endurance. Wherefore, St. Augustine says that our strength lies in knowing that we are weak and in humbly confessing that we are. And St. Jerome says that this one thing constitutes the perfection of the present life, that we should know that we are imperfect. For then we distrust our own strength and abandon ourselves to God, who protects and saves those who trust in Him. Holy David says, "The eyes of the Lord are on them that fear Him, on them that hope in His mercy." (*Ps.* 32:18). They that trust in the Lord shall be as Mount Sion; they shall not be moved for ever." (*Ps.* 124:1). Therefore, St. Augustine reminds us that, when we are tempted, we must hasten to abandon ourselves to Jesus Christ, who will not suffer us to fall, but will embrace and hold us up in the midst of our weakness.

---

# 12

## THE MERCY OF GOD

*"Mercy exalteth itself above judgment."* —James 2:13

GOODNESS is by nature diffusive—that is, it is inclined to communicate itself to others. Now God, who by nature is infinite goodness, has a sovereign desire to communicate His happiness to us, and therefore His inclination is not to punish, but to show mercy to all. Punishment, says Isaias, is a work opposed to the inclination of God: "He shall be angry that He may do His work, His strange work: His work is strange to Him." (*Is.* 28:21). And when the Lord chastises in this life, He chastises that He may show mercy in the next: "Thou hast been angry, and hast had mercy on us." (*Ps.* 59:3). He appears angry in order that we may amend and detest sin: "Thou hast shown Thy people hard things, Thou hast made us drink the wine of sorrow." (*Ps.* 59:5). And if He punishes, it is with love, that we may be delivered from eternal punishment: "Thou hast given a warning to them that fear Thee, that they may flee from before the bow, that Thy beloved may be delivered." (*Ps.* 59:6). Who can ever sufficiently admire and praise the mercy of God towards sinners, in waiting for them, in calling them and in receiving them when they return! And in the first place, oh, how great is the patience of God in waiting for our repentance! When you offended God, He might have struck you dead, but He waited for you, and instead of chastising you, He conferred benefits on you. He preserved your life, He provided for you. He feigned not to see your sins, in order that you might return into yourself: "Thou overlookest the sins of men for the sake of repentance." (*Wisd.* 11:24). But how is it, O Lord, that Thou canst not endure a single sin, and yet beholdest so many in silence? Thou beholdest the unchaste, the vindictive, the blasphemer, each day increasing their offenses against Thee, and Thou dost not punish them! And why so much patience? God waits for the sinner, that he may amend and that He may thus pardon and save him! "Therefore the Lord waiteth, that He may have mercy on you." (*Is.* 30:18).

St. Thomas says that all creatures—fire, earth, air, and water—would, through their natural instinct, punish the sinner to avenge the injuries done to their Creator, but God withholds them in His mercy: "All creation, in its service to Thee, the Creator, is enraged against the unjust." But, O Lord, Thou waitest for these impious men, that they may enter into themselves, and seest Thou not that they ungratefully make use of Thy mercy only to offend Thee more? "Thou hast been favorable to the nation, O Lord, Thou hast been favorable to the nation: art Thou glorified?" (*Is.* 26:15). And why so much patience? Because God desires not the death of the sinner, but that he be converted and live: "I desire not the death of the wicked, but that he turn from his way and live." (*Ezek.* 33:11).

The princes of the earth disdain even to look upon those rebel subjects who come to ask their pardon, but God does not act thus in our regard: "He will not turn away His face from you if you return to Him." (*2 Par.* 30:9). God cannot turn His face from those who return to cast themselves at His feet; no, for He Himself invites them and promises to receive them as soon as they come: "Return to Me, and I will receive thee." (*Jer.* 30:1). "Turn to Me, saith the Lord, and I will turn to you." (*Zach.* 1:3). Oh, the love and tenderness with which God embraces the sinner who returns to Him! This is precisely what Jesus Christ would have us understand by the Parable of the Lost Sheep, which, when the shepherd had found it, "he laid it on his shoulders rejoicing" (*Luke* 15:5), and called his friends to rejoice with him: "Rejoice with me, for I have found my sheep that was lost." (*Luke* 15:6). This was more fully explained by the Redeemer in the Parable of the Prodigal Son, saying that He is that Father, who when He beholds His lost son returning, runs to meet him, and before he can speak, embraces and kisses him, and in embracing him almost swoons away through tenderness from the consolation He experiences: "Running to him, he fell upon his neck and kissed him." (*Luke* 15:20).

"Come and accuse Me, saith the Lord: if your sins be as scarlet, they shall be made white as snow." (*Is.* 1:18). It is as if He had said, "Come, sinners, and if I do not pardon you, upbraid Me and treat Me as unfaithful to My promises." But no, God cannot despise a contrite and humble heart: "A contrite and humbled heart Thou wilt not despise." (*Ps.* 50:19).

---

# 13

## THE VALUE OF TIME

*"Son, observe the time."* —Ecclesiasticus 4:23

MY SON, says the Holy Spirit, be careful of time, for it is the greatest and most precious gift that God can bestow upon a living being. Even pagans knew the value of time. Seneca said that "the value of time is above all price." St. Bernardine of

Siena declared that a moment of time is of as much value as God, because in each moment a man may, by an act of contrition or of love, gain Divine grace and eternal glory: "In a little time man can gain grace and glory. Time is worth God Himself, because God is gained in well-spent time." Time is a treasure which is found only in this life; it is not to be found in the next, neither in Hell nor in Heaven. In Hell the lamentation of the damned is, *O, si daretur hora!*—"Oh, that an hour were given us!" They would pay any price for one hour of time to redeem the past, but never will they have this hour. In Heaven there is no weeping, but if the blessed could weep, their tears would only be shed for having in this life lost time, in which they might have acquired greater glory and because they can never again possess this time.

"Why, O miserable man," says St. Bernard, "dost thou presume upon the future, as if the Father had placed the times in thy power?" And St. Augustine says: "Dost thou count on a day, who hast not an hour?" How canst thou promise thyself the day of tomorrow since thou knowest not whether even another hour of life will be thine? St. Teresa then concludes and says: "If thou art not ready to die today, fear to die ill."

There is nothing more precious than time, but there is nothing less valued and more despised by men of the world. Lamenting over this, St. Bernard says: "The days of salvation pass, and no one reflects that for him that day vanishes and returns no more." You will see that gambler, who night and day loses his time in play. If you ask him, "What are you doing?" he replies, "We are passing away time." You will see that other vagabond loitering for whole hours in the middle of a street, looking at the passers-by, or speaking immodestly or on idle things. If you ask him, "What are you doing?" he will reply, "I am passing away time." Poor blind creatures who lose so many days, but days that return no more!

Therefore does the Prophet exhort us to remember God and to obtain His grace before the light fails us: "Remember thy Creator . . . before the sun and the light be darkened." (*Eccles.* 12:2). How great is the distress of a traveler who perceives that he has lost his way when night has already set in and it is too late to repair his mistake! Such, at the hour of death, will be his distress who has lived many years in the world, but has not lived for God: "The night cometh when no man can work." (*John* 9:4). Death will then be for him that night in which he can no longer do anything: "He hath called against me the time." (*Lament.* 1:15). Conscience will then recall to him how much time he has had and that he has spent it to the destruction of his soul; how many calls, how many graces he has received from God for his sanctification, and he has not chosen to profit by them. And then he will find the way of doing any good closed against him, upon which he will weep and say: "O fool that I have been! Oh time forever lost! Oh my lost life! Oh lost years in which I might have become a Saint but have not, and now there is no more time!" But of what avail will tears and lamentations be when the scene closes, the lamp is on the point of being extinguished and the dying man is approaching that awful moment upon which eternity depends?

---

## 14

## THE LOVE WHICH GOD REQUIRES OF US

*"Thou shalt love the Lord thy God with thy whole heart."* —Luke 10:27

THE first thing which God commands us in these words is that we love Him, not in outward appearance and with the lips, but with a true love which springs from the heart. Our Lord, speaking by the Prophets, called strongly to the children of Israel to give Him their hearts, in these and similar expressions: "Son, give Me thy heart" (*Prov.* 23:26); "Put Me as a seal upon thy heart." (*Cant.* 8:6). But when He speaks to us through His only Son, Jesus Christ, He makes use of more definite language and lays down a strict precept of love, saying, "Thou shalt love the Lord thy God with thy whole heart." The reason why God requires from us the sacrifice of our hearts above all things is plain from the following words of the Book of Proverbs: "With all watchfulness keep thy heart, because life issueth out from it." (*Prov.* 4:23). God desires that above all we should give Him our hearts because they are the fountain of life. By the sacrifice of our hearts, we offer to God not only our possessions, but ourselves, our will and our very being. Whoever, therefore, imagines that he loves God, but does not detach his heart from creatures and give himself entirely to Him, is under a great delusion. Of what use are external acts of religion, such as fasts, austerities, practices of devotion, protestations of love, sighs and tears, unless they proceed from a loving heart which lives and breathes for God alone? God has no pleasure in such worshippers who content themselves with mere appearances of piety; He hates and detests them; they are the objects of His wrath. He says of the children of Israel: "This people glorify Me with their lips, but their heart is far from Me." (*Is.* 29:13). Who were more religious in outward appearance than the Pharisees, who by their fasts, prayers and other practices had induced the people to consider them as models of virtue? But they concealed their wicked hearts under this show of sanctity, and therefore did our Saviour cut them to the heart with His tremendous reproofs. In effect He said to them: "Of what use is your exterior purity? You may, indeed, deceive men by it, because they only see what is without, but you cannot hide your true selves from God, whose eye penetrates into the most hidden recesses of the heart. You desire that he who sits at table with you should have clean hands, well-washed clothes and his body be pure and spotless, but what does this signify if his soul be full of deceit, injustice and iniquity? You think that you pay honor to God by this cleansing and believe it sufficient to make you pious and religious. But what a delusion is this! You are blind and ignorant and without any excuse. If God desires to be honored by your exterior worship, does He not desire still more that of your interior, which is the noblest part of man? Who has taught you that God receives offense by soiled hands and dirty plates, and not still more by the impurity and depraved affections of the heart? O blind and malignant Pharisees! Why not begin by purifying the interior? This would diminish your labor, for by cleansing your interior, you would also render your exterior beautiful and pleasing in the sight of God. Woe to you, Pharisees, for your piety consists in things which are of no consequence, and beneath this care about unmeaning devotions, your consciences rest under abominations which you try to hide by this devout exterior. Of what avail are your affected scruples while you trample under foot the most essential laws of justice, mercy, loyalty and, above all, charity to God and your neighbor? These things you should have done first and not have left the others undone."

To love God truly and from the heart, it is necessary that we should act in all things with great purity of intention, desiring only to satisfy and please Him in all that we do. As the eye of the body, by means of light, guides and directs the feet and the other limbs to move and act, so the intention, which is the eye of the soul, guides and governs man in all his movements and actions. This simile is from Christ Jesus Himself, who said to His disciples, "The light of thy body is the eye." (*Matt.* 6:22). If the eye be clean and bright, it will be a clear and shining lamp, safely lighting the other members in their operations; but if it be dimmed and obscured by corrupt humors, it will no longer transmit the light, but will leave the whole body in obscurity. So is it with the lamp of your soul, which is your intention. If that be directed solely to acting for the love of God and for His glory, it will be a clear and brilliant light which will direct your soul in safety in all its operations and will cause them to be pure, simple and full of merit. But if the intention is vitiated and corrupted by the deceits and the pleasures of earth, it will lose the light and will blind your soul, and all its operations will become dark and evil.

This doctrine of Jesus Christ concerning the nature of the intention and of its influence upon all the actions of our life contains a lesson of morality more sublime than can well be conceived. A man may be as exalted as possible in the eyes of the world and his greatness the theme of every tongue, but if the eye of his intention be corrupted, he is vile in the sight of God, and his actions are filthy and worthless. So, on the other hand, he may be most insignificant in the opinion of men, but if the eye of his intention be pure, he is great, and all his actions are most excellent and acceptable before God. Thus, the meanest and most obscure occupation, the daily employments of the poorest and weakest woman, of a simple country girl, of a humble artisan about whom no one concerns himself, are in the balance of God as pure gold—as gems of inestimable value—if their souls really love Him and if they endeavor to please Him alone, seeking nothing but His honor and glory. Whereas, undertakings noble in themselves and brilliant in the eyes of men, such as missions, labors and voyages for the conversion of the world, eloquent sermons, large alms, austere penances, may become not only useless and of no merit, but even sinful, if pride, self-love, the spirit of ambition or of any other passion, should enter and tarnish them.

---

## 15

## THE LOVE OF GOD—
## A NEVER-FAILING GOOD

*"The things which are not seen are eternal."*
—2 Corinthians 4:18

THE heart of man requires the possession of such goods as cannot be taken from him against his will and which shall not become corrupt by length of years, but will accompany him into that eternity to which he is destined. Now, where shall we find goods of this nature? Are they such as those which the world bestows on its followers and which it so highly appreciates? Quite the contrary, for on whatever side we behold them, or under whatever form they meet our eyes, they present nothing but decay.

They are deficient, first, because they may be torn from us at any moment. Oh, how many from the summit of wealth have fallen in an instant into the depths of poverty! How many, who once occupied lucrative posts of honor, have been plunged on a sudden into the lowest state of humiliation! Thus it happened to the proud Aman, who passed from the highest honors and richest banquets to the gallows, and so it is continually happening to thousands of unhappy men, who treading in his footsteps, follow him also in his downfall.

They are deficient, in the second place, because, even if they should not be taken from us, yet they contain within themselves the seeds of corruption by which they tend towards alteration and dissolution.

Where are now the sumptuous palaces, the famous cities and the flourishing kingdoms which of old constituted the glory of the lovers of this world? Nothing remains of them but here and there a heap of ruins and a barren remembrance. As the wood generates its worm and the cloth its moth, so does everything in this world generate its own destruction.

Earthly goods are deficient, in the third place, because, though they should not fall by themselves into dissolution nor be removed from us by the changes of fortune, yet we must leave them when we die, for nothing but our good or our evil works will accompany us to the tribunal of God and into eternity. Who among men can so bind himself to any possessions as that they shall not be torn from his grasp forever? "When a man dies, he shall take nothing away, nor shall his glory descend with him." (*Ps.* 48:17-18). Behold Herod, who, swelling with pride at the sight of his prosperity, which appeared to have reached the highest point, flattered by his ministers and the nobles of his kingdom, humbly entreated by the ambassadors of two powerful cities to grant them peace, drunk to satiety with his glories and his triumphs, began to believe himself something more than man. Behold him fallen in a moment from all this proud elevation into the lowest misery! God, who has sworn to resist the proud, sent His Angel at this hour to strike him, and with a cruel and incurable disorder, attacked him while he was in the act of haranguing the people, who regarded him as a god. Neither pain-killers nor medicines were of any avail, and at length this guilty soul passed to his eternal separation from all the grandeur and delights which he had enjoyed in this world. (*Acts* 12:23). Behold how the glories and the goods of this life depart from the hands of their lovers!

How different is the case as regards Divine love! It is in itself a treasure incorruptible and never deficient, for it includes the possession of God Himself—the eternal, the immutable Good, subject neither to change nor vicissitude. "Thou, O Lord," exclaims the Psalmist, with all his energy, "in the beginning didst found the earth, and the heavens are the work of Thy hands. They shall perish, but Thou remainest; and all of them shall grow old like a garment, and as a vesture Thou shalt change them, and they shall be changed. But Thou art for ever the same, and Thy years shall not fail." (*Ps.* 101:26).

This precious treasure of Divine love, which by itself can never fail, is also such that no created being has power to rob us of it, unless our evil will consents. Yes, in the same manner as we can, by the help of grace, acquire it by simply desiring it, so we can never be deprived of it, except by renouncing it of our own will. For if we do not give it up, who has power to rob us of it? If the whole world were to rise against the just, if it should excite all the powers of Hell to wage war against him with all their fury, what does it matter? Men may persecute him cruelly, tear his flesh, rend his limbs, pierce his body, dislocate his bones, consume his life by slow torments; the devils may be given the power to assail him grievously, to disturb his imagination with every species of temptation, to incite his flesh to evil, to heap upon his head a storm of persecutions and temporal misfortunes, worse even than those of Job. But the world and all Hell united can never tear from his heart the love of his God, unless he gives his consent. Rather, to their infinite confusion, their stratagems will only plant it deeper in his soul, and all their united endeavors will only give the just man further occasion of adding to his treasure by uniting himself still more intimately with his Beloved.

And further, death itself, which is regarded with so much horror by the lovers of earthly things and considered by them as the greatest of evils because it robs them of all they hold most dear—death, the simple thought of which clouds and embitters all their pleasures (*Eccles.* 41:1)—death itself has a very different aspect in the eyes of the lovers of God. To them it is sweet, it is even dear, for instead of separating them from their treasure, it becomes the means of uniting them, perfectly and eternally, with that which in this life they only possessed in part, and never without the danger of losing it. Wherefore, in the *Psalms,* death is denominated a sleep which God sends to His beloved children and which is followed by His blessed inheritance.

---

## 16

## THE BLESSEDNESS OF DIVINE LOVE

*"Blessed are they that dwell in Thy house, O Lord."*
—Psalm 83:5

THERE are some who are so bound up with earthly things that they fancy it would be impossible to renounce them and dedicate themselves to Divine love. "How," they say, "can we break the chains which attach us to the objects of our love? How could we exist without the things which, for so many years, formed the food and the joy of our hearts? How could we make so many sacrifices as are necessary to enable us to enter on the ways of justice and holiness?"

Thus argue men of the world, who know little or nothing of the sweetness and of the power of Divine love. But how entirely would they alter their language if they could prevail on themselves to respond to the calls of Divine grace, which is inviting them and offering to help them to give themselves to God, and how astonished would they be at the happy and profitable exchange they would have made! What man ever had a heart more tied to the love of earthly pleasure than St. Augustine? And what were his sentiments after the blissful moment in which he determined to give his whole heart to God without reserve? Listen to his own words: "For me, I find more pleasure in weeping for my sins at the foot of the crucifix than I ever experienced in attending the theatre, which formerly afforded me such delight. Oh what sweetness diffused itself through my heart in that moment when the love of God triumphed over me! Oh what streams of comfort poured over me as I trod under foot all the fascinations of this earth and consecrated my entire being to Divine love! As I emptied my heart, as it were, on one side of worthless affections, the love of God entered at the other and brought with it a sweetness, compared to which all earthly felicity became as nothing. Yes, my God, I say it, and I will repeat it forever, to the triumph of Thy love: As long as my heart was the slave of passion, it was always agitated like the waves of the sea, swelling during the tempest, but it became calm as soon as it began to taste of Thy holy love." The filthy joys which our passions make us greedy to procure may excite, but they never can satisfy us. Thou alone art the center of our hearts; Thou alone canst fulfill our desires; Thou alone art the summit of joy; Thou alone canst satiate with Thy sweetness; Thou alone canst console and support in sufferings and in labors; Thou alone art, in short, our rest, our happiness, and away from Thee all things are hard and painful." The Saint continues "O ye blind men! What is it you hope to obtain by giving your affections to creatures? Perhaps you expect to gain peace of mind?

Unhappy beings, you are mistaken! Give your heart to God, and He who is a Good containing all other goods, will bestow on it true, solid and real peace."

How many who now lead miserable lives under the tyranny of their passions would become models of virtue and spend their days in happiness if they had but the courage to break the chains which fetter them and devote themselves to the love of God! They would have, it is true, to endure privations, to undergo labor, to make sacrifices. But what then? Is there anything so hard and laborious, says St. Bernard, nay, is there anything, however impossible it may appear to human frailty, which may not become joyful and be rendered sweet and easy by the power of love? What signifies it that you are weak, when the hand which sustains you in all things is so strong? Remember the words of David when he confronted the fierce giant. It was said to him, "Thou art too weak to resist so terrible an enemy." But the valiant youth, trusting to the aid of God rather than in his own strength, did not draw back from the combat, but boldly replied: "The God of armies, in whom I trust, will give me strength to triumph over this haughty foe." Blessed are they, O Lord, who scorning all earthly vanities, desire only to please Thee and to walk in the way of Thy holy love! Let us then arouse ourselves and despise the wretched objects of this world; let us banish from our hearts every worldly affection and consecrate it entirely to God. Let us say, "Take up Thy abode, O Lord, in my heart and leave me not again. It is, I know, unworthy of Thy presence, but Thou canst make it noble and glorious. By the pleasure which Thou hast in conversing with the children of men, by Thy ardent desire to sanctify all and by the glory which will result to Thee, to the Father and to the Holy Spirit by my own sanctification, graciously listen to my prayer and grant it."

---

# 17

## MAXIMS FOR HOLY LIVING

*"The grace of our Lord Jesus Christ be with you."*
—Philippians 4:25

IN ORDER to live in peace and holiness, we have only to settle in our minds certain maxims taught us in Holy Writ.

The first maxim is that of St. Paul: "To them that love God, all things work together unto good." (*Rom.* 8:28). And in truth, since God is able and knows how to draw good out of evil, for whom will He do it, if not for those who have given themselves without reserve to Him? Yes, even the sins from which God by His mercy delivers us are turned by Divine providence to the advantage of those that are His. David would never have had such a depth of humility if he had not sinned, nor Magdalene such a love for her Saviour if He had not forgiven her so many sins; and He could never have forgiven them her if she had not committed them. What then will He not make of our afflictions, our sorrows and the persecutions that are brought upon us? If, therefore, it ever occurs that any sorrow touches us, on whatever side it may be, let us assure our soul that, if it loves God, all will turn out for good. And although we cannot see the means by which this good is to arise, let us remain so much the more assured that it will arise.

The second maxim is that God is our Father, for otherwise He would not have commanded us to say, "Our Father who art in Heaven." And what have we to fear? We are the children of that Father without whose providence not a hair of our head shall perish. (*Luke* 21:18). It is a marvel that, being children of such a Father, we have or can have any care but that of loving and serving Him well. Let us have the care which He wills we should have, and nothing more; for doing so, we shall see that He will have a care for us.

The third maxim is that which Our Lord taught His Apostles. He had sent His Apostles hither and thither, without money, without staff, without shoes, without scrip, clad in a single coat; and He says to them afterwards, "When I sent you without purse and scrip and shoes, did you want anything? But they said, Nothing." (*Luke* 22:35). I say the same to you. When you were under affliction, even at the time when you had not so much confidence in God, did you perish in affliction? You will tell me, "No." And wherefore, then, will you not have courage to succeed in all other adversities? God has not abandoned you so far; how should He abandon you now, when you are willing to be His more than before?

Let us put away all apprehensions for future evils of this world, for perhaps they will never come; but in any case, if they do come, God will strengthen us. He commanded St. Peter to walk on the waves, and St. Peter, beholding the wind and the storm, was fearful, and fear made him sink, and he asked his Master for help. But his Master said to him, "O thou of little faith, why didst thou doubt?" (*Matt.* 14:31). And stretching forth His hand to him, He encouraged him. If God wills us to walk upon the waves of adversity, we need not doubt nor be fearful, for God is with us.

The fourth maxim is to think often of eternity. Of little consequence is it to be under affliction in these passing moments, provided that we are eternally in the glory of our God. We are going into eternity; we have, as it were, one foot already there. Provided it is a happy eternity for us, what does it matter if these short moments are painful? Is it possible for us to know that our tribulations of three or four moments work for us so many eternal consolations and yet that we should not be willing to endure them? In short, what is not for eternity can be nothing but vanity.

The fifth maxim is that of the Apostle: "God forbid that I should glory, save in the Cross of Our Lord Jesus Christ." (*Gal.* 6:14). If we plant Jesus Christ in our heart, all the crosses of this world will only seem to us as roses. Those who are wounded by the thorns of the crown of Our Lord, who is our head, will hardly feel the smart of other thorns.

# 18

## THE DEATH OF THE WICKED

*"The death of the wicked is evil."* —Psalm 33:22

DEATH IS a great evil; sin is greater still; but death and sin united make the greatest of all evils. It is a universal and eternal evil and an evil without remedy. The most terrible threat that God can utter against a man is that he shall die in his sin.

The death of the wicked is, in truth, horrible beyond description! They are seized with mortal terror when, without expecting it, they find themselves on the uttermost verge of that time which they have so badly employed, ready to enter into a frightful abode from whence they will return no more forever—when they begin to see that which they have never seen, when they begin to conceive that which they have never conceived, when they begin to measure an evil which has no measure and begin to feel an evil which they have never felt. They leave a place of temporal pleasures to enter into a place of eternal torture, descend from their earthly paradise to a place of misery, pass from abundance to extreme poverty and fall from a throne of glory into an abyss of shame. Oh, terrible change!

That which constitutes the desire of the good will be the fear of the wicked. The just desire only to see God; the wicked fear nothing so much as to appear before Him. What will be the astonishment and dismay of the sinner when he finds himself before the tribunal of God, whom he has irritated, a Father whom he has outraged, a Friend whom he has betrayed, a King whom he has abandoned, a Judge whom he has offended, a SAVIOUR whom he has mocked, sold and crucified?

Then he will behold himself like a rebellious city, surrounded by devils, who besiege and lay claim to the possession of his soul and body. He will see at his head a Judge who is about to condemn him, at his feet an abyss into which he will fall, behind him the world which has betrayed and abandoned him, before him the goods and treasures that he has loved so much and of which he will soon be stripped, the devils waiting impatiently for their prey, within an enraged conscience and the sight of innumerable sins which he has committed, and around him the flesh that he has loved but which he must now abandon.

What a sweet and consoling spectacle to the dying Christian is the death of Jesus on the Cross! But while it is the hope of Christians, it fills the dying impenitent with despair. They behold all His wounds reopen at their presence and hear a voice of thunder saying to them, "Behold Him whom you have crucified! Behold the Saviour you have renounced! Behold the Wounds I have received for and from you! Behold the side which was opened for you, that you might enter into My heart, but you refused! Depart from Me, ye accursed; ye can never enter here!"

What will be our last end? How shall we die? As we have lived. If we live like the just, our death will be like theirs; if we live like the wicked, our end will be like unto theirs. If we would die in grace, we must

live in grace; if we would die in peace, we must live
in the peace of God.

--------

## 19

### CHRISTIAN PEACE

*"My peace I give unto you."* —John 14:27

PEACE, which St. Paul reckons among the fruits
of the Holy Ghost, is so desirable and precious
a blessing that one of the strongest reasons to make
us despise the esteem of the world and to be humble is that which our Saviour proposes to us. He
teaches us that humility is the only means of acquiring inward peace. But, as everything becomes more
intelligible by comparing it with its contrary, let us
see in the first place with what trouble and restless-
ness the hearts of the proud are tormented, that we
may the better comprehend the peace and tranquillity which the humble enjoy. Holy Scripture is
full of passages which show us that the wicked have
no peace. "There is no peace," saith the Lord, "unto
the wicked." (*Is.* 48:22). "Destruction and unhappiness are in their ways, and the way of peace they
have not known." (*Ps.* 13:3). Their conscience is
always at war with them, and even their very peace,
if they have any, "is full of bitterness." (*Is.* 38:17).
The proud, in particular, are in continual disquiet,
which St. Austin explains when he says that "pride
never goes without envy and that it is by these two

things that the devil is what he is." We may judge, then, what effects they produce in man, since they make the devil to be what he is.

It is impossible for a man who is possessed of pride—and envy, its inseparable companion—and who seeks to be honored by everybody, not to have a heart full of gall and bitterness and to be in continual agitation of mind. For what can more sensibly disturb a proud man than to see himself despised and others preferred to him?

Holy Scripture gives us a remarkable description of the nature and effects of pride in the person of Aman. He was the great favorite of King Assuerus, by whom he was made rich and placed above all the grandees of the kingdom. He was respected by all, and nothing seemed wanting to his wishes. Yet, nevertheless, he was so disquieted because Mardochai, the Jew who usually sat at the king's gate, did not rise up and show him respect when he passed by that he could enjoy no content. For notwithstanding the happy state of his fortune and the favors he received from the king, "Yet all this he reckoned as nothing, so long as he saw Mardochai sitting at the king's gate." (*Esther* 5:13). What trouble and disquiet does not this express? Does it not prove that pride raises many storms in the breast of man and that "the wicked are as the raging sea, which cannot rest?" (*Is.* 57:23). So great was his hatred toward Mardochai that, thinking it too little to be revenged on him, he resolved to extend his vengeance towards all the Jews and obtained an edict from King Assuerus to put them all to death. His fury, in the meantime,

not permitting him to await the day appointed for
its execution, he caused a gallows to be set up to
hang Mardochai upon and went to the king for
orders to that effect. But Divine Providence frus-
trated all his measures, covered him with confusion
and brought upon his own head the vengeance which
he contrived against an innocent man. For the king,
not being able to sleep that night, ordered the book
of records to be brought to him, where all the remarkable things of his reign were written. And as they were
read before him, there was a passage which showed
that Mardochai had discovered a plot which had
been made against his royal person. He then asked
what reward Mardochai had received for so great a
service. It was answered, "None." And then inquir-
ing who waited without, he was told, Aman, upon
which he commanded that he should be called in.
And as soon as he saw him, he asked him, "What
should be done to the man whom the king would
honor?" He, thinking that his majesty would honor
no one but himself, answered that he whom the king
had a mind to honor should be clothed with his royal
robes and seated upon his horse, and have the crown
put upon his head, and that one of the greatest
nobles of the kingdom should hold the horse by the
bridle and go before him, proclaiming through the
streets: "Thus shall he be honored, whom the king
hath a mind to honor." (*Esther* 6:9-10). "Make haste,
then," said the king, "and take the robe and the
horse and do as thou hast spoken to Mardochai the
Jew, who sitteth before the gates of the palace."
What a heartbreak was this to a man puffed up with

pride! What more terrible mortification could be thought of? But he was obliged to obey all to the letter, and to complete his punishment, he himself was hanged a little after on the same gallows he had prepared for Mardochai. This is what a man gets by giving way to the motions of pride and vanity. And then consider the cause which made Aman so furious against poor Mardochai: because he did not bow to him when he passed by! Any little trifle is enough to trouble a proud man's rest and make him pine away with vexation. We have many examples of this in people of the world, especially those who are in high posts; whatever touches their pride pierces them to the quick; the thrust of a sword would be felt less keenly by them. And because there is no favor or preferment which can protect them from the affronts of this kind, they live in continual agitation and bitterness of heart.

------------

## 20

### CONFIDENCE IN GOD

*"I have compassion on the multitude: for, behold,*
*they have now been with Me three days,*
*and have nothing to eat." —Mark 8:1*

LET US admire the devotion and confidence of these people who followed Our Lord three days and nights into the desert without giving themselves any concern about where they were going, what they were to eat or where they would lodge. They abandoned themselves to the guidance of Jesus and would rather have died at His feet than have left Him. They did not complain about the length of the road or murmur like the Jews when Moses led them into the desert. Every consideration was forgotten in the delight they felt at hearing His voice and being in His company. They went after Him, following His footsteps like a flock of sheep with their shepherd. Alas! How few follow Jesus into the desert! How few place their trust in Him and abandon themselves to His providence! On the contrary, how many complain of the past and are troubled for the future! Listen to the words of our Divine Lord: "Whosoever will be My disciple, must take up the cross and follow Me."

Jesus had compassion on the multitude who had been with Him, fasting three days in the desert. "If I send them away fasting to their own homes," saith He, "they will faint in the way, for some of them came from afar off." How full of tenderness, mildness and charity is the Sacred Heart of Jesus! He cannot see the miseries of mankind without being moved with compassion. He sees every day, every hour and moment our sufferings, and when the proper time comes, He assists us. When everything tempts us to despair, it is then we must hope the more, for it is in such straits as these that He works miracles. It was necessary for the multitude to have been three days in the desert, that His providence might be more apparent and His Divine power better known. It was necessary that the Egyptian flour should be entirely consumed before manna descended from heaven. If we do not receive heavenly consolation, it is without doubt because we seek too ardently our solace on earth. If Jesus has not done great things in our behalf, it is because we have not hoped or confided in Him. "I have compassion on the multitude," saith He, "for behold, they have been with Me three days," that is to say, they have attached themselves to Me and depend on My care. Rest then, Christian soul, on the providence of God, and you shall never want.

The man who trusts in God and casts his whole care on Him defends in a manner His Divine Providence and proves beyond dispute that he believes Him to be a good, wise and powerful God who watches over all the spiritual and corporal needs of His creatures. Alas! How many act as if there were no such thing as the Providence of God? Or as if they were afraid to abandon themselves to its guidance? One believes himself ruined unless human wisdom can be brought to aid him; he rests only on its spirit, its prudence, its suggestions and its works, all the time forgetting to cast his cares on God and depend for support on His goodness. He seeks his friends among those who have power, riches and credit, but he comes not to Jesus Christ, who alone knows all the bitterness of our miseries and has the power and will to deliver us from our difficulties. Do we follow Jesus into the desert? Do we abandon ourselves to His providence? Or are we tempted to distrust His wisdom, His power and His goodness?

———————————

# 21

## GENEROSITY IN THE SERVICE OF GOD

*"I can do all things in Him who strengtheneth me."*
—Philippians 4:13

IF humility makes us believe that we can do nothing, from a consideration of what we know of our feebleness and poverty, generosity, on the contrary, makes us say with St. Paul, in the words just quoted, "I can do all things in Him who strengtheneth me." Humility leads us to mistrust ourselves; generosity leads us to trust in God. These two virtues are so linked together that they never are or can be separated.

There are persons who give way to a false humility, which hinders them from regarding the good that God has wrought within them. They are greatly to blame, for the good that God has placed in us ought to be recognized, valued and highly honored.

That humility which does not produce generosity is undoubtedly false, for after humility has said, "I can do nothing, I am nothing," it immediately gives place to generosity, which says, "There is nothing which I cannot do, inasmuch as I put all my confidence in God, who can do everything!" And with this confidence, humility consequently undertakes everything which it is ordered to do, no matter how difficult soever, and if it applies itself to fulfill the commandment in simplicity of heart, God will rather work a miracle than fail of giving it His aid, because it is not from any confidence in its own strength that humility undertakes the work, but from the confidence which it has in God. Humility, then, does not consist only in distrusting ourselves, but in trusting ourselves with God; and distrust of ourselves and of our own strength produces confidence in God, and from this confidence springs generosity.

The Blessed Virgin furnished us with a most remarkable example on this subject when she uttered the words, "Behold the handmaid of the Lord; be it done unto me according to Thy word." In saying that she is the handmaid of the Lord, she makes the greatest possible act of humility. But observe that, directly she has discharged her duty to humility, she forthwith makes a most excellent act of generosity by saying, "Be it done unto me according to Thy word."

It is true she would say that I am in nowise capable of this grace, regard being had to what I am of myself, but so far as that which is good in me is of God, and what you say to me is His most holy will, I think that it can be done, and that it will be done.

Behold the example which we ought to follow when any duty lies before us. We ought to undertake it generously, without reckoning on ourselves, but reckoning much on the grace of God, who wills that we should obey Him implicitly.

Besides what has been said of this generosity, it ought also to be added that the soul which possesses it receives alike drynesses, as well as consolations— interior weariness, sadness, heaviness of spirit, as well as the favors and prosperity of a spirit full of peace and tranquillity—and this because it considers that He who gave it consolations is the same as He who sends it afflictions—and all by an effect of His love, in order thereby to attract it to greater perfection, which is the abnegation of itself, remaining most assured that He who deprives it here below of consolations will by no means deprive it of them eternally in Heaven above.

---

## 22

## DIVINE LOVE, THE SUBSTANCE OF THE NEW COVENANT

*"I will write My law in their hearts."*
—Jeremias 31:33

ALTHOUGH in the Old Testament men were enabled by means of a lively faith to share in the merits of the future Redeemer and to return into the way of Divine love, yet it is no less certain that this only happened by way of preparation for the New Covenant, which was intended by the Divine wisdom and goodness to be, in a special manner, the Covenant of Love. If then the spirit of that Ancient Covenant, which the Almighty made with the children of Israel through His servant Moses, is said in Scripture to be one of bondage and fear, that of the New Covenant, which God made with men by means of the Word Incarnate, is called, by excellence, the Spirit of love, because love is the truly sublime element which molds, vivifies and penetrates it throughout. Hence the great reign and triumph of Divine love on the earth is not to be sought amidst the darkness of the Old Law, but in the refulgent light of the Gospel. As regards those illustrious men who shared in the Divine love before the coming of Christ, it suffices to say that they did not attain to it by virtue of the Covenant under which they lived, but rather by virtue of the merits of Christ, the Author and Vivifier of the New Law, of which Our Lord, speaking by the mouth of the prophet Jeremias, says, "Behold the days shall come . . . and I will make a New Covenant with the house of Israel, and with the house of Juda: Not according to the covenant which I made with their fathers in the day that I took them by the hand to bring them out of the land of Egypt. . . . But this shall be the covenant that I will make with the house of Israel after those days, saith the Lord . . . I will write My law in their heart, and I will be their God, and they shall be My people." (*Jer.* 31:31-33). Here we see the difference between the Old and the New Covenant, that in the latter alone grace is bestowed and that spirit of love exists which begets sons to God and causes the law to be loved and observed. This law, which is written in the mind and in the heart of man, means the Divine love which is poured forth in our hearts by the Holy Ghost, who is given to us according to those words of St. Paul, "The charity of God is poured forth in our hearts by the Holy Ghost, who is given to us." (*Rom.* 5:5). The same Apostle, writing to the Romans, says to them, "Whosoever are led by the

Spirit of God, they are the sons of God. For you have not received the spirit of bondage again in fear, but you have received the spirit of adoption of sons, whereby we cry, Abba (Father)." (*Rom.* 8:15).

If Christians would but reflect as they ought on their happy condition in having been called to the Gospel, in belonging to the Church of Christ and in living in fact under the law of love, which has no other end than to unite them to God, to the source of all goodness, and to make them perfectly and eternally happy in possession of Him; if they thought of these things, who would be so mad as not to submit willingly to so sweet a yoke and trample underfoot all earthly vanities? Who would not consecrate himself entirely to God's love with all the affections of his heart? But, alas! The greater part of men, instead of reflecting on the blessing and privilege which they enjoy in living under the Covenant of Love and in having it in their power to enkindle in their hearts the heavenly fire of Divine charity, consider only the vain and fleeting goods of this world, and fascinated by their false splendor, love them and spare no pains to purchase them. Where there is question of obtaining temporal goods, they despise labor and fatigue and willingly endure any privation and sacrifice, while for spiritual and heavenly things, for the noble and incomparable treasure of Divine love, they have no zeal, no concern and will scarcely endure the least labor or suffer the smallest pain, or make the most insignificant sacrifice to attain it. Oh, ye sons of men, how long will you be so hard of heart? "Why will you love vanity, and seek after lying?" (*Ps.* 4:3). Who has fascinated your heart and blinded your understanding to such a degree as to induce you to renounce the possession of the Infinite Good, in order to purchase a few fleeting and deceptive pleasures? Alas, you might obtain a treasure of infinite value, and instead of seeking for it, you are only anxious for vile earth and worthless clay; you prefer the stagnant marsh to the fountains of living water which flow on unto eternal life! Ah, let us enter into ourselves and search into the inmost recesses of our hearts to discover whether God with His holy love or the world with its vanities reigns therein. Can we say with truth that our greatest study is to unite ourselves more and more closely with God and to desire nothing but to please Him? Have we any reasonable ground for hoping that we belong to the number of those happy souls who esteem nothing, desire nothing, sigh after nothing, but the great, the inestimable treasure of Divine love? If we have hitherto wasted upon the inordinate love of creatures that heart which was created to adore the Creator alone, let us humble ourselves profoundly in His sight, deploring in the bitterness of our souls and with the deepest compunction our folly and our blindness, and let us promise that we will henceforward endeavor to love Him alone who is the Infinite Good, worthy of infinite love.

St. Augustine, in order to excite his soul to center all its love in God, thus addresses it: "What thing is there in this world which can please thee and deserve thy love? Whichever way thou turnest, thou seest nothing but heaven and earth; if in all places and in all things we behold objects of praise and love, what praise and love does not He deserve from thee who created those very things which thou dost praise and love? Oh, my soul, thou hast hitherto been occupied and driven to and fro by a thousand different desires which have occupied thy heart and divided it among many objects of love, leaving thee always disturbed and dissatisfied. Enter now into thyself and ask thyself who is the author of those things which attract thy admiration and love, who but the Lord and Creator of all? If, therefore, thou dost admire the edifice, admire yet more the Architect, and be not so much absorbed in His works as to forget the hand which formed them."

---

## 23

## THE SHORTNESS OF LIFE

*"What is your life? It is a vapour, which appeareth for a little while."* —James 4:15

WHAT is your life? It is like a vapor, which is dispersed by a breath of wind and is no more. All know that they must die, but many are deceived by picturing to themselves death at such a distance as if it could never come near them. Job, however, bids us remember that the life of man is short: "Man's life is short: he cometh forth as a flower, and is destroyed." (*Job* 14:1-2). The Lord commanded Isaias to preach this very truth: "Cry," He said to him, "all flesh is grass . . . indeed the people is grass. The grass is withered, and the flower is fallen." (*Is.* 40:6-7). The life of man is like the life of a blade of grass. Death comes, the grass withers and behold life ends, and the flower falls of all greatness and all worldly goods.

"My days have been swifter than a post." (*Job* 9:25). Death comes to meet us more swiftly than a post[courier or runner], and we advance every moment towards death. In every step, in every breath we draw, we approach nearer to death. Even while I write, says St. Jerome, I approach nearer to death: "What I write is so much taken from my life." "We all die, and like the waters that return no more, we fall down into the earth." (*2 Kings* 14:14). Behold how the stream flows to the sea, and the flowing waters will return no more; thus, my brother, do your days pass away, and you approach to death; pleasures pass, amusements pass, pomp, praises, acclamations pass, and what remains? "The grave alone remains for me." (*Job* 17:1).

King Ezechias said, with tears, "My life is cut off as by a weaver; while I was yet beginning, He cut me off." (*Is.* 38:12). Oh how many, while they are busy weaving—that is, preparing and executing the worldly projects which they have devised with such care—are surprised by death, which cuts short all! All the things of this world vanish; applause, amusements, pomps and grandeurs.

Great secret of death, which makes us see that which the lovers of this world do not see! The most enviable fortunes, the most exalted dignities, the proudest triumphs, lose all their splendor when they are viewed from the bed of death. The ideas of certain false happiness which we have formed to ourselves are then changed into indignation against our own madness. The dark and gloomy shades of death cover and obscure all dignities, even royal ones. At present our passions make the things of this earth appear different from what they really are; death tears away the veil and shows them in their true light.

Let us, then, be persuaded that the proper time to prepare for the hour of death is during life. Let us hasten to do now that which we cannot do then. All passes quickly and ends. "The time is short." Therefore, let us so act that everything may serve us towards attaining eternal life.

*Absolutely Remembered This*

# 24

# SINS OF HABIT

*"Let not sin reign in your mortal body."*
—Romans 6:12

IT is a great evil to accustom ourselves to evil. A habit of sinning is a fatal chain which binds the soul and renders it a slave to crime. It blinds the spirit, hardens the heart, stifles the voice of conscience and gives a death-blow to modesty and virtue. The oftener we sin, the less pain we feel in the indulgence of it. At first we regard the sin by which we are tempted with horror, then with fear, and soon with more assurance; in a little while with complaisance; then we begin to take pleasure in it and, ere long, to glory in it; after which we sin with contempt and indifference and excite others to do the same. This last state is the profoundest abyss of iniquity and the extremest degree of malice.

A man who does not feel the miseries of a sickness which is destroying him is sick unto death. A sinner who grows old and hardened in his sins may be regarded as a diseased man whose life is almost despaired of. He is unconscious of his malady. If he desires conversion, it is only for a moment and in appearance only, and unattended by the slightest effort. His will is without effect, his desires without execution and his resolutions without perseverance. His evil inclinations come from nature, and his vices from habit.

When an evil habit gains the mastery over a soul, it is almost impossible to overcome it. It is like a torrent that sweeps away all that resists it; it is a tyrannical law which domineers over his will; it is a second nature more corrupt than the first. Grace attacks in vain the heart that sins through habit. Its most vehement blows fall disregarded and are without effect. It is insensible to the touches of Divine love, impenetrable to its arrows and impervious to its light. It would be less difficult to make an Ethiopian white than to convert an inveterate sinner. It would be easier to tear up a tree from the earth than to tear from the heart a deeply rooted vice.

How miserable is he whom habit has rendered worse than nature, more hardened, more insensible!

If such a one felt the evil that is destroying him, there would be some hope of his final restoration; but while he is callous and insensible to his miseries, he is without remedy.

But let not those despair who still desire to be saved. God does all things well and nothing in vain; it is He who inspires this salutary feeling. He expresses by it His desire to save and His will to deliver everyone who will, without delay, cooperate with Him in His designs for his salvation.

---

## 25

## SUFFERING FOR THE LOVE OF CHRIST

*"If any one will come after Me, let him deny himself, and take up his cross daily, and follow Me."*
—Luke 9:23

LET us make a few reflections on these words of Jesus Christ. He says, "If any one will come after Me." He does not say, "to Me," but, "after Me." The Lord desires that we should come close after Him; we must therefore walk the same road which He walked. He goes before and does not rest until He reaches Calvary, where He dies. Therefore, if we love Him, we must follow Him, even to death. And thus it is necessary that everyone should deny himself, that is, that he should deny himself everything which self-love demands, but which is not pleasing to Jesus Christ.

*Absolutely Remember This*

Our Lord says further, "Let him take up his cross daily, and follow Me." Let us consider these last words one by one. "Let him take up": it avails little to carry the cross by compulsion; all sinners bear it, but to bear it aright, we must embrace it voluntarily. "His cross": under this word is implied every kind of tribulation, which is called a "cross" in order that the name may render it sweet, from the thought that He died on the Cross for love of us.

He also says, "his cross." Some persons, when they receive spiritual consolations, offer themselves to suffer as great things as were endured by the martyrs—hot irons, piercing nails and tortures—but then they cannot endure a headache, the carelessness of a friend, the ill-temper of a relation. God does not ask us to endure hot irons, piercing nails and tortures, but He desires that we should suffer patiently this pain, this annoyance, this contempt. God desires that we should bear that cross which He gives us to suffer and not that which we would ourselves choose.

He says "daily." Some persons embrace the cross at the beginning, when it reaches them, but when it lasts long, they say, "Now I can bear no more." Yet God wills that we should go on to endure it with patience and even that we should bear it continually, even till death. See, then, that salvation and perfection consist in these three works: "Let him deny"—we must deny to our self-love whatever is not right; "let him take up"—we must embrace the cross which God gives us; "let him follow"—we must follow the footsteps of Jesus Christ, even to the end.

Our Saviour, because He loved us, came into this

world, not for enjoyment, but to suffer, in order that we might follow in His steps. "For unto this are ye called, because Christ also suffered for us, leaving you an example that you should follow His steps." (*1 Peter* 2:21). Let us watch Him as He goes before with His Cross to point out the road by which we must follow Him if we would be His. Oh, what a joy it is in every trouble that befalls us to say to Jesus Christ, "Lord, is it Thy will that I should endure this cross? I accept it, and I will endure it as long as it pleases Thee."

Many persons are delighted to hear of prayer, of peace, of love for Jesus Christ, but they find little pleasure in hearing of crosses or of suffering. These people are satisfied so long as the wind breathes with spiritual delights, but if it ceases and there comes some adversity or desolation in which the Lord hides Himself in order to prove them, and if He deprives them of their usual comfort, they leave off prayer, Communion and mortifications and abandon themselves to ill-humor and lukewarmness, seeking their pleasure from earthly things. But these souls love themselves more than Jesus Christ; whereas, they who do not love Him with an interested love for the sake of consolations, but with a pure love and only because He is worthy of love, do not leave their usual devout exercises for any dryness or weariness which they experience, being content to please God. And they offer themselves to suffer this desolation so long as God wills it.

O my Jesus, Thou alone hast been able to teach us these maxims of salvation, so contrary to the max-

ims of the world, and Thou alone canst give us
strength to suffer with patience. I do not pray Thee
to exempt me from suffering; I only pray Thee to
give me strength to suffer with patience and resignation. O Eternal Father, Thy Son has promised that
whatever we ask Thee in His name, Thou wilt give
it to us. Behold, we ask this of Thee: give us grace
to endure with patience the sufferings of this life;
hear us for the love of Jesus Christ. And Thou, O
my Jesus, pardon me all the offenses I have committed against Thee, in that I have not been willing
to suffer with patience the troubles Thou hast sent
me. Give me Thy love, that it may give me strength
to suffer all for love of Thee.

---

## 26

## THE HOUSE OF ETERNITY

*"In what place soever it shall fall, there it shall be."*
—Ecclesiasticus 11:3

WE err in calling this our habitation in which
we now dwell; the habitation of our body in
a little while will be a grave, in which it must rest
until the Day of Judgment. And the habitation of
the soul will be either Paradise or Hell, according
as it has deserved, and there it will continue through
all eternity.

At our burial, our corpses do not go to the grave
of themselves; they are carried thither by others, but

the soul goes itself to the place which awaits it, either of eternal joy or eternal woe. According as a man lives well or ill, so he departs himself to his habitation in Paradise or in Hell, which he shall never change.

Those who live on this earth often change their home, either to please themselves or because they are compelled. In eternity the habitation is never changed; where we enter the first time, there we abide forever. "If the wood fall to the south or to the north, in whatever place it shall fall, there shall it be." He that enters into the south, which is Heaven, will be ever happy; he that enters the north, which is Hell, will be ever miserable.

He, then, who enters Heaven, will be always united with God, always in company with the Saints, always in the profoundest peace, always abundantly contented, because every blessed soul is filled and satisfied with joy, nor will he ever know the fear of losing it. If fear of losing their happiness could enter among the blessed, they would be no longer blessed, for the mere thought of losing the joy they possess would disturb the peace they enjoy.

On the other hand, whoever enters into Hell will be forever far from God. Let us not think that the pains of Hell will be like those of earth, where through the force of habit, a trouble continually grows less; for, as in Paradise the delights never cause weariness but seem ever new, as though they were for the first time enjoyed (which is implied by the expression of "the new canticle," which the blessed are ever singing), so in Hell the pains never grow less through all eternity; habit will never diminish their torment.

O my Jesus, send us not to Hell, to that Hell in which we could no longer love Thee, but must hate Thee forever! Deprive us of everything—of property, health, life—but deprive us not of Thyself. Grant that we may love Thee and praise Thee forever, and then do with us what Thou wilt.

---

## 27

# DESIRE FOR THE PRESENCE OF GOD

*"We shall see Him as He is."* —1 John 3:2

"WHILE we are in the body, we are absent from the Lord." (*2 Cor.* 5:6). Souls who in this life love nothing but God are like noble pilgrims, destined according to their present state to be the eternal brides of the King of Heaven, but who now live far away without seeing Him; wherefore, they sigh to depart to the country of the blessed, where they know that their Spouse awaits them.

They know, indeed, that their Beloved is ever present with them, but that He is, as it were, hidden by a veil and does not show Himself. Or rather, He is like the sun behind clouds, which from time to time, sends forth some ray of its splendor, but displays not itself openly. They live, nevertheless, contented, uniting themselves to the will of the Lord, who chooses to keep them in exile and far away from Himself. Yet with all this, they cannot help continually sighing to know Him face-to-face, in order to be more inflamed with love toward Him.

Therefore every one of them often sweetly laments with her beloved Spouse because He shows Himself not, and they say, "O Thou only love of my heart, since Thou hast so loved me and hast stricken me with Thy holy love, why hidest Thou Thyself and makest me not to see Thee? I know that Thou art infinite beauty; I love Thee more than myself, though I have never yet beheld Thee; open to me Thy fair countenance; I would know Thee all revealed, in order that I may no more look to myself nor to any creature and may think only of loving Thee, my highest good."

When to these souls thus filled with love for God there appears any ray of the Divine goodness and of the love which God bears them, they would be dissolved and fade away for desire of Him. And though for them the sun is still hidden behind the clouds and His fair face is covered by a veil and their own eyes are bandaged so that they cannot gaze on Him face to face, yet what shall be their joy when the clouds shall disperse and the gate open and the covering shall be taken from their eyes and the fair countenance of their Beloved shall appear without a veil, so that in the clear light of day they shall look upon His beauty, His goodness, His greatness and the love which He bears to them!

O death, why dost thou so delay to come? It is thou that must open to us the gate, that we may enter into the palace of the Lord. O blessed country, when will the day be here when we shall find ourselves beneath thy eternal tabernacles? O Beloved of our souls, O

Jesus, our Treasure, our Love, our All, when will that happy moment arrive when, leaving this earth, we shall see ourselves united to Thee? We deserve not this happiness, but the love which Thou hast shown us, and still more Thine infinite goodness, make us hope that we shall one day be joined to those happy souls, who, being wholly united to Thee, love Thee, and will love Thee with a perfect love through all eternity.

---

## 28

## THE GOOD SHEPHERD

*"The shepherd and bishop of your souls."*
—1 Peter 11:25

THUS spoke Jesus of Himself, "I am the Good Shepherd." (*John* 10:14). The work of a good shepherd is nothing but this, to guide his flock to good pastures and to guard them from wolves. But what shepherd, O sweet Redeemer, ever had the mercy like Thee, to give his life to save his flock, which flock are we, to deliver them from the punishment they had deserved?

He Himself hath borne our sins in His own Body on the tree, that being dead to sin, we should live to justice; by whose stripes we were healed. (*1 Peter* 2:24). To heal us of our sicknesses, this Good Shepherd took upon Himself all our debts and paid them with His own Body, dying with agony upon a cross. It was this excess of love towards us His sheep which made St. Ignatius the martyr burn with desire to give his life for Jesus Christ, saying, "My love is crucified," as he wrote in his letter, saying, "What! Has my God been willing to die on a cross for me, and cannot I desire to die for Him!" And in truth, was it a great thing the martyrs did in giving their lives for Jesus Christ when He died for love of them? Oh how the death endured for them by Jesus Christ made sweet to them all their torments, stripes, piercing nails, fiery plates of iron and tormenting deaths!

When this Good Shepherd sees a sheep lost, what does He not do, what means does He not take to recover it? "If He lose one of them, He goeth after that which was lost until He find it." (*Luke* 15:4). And when He has found it, rejoicing He places it upon His shoulders, that it may be lost no more, and calling to Him His friends and neighbors, i.e., the Angels and Saints, He invites them to rejoice with Him for having found the sheep that was lost. Who then will not love with all his affections this good Lord, who shows Himself thus loving to sinners who have turned their backs upon Him and destroyed themselves of their own accord!

O my Saviour, worthy of all love, behold at Thy feet a sheep that was lost! What would have become of me if Thou hadst not thought of seeking me! And as I first fled from Thee, now I desire nothing but to love Thee and to live and die embracing Thy feet. Oh bind me, chain me with the bond of Thy holy love! "I have gone astray like a sheep that was lost! Oh, seek Thy servant!"

———————

## 29

## RESIGNATION TO THE DIVINE WILL

*"My meat is to do the will of Him that sent me."*
—John 4:34

S O said Jesus Christ, speaking of Himself. In this mortal life, "meat" is that which preserves our life, and therefore Our Lord said that it was His meat to do the will of the Father. This also ought to be the meat of our souls: "Life is in His will." (*Ps.* 29:6). Our life consists in doing the Divine will; he that does not fulfill it is dead.

God only desires that which is best for us, which is our sanctification. Let us take care, therefore, to quiet our own will, uniting it ever to the will of God, and thus we shall be able also to quiet our mind, recollecting that everything that God does is the best thing that can befall us. Whoever does not do this will never find true peace. All the perfection which can be attained in this world, which is a place of preparation and purification, consists in suffering patiently those things which are opposed to our self-love. And, in order to suffer with patience, there is no more efficacious means than a willingness to suffer in order to do the will of God. He that acquiesces with the Divine will in everything is always at peace, and nothing that happens to him can make him miserable.

The Divine will, so to say, draws out all the thorns and bitterness of the tribulations which come upon us in this world. The hymn which speaks of the Divine will thus sings: "Thou changest crosses into joys; Thou makest even death to be sweet; he that can unite himself with Thee, knows neither cross nor fear. Oh, how worthy art Thou of love, Thou, O Will of God!"

Behold the excellent counsel of St. Peter, in order to find a perfect peace in the midst of the toils of this present life, "Casting all your care upon Him, for He careth for you." (*1 Peter* 5:7). And if it is God who thus gives thought for our good, why should we weary ourselves with so many anxieties—as if our happiness depended on our own cares—and not rather give ourselves up into the hands of God, upon whom all depends. "Cast thy care upon the Lord," says David, "and He shall sustain thee." (*Ps.* 54:23).

In a word, whoever does the will of God enters into Paradise, and he that does it not, enters not. Some people trust their eternal salvation to certain devotions or to certain outward works of piety, and yet they do not give their hearts to God. But Jesus Christ says, "Not every one that saith to Me, Lord, Lord, shall enter into the kingdom of heaven; but he that doth the will of My Father, he shall enter into the kingdom of heaven." (*Matt.* 7:21).

Receive, O God of my soul, receive the sacrifice of my whole will and my whole liberty. I see that I have deserved that Thou shouldst turn Thy back upon me and refuse this gift of mine, so often have I been unfaithful to Thee. But I learn that Thou dost again command me to love Thee with all my heart, and therefore I am sure Thou wilt receive it. I resign myself, then, wholly to Thy will; make me to know what Thou wilt, that I may be able to accomplish it all. Make me love Thee, and then dispose of me and all my affairs as it pleases Thee. I am in Thy hands; do what Thou knowest to be most expedient for my eternal salvation, while I declare that I desire Thee alone and nothing else.

---

## 30

## THE JOY OF THE BLESSED

*"Thou hast established me in Thy sight for ever."*
—Psalm 40:13

"ENTER thou into the joy of thy Lord." (*Matt. 25:21*). When the soul enters the kingdom of the blessed and the barrier which hinders her sight is taken away, she will see openly and without a veil the infinite beauty of her God, and this will be the joy of the blessed. Every object which she will then see in God Himself will overwhelm her with delight: she will see the rectitude of His judgments, the harmony of His regulations for every soul, all ordained to His divine glory and her own good.

She will perceive in respect to herself the boundless love which God has entertained towards her in becoming man and sacrificing His life upon the Cross through love of her. She will perceive all the graces and favors shown to her, which until then had been hidden. She will see all the mercies He has bestowed on her, in waiting for her and pardoning her ingratitude. She will see the many calls and lights and aids which have been granted to her in abundance. She will see that these tribulations, these infirmities, these losses of property or of kindred, which she counted punishments, were not really punishments, but loving arrangements of God for drawing her to the perfect love of Him.

In a word, all these things will make her know the infinite goodness of her God and the boundless love which He deserves, for which reason, so soon as she shall have reached Heaven, she will have no other desire but to behold Him in His blessedness and content. And at the same time, comprehending that the happiness of God is supreme, infinite and eternal, she will experience a joy which is only not infinite because a creature is not capable of anything that is infinite. She will enjoy, nevertheless, a pleasure which is extreme and full, which fills her with delight and with that kind of delight which belongs to God Himself. And thus will be fulfilled in her the words, "Enter thou into the joy of thy Lord."

The blessed are not so much blessed through the delight which they experience in themselves as in the joy with which God rejoices, for the blessed love God so infinitely more than themselves that the blessedness of God delights them infinitely more than their own blessedness, through the love which they bear to Him, which love makes them forget themselves and find all their delight in pleasing their Beloved.

And this is that holy and loving inebriation which causes the blessed to lose the memory of themselves, to give themselves wholly to praise and to love the Dear Object of all their love, which is God. "They shall be inebriated with the plenty of Thy house." (*Ps.* 25:9). Happy from their first entrance into Heaven, they continue, as it were, lost and, so to say, swallowed up in love in that boundless ocean of the goodness of God.

Wherefore, every blessed soul will lose all her own desires and will have no other desire but to love God and to be loved by Him, and knowing that she is sure of ever loving Him and of being ever loved by Him, this very thing will be her blessedness, which will fill her with joy and will make her throughout eternity so satisfied with delight that she will desire nothing more.

In a word, it will be the paradise of the blessed to rejoice in the joy of God. And thus, he who in this life rejoices in the blessedness which God enjoys, and will enjoy through eternity, can say that even in this life he enters into the joy of God and begins to enjoy paradise.

---

## 31

## TRUE PEACE FOUND IN GOD ALONE

*"Peace, because we have hoped in Thee."*
—Isaias 26:3

HE that seeks peace in creatures will never find it, because no creatures are fitted for giving satisfaction to the heart. God has created man for Himself, who is the Infinite Good; wherefore, God alone can content him. Hence it comes that many persons, though loaded with riches, honors and earthly pleasures, are never satisfied; they are ever seeking for more honors, more possessions, more amusements. And however many they obtain, they are always restless and never enjoy a day of true peace. "Delight in the Lord, and He shall give thee the desires of thy heart." (*Ps.* 36:4). When any person delights only in God and seeks nothing but God, God Himself will take care to satisfy all the desires of his heart, and then he will attain the happy state of those souls who desire nothing but to please God.

Senseless are they who say, "Happy is he who can employ himself as he likes, who can command others, who can take what pleasures he pleases." It is madness; he alone is happy who loves God, who says that God alone is sufficient for him. Experience shows clearly that multitudes of persons who are called fortunate by men of the world, because they are raised up to the possession of great riches and great dignities, live a miserable life and never find rest.

"The peace of God surpasseth all understanding."

(*Philip.* 4:17). Oh, how the peace which the Lord gives to those who love Him exceeds all the delights which the world can give! "Oh, taste and see that the Lord is sweet." (*Ps.* 33:9). O men of the world, why will ye despise the life of the Saints without having ever known it? Try it, leave your worldly vanities, give yourselves to God, and you shall see how well He knows how to comfort you, more than all the greatnesses and delights of this world.

It is true that even the just suffer great troubles in this life, but they, resigning themselves to the will of God, never lose their peace. The lovers of the world seem now at times joyful, now at times sad, but in truth, they are ever restless and in a state of storms. On the other hand, the lovers of God are superior to all adversity and to the changes of this world, and therefore they live in uniform tranquillity. See how the celebrated Cardinal Petrucci describes a soul that is wholly given to God: "It beholds all creatures around change into a thousand various forms, while within, the depths of its heart, ever united to God, continue without change."

But he who would live ever united with God and would enjoy a continual peace must drive from his heart everything which is not God and separate himself from all the snares which draw him to the world.

Happy are they for whom God alone is sufficient! O Lord, give me grace, that I may seek nothing but Thee and ask for nothing but to love Thee.

## 32

# THE PATH OF THE JUST

*"He shall be like a tree which is planted near the running waters, which shall bring forth its fruit in due season. And his leaf shall not fall off; and all whatsoever he shall do shall prosper."* —Psalm 1:3

AMONG the many images under which the good man is described in Holy Scripture, perhaps there is none more vivid, more beautiful and more touching than that which represents him as some favored and thriving tree in the garden of God's planting. Our original birthplace and home was a garden, and the trees which Adam had to dress and keep, both in themselves and by the sort of attention they demanded, reminded him of the peaceful, happy duties and the innocent enjoyments which were the business of his life. A garden, in its perennial freshness and its soothing calm, is the best type of Heaven, and its separate plants and flowers are the exactest types of its blessed inhabitants. Accordingly, it is introduced into the last page of Scripture as well as into the first; it makes its appearance at the conclusion of man's eventful history, as in the record of its opening. As in the beginning we read of the Paradise of pleasure, with the great river and its four separate streams, with all manner of trees, fair to behold and pleasant to eat of, and above all, the Tree of Life, so, in the last chapter of the Apocalypse, we are told of the river of water of life, clear as crystal, proceeding from the throne of God and of the Lamb, of which he that thirsteth may drink freely, and of the Tree of Life, bearing twelve fruits, the leaves of which were for the healing of the nations. And in like manner, when we turn to that portion of the sacred volume which, more than any other, both reveals and supports the hidden life of the servants of God in every age, we find the first Psalm is that in which the obedient and just man is set before us under the self-same image—under the image of some choice specimen of the vegetable world, that innocent portion of the divine handiwork which is deformed by no fierce passions, which has no will and pursues no end of its own, and which seems created only to please the eye of man and to be his food, medicine and refreshment:

"Blessed is the man who hath not walked in the counsel of the ungodly, nor stood in the way of sinners, nor sat in the chair of pestilence: but his will is in the law of the Lord, and in His law he shall meditate day and night. And he shall be like a tree which is planted near the running waters, which shall bring forth its fruit in due season. And his leaf shall not fall off; and all whatsoever he shall do shall prosper."

This favored plant of God is placed by the running waters; it is nourished and recruited by the never-failing, the perpetual, the daily and hourly supply of their wholesome influences. It grows up gradually, silently, without observation, and in proportion as it rises aloft, so do its roots, with still less observation, strike deep into the earth. Thus it determinately takes up its habitation in one place, from which death alone shall part it. Year after year, it grows more and more into the hope and posture of a glorious immobility and unchangeableness. What it has been, that it shall be; if it changes, it is as growing into fruitfulness and maturing in its fruit's abundance and perfection. Nor is that fruit lost; it neither withers upon the branches nor decays upon the ground. Angels unseen gather crop after crop from the unwearied never-failing parent and carefully store them up in heavenly treasure houses. Its very leaf remains green to the end; not only its fruit, which is profitable for eternal life, but its very foliage, the ordinary dress in which it meets our senses, its beautiful coloring, its rich yet delicate fullness of proportion, the graceful waving of its boughs, the musical whispers and rustlings of its leaves, the fragrance which it exhales, the refreshment which it spreads around it—all testify to that majestic, serene beneficence, which is its very nature, and to a mysterious depth of life which enables it ever to give out virtue, yet never to have less of it within.

Such is the holy servant of God, considered in that condition which is both his special reward and his ordinary lot. There are those, indeed, who for the good of their brethren and according to the will of God, are exercised by extraordinary trials and pass their lives amid turbulence and change. There are others, again, who are wonderfully called out of error or of sin, and have experience of much conflict within or without them before they reach the heavenly river and the groves which line its banks. Certainly history speaks much more of martyrdom and confessorship, on the one hand, and of inquiry and conversion, of sin and repentance, on the other, than of the tranquil Christian course; yet history does but give the surface of what actually takes place in the heavenly kingdom. If we would really bring before us what is the ordinary portion of the multitude of religious men, we should find it to consist in what from its very nature cannot make much show in history—in a life barren of great events and rich in small ones; in a life of routine duties, of happy obscurity and inward peace, of an orderly dispensing of good to others who come within their influence, morning and evening, of a growth and blossoming and bearing fruit in the house of God, and of a blessed death in the presence of their brethren. This had been the blessedness of holy Job, as he sets it before us himself: "I said, I shall die in my nest, and as a palm tree shall multiply my days. My root is opened beside the waters, and dew shall continue in my harvest. They that heard me . . . to my words durst add nothing, and my speech dropped upon them. They waited for me as for rain, and they opened their mouth as for a latter shower." It is expressed also in the words of the *Canticle*, which, though belonging in their fullness to Our Lord Himself, yet in their measure apply to the benefits which any holy man extends to those who are within the range of his attraction: "As the apple tree among the trees of the woods, so is my beloved among the sons. I sat down under his shadow whom I desired, and his fruit was sweet to my mouth."

# 33

## CHARITY

*"Charity is patient, is kind: charity envieth not, dealeth
not perversely, is not puffed up, is not ambitious, seeketh
not her own, is not provoked to anger, thinketh no evil,
rejoiceth not in iniquity, but rejoiceth with the truth:
beareth all things, believeth all things, hopeth all things,
endureth all things. Charity never faileth."*
—1 Corinthians 13:4-8

"CHARITY is patient." She is not vindictive or resentful against her neighbor for any ill treatment that she may receive from him; she bears with his vices and imperfections with sweetness and excuses them as much as possible; if anyone says anything to offend her, she seems not to hear it; she returns neither railing for railing, nor injury for injury, but suffers all without a word, without complaint, without revenge and without showing any mark of resentment.

Charity is sweet to all the world; she does good to those who do her evil and ranks among her best friends those who cause her the most pain. She offends no one, either by word or by action, and if she happens to wound or excite the anger of a neighbor, she asks his pardon and expresses much sorrow for having offended him.

Charity is prompt to do good unto others; she flies to relieve the necessities of her neighbor, serves him with joy, studies his interests, alleviates his cares and takes extreme pleasure in serving him, regarding in his person Jesus Christ. She does not consult her own convenience in serving others.

Charity is not imprudent, rash or audacious, but humble, modest and respectful; she is honored by all men, even by those who do not practice her sacred laws. Her conversation is honest without affectation, sincere without dissimulation, sweet without sharpness, free without frivolity and engaging without artifice; she makes a mockery of none, hates slander, buffoonery and wit which wounds her neighbor. She always puts herself in the place of others and questions herself thus: "How should I feel were they to speak thus of me, or amuse themselves at my expense?"

Charity is not haughty or proud. She does not elevate herself above others or seek the praises of the world; she is not wounded when she sees that others are more loved and honored than herself; she is humble and regards everyone as her superior; she salutes them with respect and honors them by offering them the best places. She is willing to render them the most humble services, and that from her heart, with a tender and generous affection, regarding in them the person of Jesus Christ.

Charity is not artificial or dissimulating, but simple and candid; she is prudent in her language, but never deceives anyone; she hates lying and deceit and always speaks as she thinks; her air is simple and modest, and though she may be civil, she never flatters. Insinuations, defiances and rash judgments she regards as deadly poisons, of which she has an infinite horror. She acts with simplicity, speaks with sweetness, entertains a kind opinion of all and judges ill of none.

Charity loves mortification as the principle of her life, for she loves peace, which can only be preserved by each one's contributing to bear his part, by the mortification of his inclinations and passions, which are the cause of every disorder and evil in the world. She is not inordinately attached to the goods of this life; on the contrary, she willingly strips herself to clothe others, knowing that avarice is the devil which excites all the wars, divisions, injustices, troubles and discords on earth.

Charity is not hard and unpitying, but tender and sensible of the misery of her neighbor; she looks on him as the person of Jesus Christ. This is the reason why she delights in prisons and hospitals, where she finds the miserable, whom she assists, consoles and ministers unto. She does not envy the temporal or spiritual good of her neighbor; on the contrary, she promotes both as much as possible. She believes all, hopes for all, does all, suffers all, gives all, embraces all, submits to all. Behold the spirit of Christian charity!

# 34

## DESIRES AFTER PERFECTION

*"Who will give me wings like a dove?"* —Psalm 54:7

WE may very rightly make simple wishes which witness to our gratitude. I may say, "Alas, why am I not as fervent as the Seraphim, the better to serve and love my God?" But I must not entertain myself with forming desires—as if in this world I were to attain to that exquisite perfection. Or say I desire this perfection and set myself to attain it, and if I fail of reaching it, I am unhappy. I do not say that we ought not to put ourselves in the path of such perfection; only we must not expect to reach it in one day—that is to say, in one day of this mortal life—for this desire would be a torment to us, and a most useless one.

It is necessary in order to travel well for us to attend to the accomplishment of that part of the journey which is immediately before us, to get over the first day's ground and not to amuse ourselves with desiring to accomplish the last day's journey when our business is to make an end of the first. We sometimes amuse ourselves with the idea of being good angels when we are not laboring to make ourselves even good men.

Our imperfections will often accompany us to the grave; we cannot walk without touching the earth. We ought not to lie and grovel there; but we also ought to beware of flying. We die little by little; we must therefore make our imperfections die with us, day by day.

Let us remain at Our Lord's feet with Mary; let us practice those little virtues which are adapted to our littleness; and if there are virtues that are exercised rather in descending than in ascending, the better for our weakness. Such are patience, the bearing with our neighbor and doing him service, humility, sweetness, courage, affability, the endurance of our own imperfections and other little virtues like them.

We are to ascend by means of prayer, but it must be step by step. Let us look close before us and not at those dangers which we see afar off. We fancy they are armies; they are only trees in the distance, and while we are gazing at them, we may make some false steps.

We ought not to desire impossible things or build upon difficult and uncertain ones. It is not sufficient to believe that God can succor us by all sorts of means; but we must believe that He wills not to employ for that purpose those means which He removes far from us and that He does will to employ such as are near to us.

Let us have, then, a firm and general purpose of intending to serve God with all our heart and all our life, and this done, let us not think of the morrow. Let us only think of finishing the present day well, and when tomorrow shall have arrived, it too will be called today, and then we shall think of it. It is necessary that we have a great confidence in the Providence of God, and a resignation to it. We must make provision of manna for each day and no more; let us have no doubts; God will rain manna tomorrow, and the day after tomorrow, and all the days of our pilgrimage.

---

## 35

# THE DANGER OF NEGLECTING THE SMALLEST THINGS

*"He that contemneth small things shall fall by little and little."* —Ecclesiasticus 19:1

THE doctrine contained in these words is of great importance to all persons, for as great things carry with themselves their own recommendation, we are most exact in performing them; but it is usual to be careless in small things, as we fancy they are of no great consequence. In this, however, we are mistaken; it is very dangerous to fail in these things, as is declared in this passage of Holy Scripture. To convince ourselves, then, of this truth and to oblige ourselves to be watchful, it ought to be sufficient that God Himself says so; but in order that this may make a deeper impression on our minds, when treated more at large, let us consider what was the opinion of the Saints on this subject. "Those who run into disorders and crimes of the highest nature," says St. Bernard, "begin at first by committing small faults, and no person ever falls or plunges himself all at once into an excess of wickedness"; that is to say, commonly speaking, none ever ascend at once to the highest point of vice or virtue, but good and evil gradually insinuate themselves and grow insensibly in us. It happens in spiritual as it does in corporal diseases: both the one and the other increase by little and little, so that when you see some servant of God commit some great fault, do not imagine, says the Saint, that his disease begins at that point, for none ever falls on a sudden into any enormous sin, after having a long time led an innocent and virtuous life. But they begin first by negligence in those duties which they consider as unimportant; then their devotion growing cold, it diminishes daily more and more, so that at length they deserve that God should withdraw His hand, and no longer supported by Him, they easily yield and fall under the first great temptation that attacks them.

Cassian explains this by a very apt comparison. Houses fall not all at once, but the damage first begins by some gutters out of repair and neglected, through which the rain entering, by degrees rots the timber that sustains the building; in process of time it penetrates the wall, dissolves the cement and at last undermines the very foundation, so that the whole edifice tumbles to the ground, perhaps in one night. It is just so with us. A certain natural inclination which we have to evil first flatters our senses, surprises them, gains them and thence, insinuating itself into our soul, shakes the firmness of our good resolutions, and at last so weakens the whole foundation of our piety, that the entire spiritual edifice falls in a moment to the ground; whereas, a little care and vigilance in the beginning might have easily prevented the growth of the evil. All this happens by the wile and craft of the devil, who dares not attack those that serve God by tempting them at first to omit things very essential, but begins by those that seem of little consequence and by always insensibly gaining some slight advantage, he at length succeeds. For if at first he should propose and tempt us to mortal sin, he would be quickly discovered and repulsed; but insinuating himself by little and little, he, through our slight omissions and small faults, gets into our souls before we are aware of it. It is for this reason St. Gregory says that "small faults are in a manner more dangerous than great ones" because great faults, as soon as we reflect on them, almost oblige us to avoid them, or quickly to rise if we have fallen into them. But in small faults, the less we perceive them, the less we avoid them; and making no account of them, we fall into them so often that in time we acquire such a habit as we seldom or never are able to eradicate, so that the evil, which at first seemed nothing, becomes, by our neglect and frequent relapses, almost incurable. And so St. Chrysostom says in similar language.

"Of many small drops of rain," says St. Bonaventure, "great torrents are formed which throw down the strongest walls; a small chink, by which the water gets into a ship, oftentimes causes the loss of the vessel." Wherefore, St. Austin tells us that as when a ship springs a leak, we must immediately pump in order to get out the water and prevent her from sinking, so also by fervent prayer and a strict examination of conscience, we must continually endeavor to root out of our heart whatever imperfection or impurity had found its way into it, which if neglected, might at last cause our ruin. This should be the continual exercise of a Christian: he must incessantly labor to amend his faults and continually put his hand to the pump; otherwise, he will be in great danger of shipwreck.

---

## 36

## PURITY OF INTENTION

*"If thine eye be single, thy whole body is full of light; but if thine eye be evil, thy whole body is full of darkness."* —Matthew. 6:22

PURITY of intention consists in doing everything from a simple desire to please God. Jesus Christ has said that according to the intention, whether it be good or evil, so is our work judged before God. The "single eye" here signifies a pure intention of pleasing God; the "dark and evil eye" signifies a want of such honest and holy intention, when our actions are done from a motive of vanity, or from a desire to please ourselves.

Can any action be more noble than for a man to give his life for the Faith? And yet St. Paul says that he who dies from any motive, but that of a pure desire to do God's will, gains nothing by his martyrdom. If, then, even martyrdom shall avail nothing unless it be endured for the sake of God alone, of what value will be all the preaching, all the labor of good works, and also all the austerities of penitents, if they are done to obtain the praise of men or to satisfy our own inclination?

The prophet Aggaeus says that works, however holy in themselves, if not done for God, are nothing better than bags full of holes, which means that they are all lost immediately and that no good comes of them. On the contrary, every action done with an intention of pleasing God, of however little value in itself, is worth more than many works done without such pure intention. Again, we read in St. Mark that the poor widow cast into the alms in the temple only two mites, but yet of her the Saviour said, "See, that poor widow has cast in more than all." (*Mark* 12:43). St. Cyprian remarks on this, that she put in more than all the others because she gave those two little pieces of money with the pure intention of pleasing God.

One of the best signs by which we may know whether a person's work is done with a right intention is that, if the work have not the effect desired, he will not be at all disturbed. Another good sign is that, when a person has completed any work and then is spoken ill of for it or is repaid with ingratitude, he nevertheless remains contented and tranquil. On the other hand, if it happen to anyone to be praised for his work, he must not disquiet himself with the fear of being filled with vainglory, but should it come upon him, only let him despise it in his heart and say with St. Bernard, "I did not begin it for thee, nor because of thee will I leave it."

To work with an intention of acquiring more glory

in Heaven is good, but the most perfect is the desire
to give glory to God. Let us be sure that the more
we divest ourselves of our earthly interests, so much
the more our Saviour will increase our joy in Paradise. Blessed is he who labors only to give glory to
God and to follow His holy will. Let us imitate the
love of the blessed, who in loving God, seek only to
please Him. St. Chrysostom says, "If we can attain
to the fulfillment of God's pleasure, what more can
we desire? If thou art worthy of doing anything that
pleases God, dost thou ask any other reward?"

This is that "single eye" which pierces the heart
of God with love towards us. As He says to the holy
Spouse, "Thou hast wounded My heart, My sister,
My spouse; thou hast wounded My heart with one
of thine eyes." (*Cant.* 4:9). This "single eye" signifies
the one end that holy souls have in all their actions,
that of pleasing God. And this was the counsel that
the Apostle gave to his disciples, "Therefore, whether
you eat or drink, or whatsoever you do, do all to the
glory of God." (*1 Cor.* 10:31). The venerable Beat-
rice of the Incarnation, the first daughter of St.
Teresa, said, "No price can be put on anything, however small, which is done entirely for God." And with
great reason she said this, for all works done for God
are acts of divine love. Purity of intention makes
the lowest actions become precious, such as eating,
working or recreation, when they are done from obedience and from a desire to please God.

———

## 37

# THE HEAVENLY JERUSALEM

*"At Thy right hand are delights forevermore."*
—Psalm 15:11

HAPPY is he who is saved, who leaves this place of exile and enters into the heavenly Jerusalem and enjoys that perfect day which shall be always day and always joyful, free from all molestation and from all fear of ever losing such infinite happiness.

Jacob said, "The days of the years of my pilgrimage are a hundred and thirty; few, and evil." (*Gen.* 47:9). The same may be said of us miserable pilgrims while we remain on this earth to endure the toils of our exile, afflicted by temptations, torn by passions and tormented by miseries, and still more by the fear of losing at last our eternal salvation. And thus, living detached from this earth, we ought always to aspire towards Paradise, saying, "When shall it be, O Lord, that I shall be delivered from all these distresses and think only of loving Thee and praising Thee? When will it be that Thou wilt be all to me in all things, as the Apostle writes, "That God may be all in all?" When shall I enjoy that unchanging peace, free from all affliction and from all danger of being lost? When, my God, shall I find myself dwelling with Thee and enjoying the sight of Thine infinite beauty face to face and without veil? When shall I attain to the possession of Thee, my Creator, in such a manner that I may say, My God, I cannot lose Thee more?

O my Saviour! while Thou seest me an exile and full of trouble in this land of enemies where I live in continual warfare, help me with Thy grace and console me in this sorrowful pilgrimage. Whatever the world may offer me, I know that nothing in it can bring peace; but yet I fear lest, if I have not help from Thee, the pleasures of the world, joined to my evil inclinations, should draw me on to some terrible precipice.

Exile as I am in this valley of tears, I would think of Thee continually, O my God, and have part in that infinite happiness which Thou enjoyest; but the evil appetites of sense make themselves heard within me and disturb me. I would that my affections were ever occupied in loving Thee and thanking Thee, but I am constrained to exclaim with St. Paul, "Unhappy man that I am, who shall deliver me from the body of this death?" (*Rom.* 7:24). Miserable man that I am, in continual combat, not only with external enemies, but with myself, whence I am weighed down and a trouble to myself.

Who then shall deliver me from the body of this death, that is, from the danger of falling into sin, from that peril, the fear only of which is to me a continual death, which torments me and will not cease to torment me all my life through? "O God, be not then far from me; my God, make haste to my help." (*Ps.* 70:12).

My God, go not far from me, because if Thou goest from me, I fear that I shall displease Thee. Therefore, draw nearer to me with Thy powerful help; succor me continually, that I may be able to resist the attacks of my enemies. Remain beside me, then, my beloved Saviour, and give me that patience and courage which I need to overcome the continual attacks by which I am tormented.

O house of my God, prepared for those that love Thee! For thee do I sigh from this land of misery. "I have gone astray as a sheep that is lost! Oh, seek Thy servant." O beloved Shepherd of my soul, who didst descend from Heaven to seek and to save the lost sheep, behold me, one of these who has turned from Thee and lost itself! Seek Thy servant, O Lord! Abandon me not, as I deserve; seek me and save me; take me and keep me safe within Thine arms, that I may not leave Thee ever more.

---

# 38

## FERVOR OF SPIRIT

*"Fervent in spirit."* —Romans 12:11

THE spirit of devotion relaxes, grows cold and weary, even in the greatest Saints, if they use no means to preserve and increase fervor. 1) This inclination to tepidity arises from our nature, which being come from nothingness, always tends to its origin; it is like water, which grows cold if it is not always kept on the fire. 2) It arises from the nature of grace, which is in our soul as in a strange soil, surrounded by thorns and noxious weeds which impede its growth, exposed to winds and tempests, which root it up, and combating with the cold and frost, which will kill it if we do not take care. 3) It is caused by the inconstancy and frivolity of man, whose mind is as variable as the winds, whose soul is forever agitated and in motion like the sea and filled with impetuosity and instability. 4) It is the effect of the temptations of the devil, who is unwearied in tempting, but whom one grows weary of resisting. 5) It is the result of the passions, which shake the foundations of virtue, of wicked habits, which it is necessary to combat unceasingly and which we too soon grow weary of repressing.

Why is it necessary to serve God with fervor? Because He loves us, and the love He bears us is infinite and eternal; because He is infinitely amiable, and weighs us down with undeserved blessings; because we are under the most important obligations to love Him with a love which never says, "It is enough"; because we never love Him in a manner worthy of His adorable perfections or as much as we are capable of loving Him. It is necessary, then, to love Him more and more and never to grow cold in His love. God will not tolerate a service which is rendered with unwillingness. He holds accursed all those who do His will with negligence; He would rather they should abandon His service entirely than serve Him so basely and He prefers coldness to lukewarmness. These base and slothful servants burden His heart and compel Him to vomit them forth. There is no stopping place in the road of virtue, no place of easy repose where the soul can rest from her labors. Life is a restless stream, and our passions are the torrents which will sweep us away with resistless force if we do not oppose them. In the road of virtue, if we do not advance, we retrograde; if we are not ascending, we are descending; and if we are not growing better, we are becoming worse.

Who ought to serve God with fervor? The obligation rests equally on all, the young and the old. The young, because they have strong passions and strength to practice self-denial and mortification. Great results depend on small beginnings; the safety of the edifice depends on its foundation; the life of the tree on its roots; the fullness of a stream on its source; and the tranquillity of old age on its youth. An edifice whose foundation is bad will certainly fall; a tree whose roots are diseased will never bear good fruit; if water is poisoned at its source the stream will also be the same; and if a man's youth has been spent in corrupt pleasures, his age will be also corrupt. Youth is nature's spring time, and the flowers produced then are infinitely pleasing to God. Jesus Christ called children to Him; He embraced and blessed them. The young have need of many powerful graces to enable them to resist their passions. He who goes astray in the commencement of a voyage finds great difficulty in retracing his way. Commonly speaking, man's salvation depends on the manner in which he has spent the years of his youth.

Who can explain the extent of the peril incurred by both old and young when they become lax in the service of God? Nature presumes on a little indulgence, craves still more, and becomes exacting and insolent. The passions revolt and insensibly destroy the empire of grace. Sins become more frequent and malignant, for the injuries that we receive from a friend are much more painful and unpardonable than those which are inflicted by an enemy. God will not protect or defend a base and unfaithful soul, as He did when it was in grace and fervor. The few graces it receives it does not co-operate with. It commits great sins and does not perceive their enormity. Then, when grace withdraws, it conceives a great disgust for devotion; it is distracted and dissipated from without because it can find no satisfaction within. This disgust is followed by hardness and insensibility to all the touches of grace: to the advice of confessors, to the reproofs of superiors, to admonitions and threats from the pulpit, to the influence of all pious reading, all good example, and finally to remorse of conscience. From insensibility it passes to contempt, which is the very bottom of iniquity, the character of reprobation and the last degree of impenitence, which attracts and induces mortal sins, a sudden and unprovided death and the perdition of the soul.

Let us then attend to these words uttered by Jesus Christ: "Be mindful, therefore, from whence thou art fallen: and do penance, and do the first works. Or else I come to thee, and will remove thy candlestick out of its place, unless thou shalt have done penance." (*Apoc.* 2:5). Let us imitate St. Paul and other great Saints who increased in fervor as they advanced in years, being afraid that, after having saved others, they should themselves become castaways. Let us renew in our heart a spirit of devotion, charity and mortification, of devotion towards God, charity towards our neighbor, and mortification towards ourselves.

---

## 39

## THE PERFECTION OF DIVINE LOVE IN HEAVEN

*"When that which is perfect is come, that which is in part shall be done away."* —1 Corinthians 13:10

THE Angelic Doctor, St. Thomas, teaches us that the charity which Our Lord infuses into our souls in this life, by means of His Holy Spirit, is consummated and receives its plenitude in the life to come. "The path of the just," says the Holy Ghost, "as a shining light goeth forward, and increaseth even to perfect day." (*Prov.* 4:18). While we live in this miserable pilgrimage, encumbered with the burden of the flesh, we cannot see God but as it were through a glass, that is, through the veil of faith; and we can only love Him in proportion to our knowledge of Him. But we shall no sooner be released from this mortal body and admitted into the region of eternal glory than we shall see God without a veil, face-to-face, and at that sight we shall be filled with the plenitude of love, and forgetting ourselves, we shall put forth all our strength to magnify His infinite goodness. And our souls will be inflamed to the utmost by the fire of His holy and ineffable charity. Of this

St. Paul speaks when, writing to the faithful at Corinth, he says: "But when that which is perfect is come, that which is in part shall be done away. When I was a child, I spoke as a child, I understood as a child, I thought as a child; but when I became a man, I put away the things of a child." (*1 Cor.* 13:10). Upon these words St. Thomas writes: "The Apostle compares the charity of our present life to the age of childhood, which is weak and imperfect; and the charity of the future life to the age of manhood, which has attained to its perfection—to signify that our charity is imperfect, like an infant which is just beginning to live and that the charity of the blessed resembles manhood, which has reached its fullness and its consummation."

Although in this world we may be continually advancing in divine love and increasing the fire of charity in our hearts, yet we can never reach to the height of that love which belongs to the blessed in Heaven; for it is not possible that the divine sun, which upon this earth we behold only through the veil of faith, should inflame our will as it does that of the blessed, to whom it is manifested clearly and without a cloud; so that, if we may say that the love of those souls who are entirely consecrated to God is perfect, considering the weakness and frailty of this life, yet it must certainly still be considered as very imperfect and deficient in brightness and splendor when compared to that of the future life.

Thus, we behold the place then, where the perfect love of God reigns with sovereign power! This most sublime and happy kingdom, which is the masterwork of divine goodness, is not to be found here on earth, but in Heaven, where the charity of God dwells in all its fullness, continually enveloping the happy souls in flames of ardent love and transforming them into the likeness of God. "We shall be like Him, for we shall see Him as He is." (*1 John* 3:2).

But what must the Christian do to obtain possession of this kingdom of love? The way is plain. Provided a Christian love God in this life, he cannot fail to attain to the perfect consummation of His charity in the life to come. What indeed is the charity of the present life but the first germ and beginning of that which shall be completed in the next? Charity, as the Scripture informs us, signifies the union of the soul with God. "He that abideth in charity," says St. John, "abideth in God, and God in him." (*1 John* 4:16). "Now, this union," says St. Thomas, "begins in this life by grace and is perfected in the next by glory." And in another place the same holy Doctor expressly declares that eternal life commences in the Sacrament of Baptism, in which we receive the spirit of love, and is completed in glory.

Why, then, do we afflict ourselves about our future lot? Let us love the Lord with sincerity, and nothing can prevent our future blessedness. And what shall hinder our entrance into the joy of Our Lord, if we are careful in life and in death to preserve in ourselves the holy love of God? And what is future glory but a consummation of that love which we are acquiring while we live on the earth? Let us but be careful to die with the love of God in our hearts, and we need fear nothing, for that holy seed which we carry with us to eternal life cannot fail to receive its development and to produce its perfect fruit in our consummate love and perfect happiness.

---

## 40

## CHRISTIAN HOPE

*"Against hope he believed in hope."* —Romans 4:18

AMONG the praises given by the Saints to Abraham, St. Paul ranks this above all the rest, that he hoped against all hope. God had promised him to multiply his posterity like the stars of heaven and the sand of the sea; and notwithstanding his receiving the commandment to sacrifice to Him his only son, Abraham did not on that account lose hope; and he believed that while he obeyed the commandment which had been given him to sacrifice his son, God would not fail to keep His word. Great, assuredly, was his hope, for he saw nothing on which to base it except the word of God. Oh, how true and solid a foundation is that word, for it is infallible!

Abraham, therefore, went his way to accomplish the commandment of God with a simplicity beyond compare, for he took no more thought nor made any more reply than he did when God told him he must depart out of his country and from among his kindred. Journeying, then, three days and three nights with his son, without precisely knowing whither he went, his son, who was carrying the wood of the sacrifice, asked him where was the victim for the holocaust. Abraham said, "God will provide Himself a victim for a holocaust, my son." (*Gen.* 22:8).

Oh, how happy should we be if we could accustom ourselves to make this answer to our hearts when we are in anxiety about anything: "Our Lord will provide for it," and thenceforward to have no more care and trouble, after the example of Isaac, who held his peace after that, believing that the Lord would provide a victim, as his father had told him.

Great, assuredly, is the confidence which God requires us to have in His fatherly care and in His Divine providence, but wherefore should we not have it, seeing that no one can ever be deceived in it and that no one puts his trust in God who does not reap the fruits of his confidence?

Consider that Our Lord says to His Apostles, in order to settle in them this holy and loving confidence: "When I sent you without purse, and scrip, and shoes, did you want anything?" (*Luke* 22:35). But they said: Nothing. "Be not solicitous," He said to them, "saying, What shall we eat, or what shall we drink, or wherewith shall we be clothed?" (*Matt.* 6:31). "And when they shall bring you before magistrates and powers, be not solicitous how or what you shall answer, or what you shall say. For the Holy Ghost shall teach you in the same hour what you must say." (*Luke* 12:11-12).

He who takes care to provide for the nourishment of the birds of the air, which neither sow nor reap, will not fail to provide all that is necessary for those who confide fully in His providence and who are capable of being united to God, who is the Sovereign Good. (*Matt.* 6:26).

Let us then keep our eyes lifted up unto God and not allow any apprehensions to enter into our hearts. Each day will give us the knowledge of what we shall best do the next. We have ere now got over many a difficulty, and this was by the grace of God; the same grace will be present to us on all succeeding occasions and will deliver us from obstacles and difficult roads, one after the other; yes, though it were necessary for Him to send an angel to help us over the most dangerous steps.

---

# 41

## HOW WE MAY FULFILL THE PRECEPT OF DIVINE LOVE

*"In the fear of the Lord is confidence and strength."*
—Proverbs 14:26

AMONG men we sometimes meet with hard and unreasonable masters who lay heavy burdens on the shoulders of their servants without affording them the least assistance in bearing them. But very different is the conduct of our heavenly Master towards His servants. He is so gentle and tender that He never fails to lend His helping hand to assist us in fulfilling His commands, and Holy Scripture is full of facts which prove this. When He commanded Jacob to return toward his own country, He promised him His assistance, saying to him, "Fear not, I will give strength to thy steps." When He sent Moses to deliver the people of Israel from their hard servitude in Egypt, He said to him, "Fear not, I will give power to thy word." When Josua was charged to bring His people into the land of promise, He added, "Fear not, for I will give strength to thy arm." When He confided to His Apostles the most difficult and important office of preaching the Gospel throughout the world, of overthrowing the heathen temples, of destroying the sacrilegious altars and establishing the kingdom of the Cross upon the ruins of idolatry, He said to them, "Fear nothing, neither the persecutions of the wicked, nor the false wisdom of the philosophers, nor the armies of the emperors, nor any other danger, for I will be ever with you and will watch over you to the consummation of ages." This wonderful conduct of God in so uniting His grace to His commands, as to enable men to fulfill them, appears conspicuously in the extraordinary aid which He imparted to the first Christians, by which they obtained power to follow with perfection the evangelical precept of His love. That we may somewhat comprehend this truth, let us reflect that charity is the fulfilling of the law (*Rom.* 13:10), that she contains within her bosom all other virtues (*Col.* 3:14), that, in short, she constitutes the essence of Christianity and of all perfection.

Passing over in silence the supernatural lights with which the Lord vouchsafes to visit our souls, the sentiments of piety, the feelings of penitence, the holy inspirations which He so frequently causes to arise in our hearts—how shall we speak of the copious graces which we draw from those holy fountains which our blessed Saviour Jesus Christ has graciously opened for us in the bosom of His holy Church? I mean the Sacraments. Are they not so many perennial sources from which continually flow in plentiful streams the waters of eternal life? Woe to the Christian who, having within his reach such efficacious means of enkindling and increasing the fire of Divine love in his heart, refuses to profit by them, or, which is still worse, makes use of them for his eternal ruin. If the heathen philosophers were inexcusable for not adoring the true God according to the knowledge which they had of Him (*Rom.* 1:21), what will become of those Christians who, well aware of their obligation to give to Him their whole hearts and having within their reach the means of fulfilling this duty, have stifled the voice of conscience and violated their obligations? Oh, let him who has any wisdom provide for his own soul. Let the man who is given to the love of earthly things, and feels he has not strength to break his chain, approach and drink of the waters which flow from the fountains of the Saviour (*Is.* 12:3). "If any man thirst," says Jesus Christ, "let him come to Me and drink." (*John* 7:3). The water that I give is a spring of paradise, and whosoever drinketh of it will be so refreshed that the yoke of My law will appear sweet, and its burden light.

Let us then correspond to the Divine bounty, and

let us make good use of all the graces which the Lord imparts so lovingly to us. Let us unite ourselves to Christ and center in Him all our wishes and all our hopes. What would the world avail us without Jesus? To be without Jesus is a bitter hell, but it is a sweet paradise to be with Him.

O Lord, what is man that Thou shouldest be mindful of him, and the son of man that Thou visitest him? What merit has he that Thou shouldest give him Thy grace and draw him to Thy holy love? Let us listen to the voice of the Beloved and prepare our hearts, that He may deign to come to us and to remain with us. With Christ we shall be rich enough, for He will Himself faithfully provide and procure all things for us. Men easily change and fail us in our time of need, but Christ lives forever and remains immutable unto the end.

---

## 42

## ADVANCEMENT IN PERFECTION

*"You shall be holy, for I am holy."*—1 Peter 1:16

BE YE perfect, as your heavenly Father is perfect" (*Matt.* 5:48), says our blessed Saviour in that admirable sermon He preached to His disciples on the Mount. St. Cyprian, in his discourse on these words, says: "If men feel great pleasure in seeing their children resemble them, and if a father is never better pleased than when all his son's features are like his own, how much greater joy will our eternal Father feel when we are so happily regenerated in spirit, that, by all our actions and by our good behavior, we are known to be truly His children. What palm of justice and what crown of glory will it not be to you when God shall have no cause to say, 'I have brought up children and exalted them, but they have despised Me' " (*Is.* 1:2), but, on the contrary, that all your actions shall tend to the glory of your heavenly Father? For it is truly His glory to have children who resemble Him in such a manner that, by them, He may come to be honored, known and glorified.

But how is it possible for us to render ourselves like to our heavenly Father? St. Austin teaches us in these words: "Let us remember," says he, "that the more holy and the more perfect we are, the greater resemblance we shall have to our heavenly Father." And it is for this reason that our Saviour so earnestly desires our holiness and perfection and so often recommends it to us; sometimes He does so directly, as in St. Matthew, in the passage we have already quoted; at other times He tells us the same thing by the mouth of St. Paul, "This is the will of God, your sanctification" (*1 Thess.* 4:3); and also by the Prince of the Apostles, saying, "Ye shall be holy, because I am holy." (*1 Ptr.* 1:16). It is a very great comfort to parents to have wise and discreet children, which truth the Holy Ghost tells us by Solomon, who says, "A wise son maketh his father glad; but a foolish son is the sorrow of his mother." (*Prov.* 10:1). If then, by doing so, we attained no other end than to please Almighty God, whose pleasure, honor and glory should be the chief motive of all our actions, we ought continually to aspire to perfection. But that we may be still more forcibly urged to embrace it, I shall suggest several other means, which may help us in attaining it.

The reason why in Holy Scripture we are so often called the children of God by the mouth of the prophets, who very often repeat this saying, "I will be your Father, and ye shall be My children," and by St. Paul, who exhorts us to be "followers of God, as most dear children" (*Eph.* 5:1), and by St. John, when he tells us, "Behold what manner of charity the Father hath bestowed upon us, that we should be named, and should be the sons of God" (*1 John* 3:1), and also in many other places to the same purpose—the reason, I say, why this is repeated to us so often in Holy Scripture is, as St. Austin says, "To the end that, seeing and considering the dignity and excellence of our origin, we may conceive a greater esteem and higher value of what we are and take greater care not to do anything unworthy of our noble extraction. We use great care to preserve a rich suit of clothes and to see that it be not stained, and we look carefully to our jewels and other things of great value; so also, when Holy Scripture tells us of our dignity, when it reminds us that we are the sons of God and that God Himself is our Father, it is to the end that we should take great care to preserve our hearts pure and clean and that we behave ourselves in all our actions as becomes those who have the honor to bear the character of the sons of God." So also Pope St. Leo says: "Consider, O Christian, what thy dignity is, and seeing thou art made partaker of the divine nature, suffer not thyself to fall back into thy former baseness by attaching thyself too much to the things of this life. Reflect on that Head and body whereof thou hast the honor to be a member." St. Paul represented the same thing to the Athenians when he said that we are the "offspring of God" (*Acts* 17:28, 29), thereby wishing to inspire them with sentiments worthy of their noble extraction.

Let this therefore serve to augment in us daily a desire of acquiring the virtue still wanting in us, for "Blessed are they that hunger and thirst after justice" (*Matt.* 5:6), that is to say, as St. Jerome explains it, such as never think themselves perfect enough, but always labor to improve in virtue. Thus did the royal prophet, when he said to Almighty God, "Wash me yet more from my iniquity, and cleanse me from my sin" (*Ps.* 50:4); as if he would have said, "It is not enough, O Lord, that I should be washed; an ordinary washing and cleansing is not sufficient for me." "Thou shalt wash me, and I shall be made whiter than snow." (*Ps.* 50:9). Let us cry to Almighty God in the same manner: "Wash me, O Lord, still more and more." Give me more humility, patience and charity, more mortification and a more perfect and absolute resignation to Thy holy will in all things.

## 43

# THE PRESENCE OF GOD IS THE JOY OF THE BLESSED IN HEAVEN

*"When Thy glory shall appear, I shall be satisfied."*
—Psalm 16:15

LET US see what it will be in Heaven that will make those holy citizens completely happy. The soul in Heaven, when she sees God face-to-face and knows His infinite beauty and all His perfections which render Him worthy of infinite love, cannot but love Him with all her powers, and she loves Him far more than herself. She even, as it were, forgets herself and desires nothing but to behold Him satisfied and loved, who is her God. And seeing that God, who is the only object of all her affections, she enjoys an infinite delight; this joy of God constitutes all her Paradise. If she were capable of anything that is infinite, in seeing that her Beloved is infinitely content, her own joy thereupon would also be infinite; but since a creature is not capable of infinite joy, she rests satisfied at least with joy to such an extent that she desires nothing more. And this is that satisfaction which David sighed for when he said, "I shall be satisfied when Thy glory shall appear."

Thus also is fulfilled what God says to the soul when He admits her into Paradise: "Enter into the joy of Thy Lord." (*Matt.* 25:21). He does not bid His joy to enter into the soul because His joy, being infinite, cannot be contained in the creature; but He bids the soul enter into His joy, that she may receive a portion of it, and such a portion as shall satisfy her and fill her with delight.

Therefore, in meditation, among all acts of love towards God, there is none more perfect than that of taking delight in the infinite joy of God. This is certainly the continual exercise of the Blessed in Heaven, so that he who often rejoices in the joy of God begins in this life to do that which he hopes to do in Heaven through all eternity.

The love with which the Saints in Paradise burn towards God is such that, if ever a fear of losing it were to enter their thoughts or they were to think that they should not love Him with all their powers as now they love Him, this fear would cause them to experience the pains of Hell. But it is not so, for they are as sure, as they are sure of God, that they will ever love Him with all their powers and that they will be ever loved by God, and this mutual love will never change throughout eternity. O my God, make me worthy of this through the merits of Jesus Christ!

This happiness, which constitutes Paradise, will be further increased by the splendor of that delightful City of God, the beauty of its inhabitants, the Angels and Saints, especially by that of the Queen of all, Mary, who will appear fairer than all, and by that of Jesus Christ, whose beauty again will infinitely surpass that of Mary.

The joy of the blessed will be increased by looking back upon the dangers which they have passed through in this life. What will be the thanksgivings which they offer to God when they now find themselves there on high and sure of not losing God, being destined to enjoy eternally those boundless delights in Heaven of which they will never grow weary? In this life, however great and continual be our joys, with time they always weary us; but for the delights of Paradise, the more they are enjoyed the more they are desired. And thus the blessed are ever satisfied and filled with these delights and ever desire them; they ever desire them and ever obtain them. Wherefore, that sweet song with which the Saints praise God and thank Him for the happiness He has given them is called a new song: "Sing to the Lord a new song." (*Is.* 42:10). It is called "new" because the rejoicings of Heaven seem ever new, as though they were experienced for the first time, and thus they ever rejoice in them and ever ask for them; and as they ever ask for them, they ever obtain them.

Let us, then, give heed to suffer joyfully the crosses which God sends us because they all will become for us eternal joys. When infirmities, pains or any adversities afflict us, let us lift up our eyes to Heaven and say, "One day all these pains will have an end, and after them I shall enjoy God forever." Let us take courage to suffer; it is Jesus who awaits us and stands with the crown in His hands to make us kings in Heaven, if we be faithful to Him.

O my God and Redeemer, give me help to be faithful to Thee; Thy kingdom come; through the merits of Thy Blood grant me one day to enter into Thy Kingdom; and in the meantime, until death shall come, enable me perfectly to fulfill Thy will, which is the greatest good and is that paradise which is possessed upon earth by him who loves Thee.

Therefore, O ye souls who love God, while we yet live in this vale of tears, let us ever sigh for Paradise and say, "O fair country, wherein love bestows itself upon love, I sigh for thee hour by hour! When, O my God, when will it be here?"

---

## 44

## ADVANCEMENT IN HOLINESS

*"Not as though I had already attained."*
—Philippians 3:12

IT is a common maxim of all the Saints that not to advance in the way of God is to go back. Who is there that, after having travelled homeward several days, would feel inclined to go back, particularly when he calls to mind the sentence which the Saviour of the world pronounces against such a one: "No man, putting his hand to the plough and looking back, is fit for the kingdom of God"? (*Luke* 9:62). These are words which should make us tremble, and the great St. Austin says of them: "We cannot possibly prevent ourselves from descending but by always striving to ascend, for as soon as we begin to stop, we descend. Not to advance is to go back, so that if we wish not to go back, we must always run forward without stopping." St. Gregory, St. Chrysostom and St. Leo, as well as many other Saints, say the same and express themselves almost in the same words. But St. Bernard enlarges on this subject in two of his epistles, wherein, addressing himself to a negligent and tepid religious who contents himself with leading an ordinary life and struggles not for his advancement, he discourses with him in the following dialogue: Well! will you not advance? No? What then? Will you go back? By no means! What will you do, then? I will remain as I am and grow neither better nor worse. Then you will do what is impossible, for in this life there can be no state of permanence. This is a privilege appertaining to God alone, "with whom there is no change nor shadow of vicissitude." (*James* 1:17). "I am the Lord," says He, "I change not." (*Mal.* 3:6). But all things in this world are subject to a perpetual change. Jesus Christ Himself, as St. Bernard adds, as long as He lived here on earth and conversed with man, was never stationary: "He grew in wisdom, and age, and grace with God and men." (*Luke* 2:52). That is to say, as He grew in age, He gave more signal proofs of His wisdom and holiness and prepared Himself as a champion to run His race of labor and suffering. St. John also declares that "he that saith he abideth in Him, ought himself to walk even as He walked." (*1 John* 2:6). But if, while our Saviour runs on, you stop, is it not clear that you will remain behind Him, instead of approaching near Him? Holy Scripture (*Gen.* 28:12) tells us that Jacob saw a ladder reaching from earth to Heaven, on the top of which Almighty God leaned, and that it was full of Angels ascending and descending perpetually without ever resting. Now, according to St. Bernard, this is to show us that in the way of virtue, there is no medium between ascending and descending, between advancing and going back.

Cassian explains this by a very just comparison, which St. Gregory likewise makes use of: Those who lead a spiritual life, he says, are like a man in the midst of a rapid river: if he stops but for a moment and strives not continually to bear up against the stream, he will run great risk of being carried down. Now the course we ought to take is so directly opposite to the current of our nature, corrupted by sin, that unless we labor and force ourselves to go on, we shall certainly be hurried back by the impetuous torrent of our passions. "The kingdom of heaven suffereth violence, and the violent bear it away." (*Matt.* 11:12). And as, when you go against the tide, you must always row without ceasing, and when you stop but for awhile, you find yourself drifted far from the spot you had rowed to, so here below you must still push forward, and make head against the current of your depraved passions, unless you be content to see yourself quickly carried far back from that degree of perfection which you had before attained.

Another comparison is also made use of which suits the present purpose and strongly confirms what has been already said. As sailors on the ocean main dread nothing so much as a profound calm, because then they consume all their provisions and afterwards feel themselves in want of the necessaries of life, so by those who navigate the tempestuous sea of this world and steer towards Heaven, there is nothing more to be dreaded than an unhappy calm, which stops them in the midst of their course and prevents them from making sail. Because the small provision they had laid in for their voyage is soon consumed and the little virtue they had begins to fail them, and afterwards amidst the storms and temptations which assail them on all sides, they find themselves, even in their deepest distress, destitute of all help and in the greatest danger of perishing. Woe to such as are surprised by a calm so dangerous! "You did run well," says the Apostle; "who hath hindered you that you should not obey the truth?" (*Gal.* 5:7). You went at first in full sail; what calm or sand-bank has stopped you? Certainly "now you are satiated, you are become rich." (*1 Cor.* 4:8). You fancy you have done enough; finding yourself tired, you think yourself entitled to repose; you imagine that what you have acquired is sufficient. But reflect and consider well that you have still a great way to go. Remember that many occasions will still offer themselves wherein you will have need of more perfect humility, more courageous patience, more absolute detachment and more complete mortification, and perchance you will be surprised and found unprovided for in the time of your greatest need.

———————

# 45

## THE WISDOM OF THINKING ABOUT WHAT WE ARE DEFICIENT IN RATHER THAN OF WHAT WE HAVE ACQUIRED

*"Forgetting the things that are behind."*
—Philippians 3:13

ST. JEROME and Venerable Bede tell us that our Saviour, in saying, "Blessed are they that hunger and thirst after justice, for they shall be filled" (*Matt.* 5:6), wished to teach us that we must never think we are holy enough, but must always aspire to become still more so. To this effect St. Paul proposes to us an excellent means, which he himself made use of: "Brethren," said he, "I do not count myself to have apprehended. But one thing I do: forgetting the things that are behind, and stretching forth myself to those that are before, I press towards the mark, to the prize of the supernal vocation of God in Christ Jesus." (*Phil.* 3:13-14). If then the Apostle of the Gentiles, the vessel of election, does not believe himself perfect, who will dare think himself so? He believes not that he has attained perfection, but endeavors with all his power to acquire it, and for this purpose he forgets all he has done; he only looks at what he is deficient in, and it is to obtain this that he incites and encourages himself so strongly. All the Saints have very much extolled and earnestly recommended this means, as having been prescribed and practiced by the Apostle. Hence St. Basil and St. Jerome teach that whoever wishes to be a saint must forget what he has done and constantly think about what he has still to do and that he is truly happy who advances daily and who never thinks on what he did yesterday, but what he has to do today in order to make new progress.

Human weakness ordinarily fixes its eye on the good it has done. But St. Bernard says that there is extreme danger in this. For first, if you only look to the good works you have done, you will readily yield to vainglory, preferring yourself to others; and second, you will not endeavor to ascend, believing yourself already arrived at a high degree of perfection; on the contrary, you will begin to grow tepid, and from tepidity falling to negligence, you will quickly fall lower and lower. The example of the Pharisee in the Gospel shows us plainly what must befall those who act in this manner. He casts his eyes on the good works he had done and then enumerating them, he says, "I give Thee thanks, O God, that I am not as the rest of men, extortioners, unjust, adulterers, as also is this publican. I fast twice in the week; I give tithes of all that I possess. And the publican, standing afar off, would not so much as lift his eyes towards heaven; but struck his breast, saying, O God, be merciful to me a sinner. I say to you," says our Saviour, "this man went down to his house justified rather than the other." (*Luke* 18:11-14). Thus the one, by humbling himself, was justified; while the other, by his criminal presumption, drew upon himself the sentence of condemnation and death. This is the plan the devil has formed against us, in always placing before our eyes the good we have done; his design is to instill in us a high esteem of ourselves and a contempt of our neighbor, that by yielding to pride, we may bring on our own condemnation.

There is also the danger which St. Bernard says we fall into in looking only at our good works. We shall make no effort to advance in virtue; we shall grow cold in the things of Heaven, and at length, fancying that we have labored enough, we shall think only of resting ourselves. As travellers, when they begin to grow weary, look behind and consider how far they have travelled, so when those on the road of perfection begin to get tired, they look back upon the journey they have made, and, imagining they have advanced a great way, they content themselves, and through shameful sloth, stop halfway.

In order to avoid these evils, we must always think, not on what we have already done, but on what still remains to be done. The former tempts us to repose, the latter incites us to go on. This is the second means which the Apostle teaches us—to have our eyes fixed on what we are deficient in, that we may be encouraged to attain it.

St. Bernard says that we ought to imitate merchants who, though they have acquired considerable property and encountered much hardship and pain, yet so far from being content with their gain or discouraged by their losses, constantly endeavor to acquire additional property, as if hitherto they had neither done nor gained anything. In the same manner, says he, we ought constantly to endeavor to increase our store and to enrich ourselves in humility, charity, mortification and in all the other graces, and, in a word, like good merchants for Heaven, we ought to make no account of the labors we have already undergone, nor of the riches we have acquired. For this reason our blessed Saviour compares the Kingdom of Heaven to a merchant, and commands us "to trade till He comes." (*Luke* 19:13). Consider the ardor and application of a merchant in everything which can promote his gains: how he thinks of nothing else and how ardently he undertakes any affair wherein there is the least hope of success, whether he is at table, whether he lies down or gets up, whether he is asleep or awake; in short, wheresoever he is, or whatsoever he does, this care engages his thoughts and allows him no repose. In the same manner we must proceed in the great business of our salvation, having our mind and heart entirely engaged in it, and ever attentive to derive some spiritual profit from the least occasion that presents itself. This is the thought which should always accompany us, at table, at our going to bed and getting up, in all our actions and in all our exercises, at all times and in all places during our whole life. This is our only business. If we do this well, we need desire nothing besides, nor is it worth our while to trouble ourselves for a moment about anything else.

We read of St. Francis Xavier that he was ashamed and extremely troubled on seeing that merchants had arrived before him in Japan and that they had been more diligent to sail there to sell their merchandise than he had been to carry there the treasure of the Gospel, to propagate the Faith and to increase the Kingdom of God. Let us adopt the same sentiments and be filled with a holy confusion on seeing that "the children of this world are wiser" (*Luke* 16:8) and more careful in the concerns of this life than we are in the affairs of Heaven, and let this prevent us from remaining any longer in our sloth and tepidity.

———————

## 46

## THE CHRISTIAN'S AIM

*"I show you a more excellent way."*
—1 Corinthians 12:31

IT will conduce much to our spiritual advancement that we propose to ourselves as objects the highest things and such as are of the greatest perfection, according to the counsel of the Apostle: "Be zealous for the better gifts. And I yet show to you a more excellent way." This means is without doubt of great importance; for our desires must necessarily soar high if we wish to elevate our actions to that perfection with which even our indispensable duties should be performed. This may be easily explained by a familiar comparison: When your bow is too feebly bent, you will never be able to hit the mark unless you aim considerably higher; because the looseness of the string gives to the arrow a downward direction. It is precisely so with us. Our nature is so feeble and we are so relaxed by the evil habits we have contracted

that we must take our aim considerably higher than
the mark if we wish to reach it. Man is become so
weak by sin, that to attain an ordinary degree of
virtue, his thoughts and desires must soar much
higher. But some will say, "All I propose is to avoid
mortal sin; this is the only perfection I aspire to." It
is much to be feared that you will not reach this point
you propose to yourself, for the string of your bow
is slack. Perhaps you would have reached this point
had you directed your thoughts higher, but not having done so, it is probable you will never reach it,
but that you will fall into mortal sin.

St. Jerome, explaining these words of the
Psalmist—"Blessed is the man, O Lord, whose help
is from Thee; in his heart he hath disposed to ascend
by steps" (*Ps.* 83:6)—says, the just man's heart is
always towering aloft, and the sinner's heart is perpetually sinking. The just man has his eyes continually raised to the things most sublime in virtue; he
aspires to increase in perfection; it is this which he
has perpetually in his mind, according to the saying
of the Wise Man: "The thoughts of the industrious
always bring forth abundance." (*Prov.* 21:5). But no
thought is less present to the mind of the sinner than
this; he is content to live like the rest of the world;
at the utmost, he proposes to himself but an ordinary degree of virtue; he grows tepid, his spirits sink
and he attains not his object. This, says Gerson, is
the language used by many: "It is enough for me to
live as people in general live; I desire only to be
saved; the sovereign degree of perfection and glory
I leave to the Apostles and martyrs; I do not pre-

tend to soar so high, but I am content to walk upon the plain ground." Such is the language of sinners and imperfect men, who in number far exceed the just and perfect. "For many are called," says our Saviour, "but few are chosen." (*Matt.* 20:16). And "wide is the gate and broad is the way that leadeth to destruction, and many there are who enter by it. How narrow is the gate and strait is the way which leadeth to life, and few there are who find it." (*Matt.* 7:13). St. Austin, speaking of such as walk on the broad beaten way of a loose life, says that those are the men whom the prophet calls "beasts of the field" (*Ps.* 8:8) because they always range in a spacious place, and will not be confined by rule or discipline. And Gerson says that by this kind of language—"It is enough for me to live as others do; if I be but saved, it is sufficient. I aspire to no greater perfection"—a man readily manifests the imperfect and bad state of his own heart, since he is not willing to enter by the narrow gate. He adds, moreover, that persons who, through sloth and tepidity, think it sufficient to obtain the lowest seat in Heaven have great reason to fear that they will be condemned with the foolish virgins who fell asleep without having made any provision, or with the negligent servant who buried the talent he had received and took no pains to improve it. He was cast into exterior darkness, and yet we read not in the Gospel that he was condemned for anything else than for having neglected the talent his master had entrusted him with.

But to show still more clearly the shameful and deplorable state of these men, Gerson gives this example. Imagine to yourself, says he, the father of a family, rich and noble, having many children, all of whom are capable of advancing the interest and honour of the family by their good qualities. All apply with zeal to the performance of their respective duties except one, who, through sloth, leads a loose and shameful life, though, provided he did but apply himself, he is as well qualified as the rest for performing virtuous actions. Still he does nothing worthy of his birth and talents, but contents himself, as he says, with a small fortune; and since he has the wherewithal to live at ease, he will take no pains to increase his property, nor will he entertain any honorable ambition. His father calls upon him, exhorts and entreats him to adopt more noble sentiments, reminds him of his good qualities and noble birth, proposes to him the example of his ancestors and of the rest of his brothers. But when he sees that, notwithstanding all he does, he cannot prevail on him to rise out of his sloth and to lead an active life, he must needs conceive against him a very just indignation. It is the same with God. We all are His children and brothers of Jesus Christ. He would not have us content ourselves with an idle life, but exhorts us to perfection in these words, "Be you therefore perfect, as also your heavenly Father is perfect." (*Matt.* 5:48). Consider how holy and perfect He is; think on what your birth obliges you to and endeavor to show by your actions that you are the true children of such a Father; take example from your brothers also, and if you will, look upon your eldest brother, Jesus Christ, who most freely gave His

Blood and life to repair the losses of our race and to restore it to its former splendor. But if so great an example dazzles you, look upon your other brothers as weak as yourself, like you born in sin and subject to like passions, temptations and evil inclinations. They fought against them unremittingly; they conquered and gained the crown of glory; and our holy mother the Church sets before us their example and celebrates their feasts, in order to encourage us to imitate them.

---

## 47

## JESUS THE MEDIATOR

*"And therefore He is the Mediator of the New Testament, that by means of His death . . . they that are called may receive the promise of eternal inheritance."*
—Hebrews 9:15

ST. PAUL speaks of the New Testament, not as a covenant, but as a promise or testamentary disposition by which Jesus Christ left us heirs of the Kingdom of Heaven. And because a testament is not in force until the death of the testator, therefore it was necessary that Jesus Christ should die, that we might become His heirs and enter into the possession of Paradise. Wherefore, the Apostle adds, "For where there is a testament, the death of the testator must of necessity come in. For a testament is of force after men are dead; otherwise, it is as yet of no strength whilst the testator liveth." (*Heb.* 9:16).

Through the merits of Jesus Christ our Mediator, we have received grace that we might become the sons of God—unlike the Jews, who, under the old covenant, though they were the elect, were yet all servants. Whence, the Apostle writes that there are two covenants, of which one on Mount Sinai gendereth to bondage. (*Gal.* 4:24). The first mediation was made with God by Moses on Mount Sinai when God, through Moses, promised to the Jews the abundance of temporal blessings if they observed the laws which He gave them; but this mediation, says St. Paul, only produced servants, unlike the mediation of Jesus Christ, which produces sons: "We, brethren, like Isaac, are the children of promise." (*Gal.* 4:28). If, then, being Christians we are the sons of God, by consequence, says the Apostle, we are also heirs, for a portion of the father's inheritance is given to all sons, and this is the inheritance of eternal glory in Paradise, which Jesus Christ has merited for us by His death.

St. Paul nevertheless says that if we suffer with Him, we shall also be glorified with Him. (*Rom.* 8:17). It is true that, by our sonship to God which Jesus Christ has obtained for us by His death, we have acquired a right to Paradise, but this is on the supposition that we are faithful to correspond to the divine grace by our good works, and especially by holy patience. Therefore, the Apostle says that in order to obtain eternal glory, as Jesus Christ has obtained it, we must suffer upon earth as Jesus Christ suffered. He goes before as our Captain, with His Cross; under this standard we must follow Him, each bearing his own cross, as the same Lord admonishes us: "He that will come after Me, let him deny himself, and take up his cross, and follow Me." (*Matt.* 16:24).

St. Paul also exhorts us to suffer with courage, strengthened by the hope of Paradise, reminding us that the glory which will be given us in the next life will be infinitely greater than all our sufferings, if we suffer here with good will, in order to fulfill the divine pleasure: "I reckon that the sufferings of this present time are not worthy to be compared with the glory to come that shall be revealed in us." (*Rom.* 8:18). What beggar would be so foolish as not to give gladly all his rags for a great kingdom? We do not as yet enjoy this glory, because we are not yet saved, not having finished our life in the grace of God. But hope in the merits of Jesus Christ, says St. Paul, will save us: "We are saved by hope." (*Rom.* 8:24). He will not fail to give us every help to save ourselves, if we are faithful to Him and continue to pray, and the promise of Jesus Christ assures us that He hears everyone who prays: "Every one that asketh, receiveth." (*Matt.* 7:8). Some may say, "I fear, not that God will refuse to hear me if I pray to Him, but I fear for myself, that I should not know how to pray as I ought." No, says St. Paul, fear not this, for when we pray, God Himself aids our weakness and makes us pray so as to be heard: "The Spirit helpeth our infirmity, and asketh for us." (*Rom.* 8:26). He asks, explains St. Austin, i.e., He helps us to ask.

The Apostle would still further increase our confidence: he says, "We know that all things work together for good to those that love God." (*Rom.* 8:28). By this he teaches us that shame, sickness, poverty, persecutions, are not evils, as men of the world account them, for God turns them all into blessings and glory for those who suffer with patience. Finally, he says, "Those whom He foreknew, He also predestinated to be conformed to the image of His Son." (*Rom.* 8:29). With these words he would persuade us that, if we would be saved, we must resolve to suffer everything rather than lose the Divine grace, for no one can be admitted to the glory of the blessed, unless at the Day of Judgment his life be found conformed to the life of Jesus Christ.

And that because of these words, sinners may not abandon themselves to despair, on account of their guilt, St. Paul encourages them to hope for pardon, telling them that for this end the Eternal Father has not spared His own Son, who was offered to satisfy for our sins, but gave Him up to death, that He might pardon us sinners. And to increase still further the hope of penitent sinners, he says, "Who is he that shall condemn? Is it Jesus Christ who died?" (*Rom.* 8:34). This is as though he had said, "Sinners, you who detest your sins, why do you fear to be condemned to Hell? Tell me, who is your judge—who is to condemn you? Is it not Jesus Christ! How, then, can you fear that you will be condemned to death by this loving Redeemer, who that He might *not* condemn you, has been willing to condemn Himself to die as a malefactor upon the infamous gibbet of the cross!"

---

# 48

## THE JOYS OF HEAVEN

*"Eye hath not seen, nor ear heard, neither hath it
entered into the heart of man to conceive what things
God hath prepared for them that love Him."*
—1 Corinthians 2:9

LET US lift up our hearts and souls to the highest Heaven and enter into the glorious palace of the Divinity. Let us contemplate the great and resplendent company of Saints therein and consider the happiness which they enjoy.

Heaven is a place exempt from every evil and filled with an infinity of delights, where the souls and bodies of the Saints will enjoy unchanging rest. St. Paul says that "Eye hath not seen, nor ear heard, neither hath it entered into the heart of man, what God hath prepared for them that love Him." (*1 Cor.* 2:9). Have we seen all the splendors and magnificence of this earth? Have we imagined all that the human mind is capable of conceiving of their splendors? Still it is all nothing compared to Heaven. It is there that God reveals in splendor His power and magnificence. What cannot God do? Is there anything more admirable than this world? And after all, it is but the dim shadow of that celestial land, the distant outpost of that glorious palace!

Is not God more liberal in His rewards than in His chastisements? What is there more miserable than a lost soul? Contrast with its unavailing and unutterable woe the happiness of the Saints! They shall, says David, be inebriated with a torrent of delights; they shall be loaded with joy and contentment; they shall have all that they desire and nothing that they can fear. Their good shall be unmixed with evil, their pleasure unalloyed with grief; their abundance unsullied with poverty; their rest shall be without inquietude; their life without death, and their felicity without end. "Without end!" Happy, O Lord, are those who abide in Thy house; they will praise Thee in the highest Heaven forever and ever!

The object of our happiness shall be God, who is the essence of all beauty, of all goodness and of all pleasures. He will fill our souls with the plenitude of His light, our wills with the abundance of His peace, our memories with the extent of His eternity, our subsistence with the purity of His being and all our senses and powers with the immensity of His benefits and the infinitude of His riches. We shall see Him as He is. We shall love Him without defect. We shall behold Him, the Source of all beauty, and the sight will ravish our minds; we shall see Him, the Source of all goodness, and the contemplation thereof will satiate our souls with enjoyment.

How shall we enjoy God? By a peaceable possession, as of an inheritance which can never be disputed and by an intimate union with Him, without the fear of ever being separated from Him. In virtue of this union, we shall become like to God, says St. John, that is to say, pure, holy, wise and happy, as He Himself is. He will transform us into Himself, not by the destruction of our being, but by uniting it to His. He will communicate to us His own nature,

His greatness, His strength, knowledge, sanctity, riches and felicity. We shall exclaim, in the plenitude of our joy, "It is good for us to be here." (*Matt.* 17:4). Oh, who can describe the joy of a soul which, on entering into Heaven, discovers its Sovereign Good! What love! What ecstasy! What delight!

The body shall share in the felicity of the soul, which felicity consists of four things: *first,* the beauty and splendor of the place it is in, which is the house of God; *second,* the glorious company of the Saints, who all being united by an inviolable charity and exchange of love, enjoy their treasures, their delights and happiness in common; *third,* the gifts of glory with which the body shall be clothed, which are impassibility, brightness, agility and subtilty; *fourth* and finally, in the pleasures of the senses, which shall know a satisfaction that is pure and without alloy, disgust or fatigue. Behold what is prepared for us, provided we refuse the forbidden pleasures of this life.

But that which shall fill up the measure of our happiness is "that it will never end!" Eternity is a permanent duration, which has neither past nor future, but is always present. Thus the Saints enjoy each moment all the joys of eternity, though not all in full, for they each moment discover some new delight in the contemplation of God, some new beauty and additional cause for rejoicing. O holy Zion, where all remains and nothing passes away, where all is found and nothing is wanting, where all is sweet and nothing is bitter, where all is calm and nothing is agitated! Oh happy land, whose roses are

without thorns, pleasures are without griefs, whose
peace is without combats, and whose life is without
end! Oh holy Thabor! Oh palace of the living God!
Oh celestial Jerusalem! where we shall sing eternally
the beautiful canticles of Sion! Who can find difficulty in working out his salvation, knowing that this
will be the recompense of his labors? Who will refuse
to persevere in the conflict, seeing the glorious
crowns which are prepared for those who win?

"How lovely are Thy tabernacles, O Lord of
hosts! My soul longeth and fainteth for the courts of
the Lord!" (*Ps.* 33:1).

---

## 49

## DETACHMENT FROM CREATURES

*"Thou shalt love the Lord thy God
with thy whole heart."* —Mark 12:30

IN order to attain to loving God with all our heart,
we must separate it from everything which is not
of God—which does not tend towards God. He
chooses to be alone in the possession of our hearts,
and with reason, because He is our only Lord, the
One who has given us everything. Still further, He
is our only Lover, who has loved us, not for His own
interest, but solely from His goodness. And because
He thus exceedingly loves us, He desires that in
return we should love Him with all our hearts.

To love God with our whole heart implies two

things: The *first* is to drive from it every affection which is not for God, or not according to the will of God. "If I knew," said St. Francis de Sales, "that I had one fiber in my heart which did not belong to God, I would instantly tear it out." The *second* is prayer, by which holy love introduces itself into the heart. But if the heart does not fly from the earth, love cannot enter, for it finds no place for itself. On the other hand, a heart detached from creatures instantly becomes inflamed and increases in divine love at every breathing of grace.

"Pure love," said the same holy bishop, "consumes everything which is not God, in order to change it into itself, because everything which is done for God is the love of God." Oh how God is full of goodness and liberality to those souls who seek nothing but Him and His will! Happy is he who, living still in the world, can truthfully say with St. Francis, "My God and my all" and thus can hold in contempt all the vanities of the world! "I have despised the kingdom of the world and all the glory of this life for the love of Jesus Christ my Lord."

To attain to perfect love, we must deny ourselves, above all, embracing that which is distasteful to self-love and rejecting that which self-love demands. A certain medicine is disagreeable because it is bitter; we must take it for the very reason that it is bitter. It is unpleasant to us to do good to a certain person who has been ungrateful to us; we must by all means do him good, for the very reason that he has been ungrateful.

Further, St. Francis de Sales has said that we must

love even virtues with a detachment of heart; for example, we ought to love meditation and retirement, but when they are forbidden to us, through the calls of obedience or of charity, we must leave both the one and the other without being disquieted. And thus it is necessary to embrace with equanimity everything which happens to us through the will of God. Happy is he who wishes to have, or refuses to have whatever happens without inclining to either side, because God wishes it or refuses it. And therefore we must beseech the Lord to enable us to find peace in everything which He appoints for us.

---

## 50

## THE DEATH OF THE JUST

*"Precious in the sight of the Lord is the death of His saints."* —Psalm 115:15

WHY is the death of the Saints called precious? "Because," replies St. Bernard, "it is so rich in blessings, which deserve to be purchased at any cost."

Some persons, who are attached to this world, would wish that there was no such thing as death, but St. Augustine says, "What is it to live long upon this earth, except to suffer long?" "The miseries and difficulties which constantly weary us in this present life are so great," says St. Ambrose, "that death seems rather a relief than a punishment."

Death terrifies sinners because they know that from the first death, if they die in sin, they will pass to the second death, which is eternal. But it does not terrify those who, trusting in the merits of Jesus Christ, have sufficient signs to give them a moral assurance that they are in the grace of God. Wherefore, those words, "Depart, Christian soul, from this world," which are so terrible to those who die against their will, do not afflict the Saints, who preserve their hearts free from worldly love and with a true affection can continue repeating, "My God and my all!"

To these, death is not a torment, but a rest from the pains they have suffered in struggling with temptations and from their fear of offending God, so that what St. John writes of them is fulfilled: "Blessed are the dead who die in the Lord! Yea, saith the Spirit, that they may rest from their labors." (*Apoc.* 14:13). He who dies loving God is not disturbed by the pains which death brings with it, but rather, it is delightful to such persons to offer them to God as the last remains of their life. Oh what peace is experienced by him who dies when he has abandoned himself into the arms of Jesus Christ, who chose for Himself a death of bitterness and desolation, that He might obtain for us a death of sweetness and resignation!

What else is this present life but a state of perpetual peril? "We walk amidst snares," says St. Ambrose, amidst the deceits of enemies who seek to cause us to lose the divine grace. Therefore, St.

Teresa, every time that the clock struck, gave thanks to God that another hour of struggle and peril had passed without sin, and therefore she was so rejoiced at the tidings of her coming death, considering that her struggles were over and the time was near for her to depart and behold her God.

It was this same thought which, at the time of death, gladdened Father Vincent Carafa, when he said, "Now that I finish my life, I cease to displease God." A certain man gave directions to his attendants, that at the time of his death they should often repeat to him these words, "Comfort thyself, because the time is near when thou wilt no more offend God."

And what else is this body to us but a prison in which the soul is incarcerated, so that it cannot depart to unite itself with God? On this account, St. Francis, inflamed with love, at the hour of his death cried out with the prophet, "Take my soul out of prison!" O Lord, deliver me from this prison, which prevents me from seeing Thee! O death, worthy of love, who can fear thee and not desire thee, since thou art the end of all toils and the beginning of eternal life! We read too of St. Pionius the martyr who, standing by the instruments of death, showed himself so full of joy that the people who stood by wondered at his delight and asked him how he could be so happy when he was just about to die. "You are mistaken," said he, "you are mistaken; I am not hastening to death, but to life."

---

## 51

## TRUST IN JESUS CHRIST
## FOR SALVATION

*"Looking to Jesus, the author and finisher of faith."*
—Hebrews 12:2

**B**UT let us consider the confidence we ought to have in Jesus Christ for our salvation. St. Augustine encourages us, saying that this Lord, who has delivered us from death by shedding all His Blood, desires not that we should perish. And that if our sins separate us from God and make us worthy of being rejected, our Saviour, on the other hand, cannot reject the price of the Blood which He has shed for us. Let us, then, follow with boldness the counsel of St. Paul, who says, "Let us run by patience to the fight proposed to us, looking on Jesus, the author and finisher of faith, who, having joy set before him, endured the cross, despising the shame." He says "Let us run with patience the race before us" because it profits little to begin if we do not struggle to the end, while patience in enduring labor will obtain for us the victory and the crown that is promised to him who conquers.

This patience will be the armor which will defend us from the swords of our foes, but how shall we obtain it? "By looking," says the Apostle, "to Jesus, the Author and Finisher of the faith," who, says St. Augustine, despised all earthly goods that He might show that they are to be despised; who endured all earthly evils, which He taught us were to be endured, that in these we might neither seek happiness nor fear unhappiness. Then with His glorious resurrection He animated us not to fear death because, if we are faithful to Him even to death, after it we shall obtain eternal life, which is free from all evil and full of every good thing. This is signified by the Apostle's words, "Jesus, the Author and Finisher of faith," for Jesus Christ is the author of the Faith, in teaching us what to believe and giving us grace to believe it, and so also is He the Finisher of faith, by promising that we shall one day enjoy that blessed life which now He teaches us to believe in. And that we may be sure of the love which this Saviour bears to us and of the will He has that we should be saved, St. Paul adds, "Who for the joy set before Him, endured the Cross," on which words St. John Chrysostom remarks that Jesus might have saved us by leading a life of joy upon earth, but that to make us more certain of the love He bears to us, He chose a life of pain and a death of shame—dying as a malefactor upon a cross.

Let us, then, during the life that remains to us, give ourselves to our utmost power, to love this loving Redeemer, so worthy of love, and also to suffer for Him because He has been willing to suffer for love of us. And let us not cease to ask Him continually to grant us the gift of His holy love. Happy are we if we attain to a great love for Jesus Christ! The venerable Father Vincent Carafa, an eminent servant of God, in a letter which he wrote to some studious and devout young men, said as follows: "To reform ourselves in our whole life, we must give all our study to the exercise of the divine love. The love of God alone, when it enters a heart and obtains possession of it, purifies it from all inordinate love and makes it at once obedient and pure." St. Augustine says, a pure heart is a heart emptied of every desire; and St. Bernard, he that loves, loves and desires nothing more, meaning that he who loves God desires nothing but to love Him and banishes from his heart everything which is not of God. And thus it is that, from being empty, the heart becomes full, that is, full of God, who brings with Himself every good thing; and then earthly blessings, finding no place in such a heart, have no power to move it. What power can earthly pleasures have over us if we enjoy divine consolations? What power is there in ambition for vain honors and the desire of earthly riches if we have the honor of being loved by God and begin to possess in part the richness of Paradise? To measure, therefore, the advance we have made in the ways of God, let us observe what advance we have made in loving Him—whether we often during the day make acts of love towards God, often speak of the love of God, whether we take pains to produce it in others, whether we perform our devotions solely to please God, whether we suffer with full resignation all adversities, infirmities, pains, poverty, slights and persecutions in order to please God. The Saints say that a soul that truly loves God ought not to breathe more than to love since the life of the soul, both in time and eternity, consists in the love of our Sovereign Good, which is God.

But let us be sure that we shall never attain to a

great love for God except through Jesus Christ and unless we have a special devotion to His Passion, by which He procured the divine grace for us. The Apostle writes, "Through Him we have access to the Father." (*Eph.* 2:18). The way to ask for grace would be closed to us sinners, were it not for Jesus Christ; He opens the gate to Heaven. He introduces us to the Father, and by the merits of His Passion, He obtains for us from the Father pardon for our sins, and all the graces we receive from God. Miserable we should be if we did not possess Jesus Christ. And who can ever sufficiently praise and thank the love and goodness which this merciful Redeemer has shown to us poor sinners in being willing to die to deliver us from eternal death? The Apostle says, "Scarcely, for a just man will one die; yet perhaps for a good man some one would dare to die. But . . . when as yet we were sinners . . . Christ died for us." (*Rom.* 5:7-9).

---

# 52

## DESIRE FOR SPIRITUAL THINGS

*"They that eat Me shall yet hunger, and they that drink Me shall yet thirst."* —Ecclesiasticus 24:29

ST. GREGORY tells us that there is this difference between the pleasures of the body and the pleasures of the soul, that we desire the former with great impatience when we have them not, and when we have possessed them, we set but little value on them. For example, in the world every man, according to his birth, quality and profession, desires some civil, military or ecclesiastical dignity. Hardly, however, has he attained the object of his desire when he begins to disregard it and to fix his eyes on something else, of which, when obtained, he is, in like manner, as soon wearied. In short, unable to regulate his ambition or to set bounds upon his desires, he still aspires after something new and never rests satisfied with what he has. But it is not so in spiritual things. For while we do not have them, we feel disrelish and aversion for them; but when we come to possess them, then we know better their value. And the more we taste them, the more ardently we seek after them. The reason for the difference, says this great Saint, is that the enjoyment of temporal goods and pleasures teaches us their vanity and imperfection, so that not finding in them the satisfaction we hoped for, we lose attraction for what we possess; and expecting to find in something else the content we seek after, we allow ourselves to be motivated by new desires. But we deceive ourselves: these last desires will yield the same result as the others because we are not born for this world, and so there is nothing in it which can fully satisfy us. This is what our Saviour taught the Samaritan woman when He told her, "Whoever drinketh of this water shall thirst again" (*John* 4:13), because all the "water" of the pleasures and enjoyments of this life can never quench the thirst of man, who is created for Heaven.

But as to spiritual riches and pleasures, we never love or desire them so much as when we possess

them, because then we best know their value, and
the more perfectly we possess them, the more ardent
is our thirst after them. It is not to be wondered at,
says the same St. Gregory, that we do not desire spiritual things when, so far from having experienced
how sweet they are, we have not even begun to taste
them. "For how can one love that of which he is
ignorant?" The Apostle St. Peter also says, "If so
be, you have tasted that the Lord is sweet" (*1 Peter*
2:3), and the Royal Prophet, "O taste and see that
the Lord is sweet" (*Ps.* 33:9), for when once we begin
to taste the Lord and to relish spiritual things, we
shall find such sweetness in them as to render our
desires for them insatiable. By these words, then,
"They that eat Me shall yet hunger, and they that
drink Me shall yet thirst," we must understand that
the more assiduously we apply ourselves to heavenly
things, the more frequently and fervently shall we
feel the desire to possess them.

But you will ask me, how can this accord with
what our Saviour says to the Samaritan woman, "He
that shall drink of the water that I shall give him
shall not thirst for ever"? (*John* 4:13). Here the Son
of God says that we shall never thirst if we drink
of the water He shall give, and the Holy Ghost, by
the mouth of the Wise Man, says that the more we
drink the more we shall thirst. How shall we reconcile such different assertions, one with the other?
The holy Fathers reply that by the words of Jesus
Christ to the Samaritan woman we are to understand that whoever drinks of the living water therein
described "shall never thirst after earthly pleasures"

because the sweetness of spiritual things will give him an absolute disrelish for things of the world and will render them quite unsatisfying. But as to the words of the Wise Man, we must consider them to relate to spiritual things, and we must understand that the more we taste of them, the more we shall feel our hunger and thirst for them to increase.

But again, how can this accord with what our Saviour says in the Gospel, "Blessed are they that hunger and thirst after justice, for they shall be filled"? (*Matt.* 5:6). Here He says that He will fill those who shall hunger and thirst after justice, and there the Wise Man assures us that such as shall eat and drink of wisdom shall always find the same hunger and thirst as before. How is it possible to reconcile assertions so different? It is very easy. It is the privilege and the excellence of spiritual things to satisfy and at the same time to excite our appetite; to quench and still to excite our thirst; and in a word, to cause that the more we eat and drink of them, the more we hunger and thirst after them. But then, it is a hunger which, instead of making us faint and weak, renders us strong and hearty; and it is a thirst which, instead of pain, imparts great pleasure to us. It is true that it is only in Heaven that we shall be perfectly satisfied, according to these words, "I shall be satisfied when Thy glory shall appear" (*Ps.* 16:15), and those others, "They shall be inebriated with the plenty of Thy house." (*Ps.* 35:9). However, the above words of the Wise Man must be understood according to the interpretation of St. Bernard, who says, we shall never be in such manner satisfied with the

sight of God as to be without a thirst and a longing desire because, instead of giving us weariness, it
will excite in us perpetually a new desire of seeing
and enjoying Him. It is exactly the same with spiritual things here below, for being an emanation from
those above, they in consequence participate in their
qualities and virtue. On the one hand, they satisfy
and fill our hearts, and on the other, they excite in
us hunger and thirst. The more we devote ourselves
to them, the more we relish them; and the more we
enjoy them, the more we continually hunger and
thirst after them. But then, this very hunger will be
a kind of satiety, and this thirst a most sweet and
agreeable refreshment to the soul. All this ought to
excite in us a high idea of spiritual things; it ought
to make us set a great value on them and devote
ourselves to them with such zeal and fervor that,
regardless of and scorning all the allurements and
vanities of this world, we may say with the Prince
of the Apostles, "Lord, it is good for us to be here."
(*Matt.* 17:4).

## 53

## ON DOING WELL OUR
## ORDINARY ACTIONS

*"Whatsoever ye do, do it from the heart
as to the Lord."* —Colossians 3:23

"FOLLOW justly that which is just" (*Deut.* 16:20),
says Our Lord in Deuteronomy to His elect people. It is not sufficient for our advancement and perfection that we simply perform our actions; we must
likewise perform them well. "He hath done all things
well" (*Mark* 7:37), said the people, speaking of Jesus
Christ, and it is truly in this "well" that all our good
consists.

It is certain that the good or bad state of our souls
depends upon our good or bad works because such
as our works are, such also shall we be, since they
alone show what we are. "Man," says St. Austin, "is
a tree, and his works the fruit; and therefore, by the
fruit of his works we may soon perceive what every
man is." Our Saviour, also, speaking of hypocrites
and false prophets, says, "By their fruits you shall
know them" (*Matt.* 7:6), and speaking of Himself,
on the other hand, "The works that I do in the name
of My Father, they give testimony of Me; and
though you will not believe Me, believe the works."
(*John* 10:25, 38). But our actions discover not only
what we are in this life, but also foretell what we
must be in the next, for as we are in this life, such
shall we forever be in the life to come because God,

will recompense every one according to his works, as Holy Scripture teaches us. "Thou, O Lord," says the Psalmist, "wilt render to every man according to his works" (*Ps.* 61:13), and St. Paul, "What things a man shall sow [in this life], those also shall he reap [in the next]." (*Gal.* 6:8).

But let us descend to particulars and see what those actions are upon which all our goodness and our advancement in perfection depend. I say they are none other than the ordinary actions we perform every day. It is in acquitting ourselves well of our charge and of all that obedience imposes upon us—in short, in performing well the most common and familiar actions of our life—that our advancement and perfection consist. We shall become perfect if we perform these perfectly; we shall be imperfect if we perform them imperfectly. And this is all that properly makes the difference between a perfect and an imperfect Christian. For perfection arises not from our doing more things than another does, but from our doing them better; and in proportion to the manner in which a man does these works, will he become more or less perfect.

The Son of God tells us in the Parable of the Sower, "That the grain which was sown on good ground, in one place rendered a hundred, in another sixty, and in another thirty-fold." (*Matt.* 8:8). By this, as the Saints expound it, our Saviour would manifest to us the three different degrees of those that serve God: that is to say, those that begin, those that have made some progress and those that have arrived at the height of perfection. We all sow the same grain, because we all perform nearly the same duties. Yet what a difference there is between one man and another. In some, the works they sow produce a hundredfold because they perform them with an extreme fervor of spirit and a very great purity of intention, and these are such as are perfect. In others they render sixty, and these are they who are still advancing in the way but have not yet arrived at perfection. And others reap but thirty, and these are only beginners in God's service. Let every one, therefore, see to which of these degrees he has arrived; see if you be not amongst those who render only thirtyfold; and God grant that none of us find ourselves of the number of them of whom the Apostle St. Paul makes mention, who have built upon the foundation of faith, with "wood, hay" and "stubble"; to be burned in the day of Our Lord. (*1 Cor.* 3:12). Take care that you do nothing out of ostentation or human respect, to please men or to gain their esteem, for this were to make a building of wood or straw, to burn, at least in Purgatory. But endeavor to perform all your actions with the greatest perfection you are able, whereby you will, as St. Paul says, erect a structure of "gold, silver" and "precious stones." (*1 Cor.* 3:12).

It is related in the Chronicles of the Cistercian Order that St. Bernard, being with his religious at Matins, saw a great many Angels, who noted and wrote down the actions of each one and the manner in which they performed them, and according to the greater or less attention shown in their singing and praying, they noted the actions in letters of gold or silver, or else with ink or water. But they wrote nothing at all of some, who being present only in body but absent in spirit, let themselves be carried away with vain and unprofitable thoughts. He perceived also that the Angels, chiefly at the *Te Deum*, were very desirous that the religious should sing it devoutly, and he saw, as it were, flames issuing from the mouths of those who performed it with fervor. Let each one, then, reflect upon himself and take notice of the manner in which he makes his prayer, to see whether it deserves to be written in gold or silver letters, or with ink or water—or lastly, to see whether it deserves to be noted at all. Let him observe whether flames issue from his heart and mouth, or whether he yawns through laziness and disgust; and let him reflect whether he be there present in body only, having his mind dissipated or occupied with thoughts of study or business, or with other things still more to be condemned.

---

# 54

## THE PERFECTION OF OUR ACTIONS

*"The Lord beholdeth the heart."* —1 Kings 16:7

LET us consider in what the goodness of our actions consists, that thereby we may better know the means of performing them well. It consists in two things, of which the first and chief is that we act strictly for God. St. Ambrose asks the reason why God, in the creation of the world after He had created the living creatures and all other corporal things, praised them at the same instant. "He created the plants and trees, and He saw that it was good. He created the beasts upon the earth, the birds also, and fishes; and He saw that it was good. He created the heavens and stars, the sun and moon; and He saw that it was good" (*Gen.* 1:10, 12 ff.); in fine, He praised everything He created as soon as He had effected its creation. But as soon as He had created man, He seems to leave him the only one without praise because He did not presently add, "He saw that he was good," as He had said of the rest. What mystery is there in this? What can be the cause of this difference? The cause, says the Saint, is this: "That the beauty and goodness of beasts and corporal things consist entirely in their external appearance, and that there is nothing but what appears externally to the eye that is perfect in them, and therefore they may be praised as soon as they are seen. But the goodness and perfection of man consist not in the exterior, but in what lies inwardly hid: 'all the glory of the king's daughter is within' "(*Ps.* 44:14). It is this which is pleasing in God's sight. "For man sees only those things that appear, but the Lord beholdeth the heart." (*1 Kings* 16:7). He sees with what intention every one performs each action, and it is upon this account that He did not praise man, as He did all other creatures, as soon as He had created him. The intention is the foundation of the goodness of all our actions; the foundations of a building are not seen, and yet they alone sustain the whole edifice; our intention also does the same.

But it is not enough that our intention be good, nor to say that we do this for God. But the better to please Him, we must strive to perform it after the best manner possible. For though our superiors do not behold us and though men cannot see everything we do, yet the desire we have to please God will oblige us to perform our actions with all the perfection we are able to and to imitate those who truly labor for God. St. Ignatius once asked a brother whom he saw perform his office very negligently, "Dear brother, for whom do you do that?" "For the love of God," answered the brother. "Then I assure you," replied the Saint, "if you do so hereafter, I shall give you a severe penance, for if you did it for men, it were no great fault to do it with so little care as you do, but since you do it for so great a Master with so great carelessness, it cannot be excused."

The second means which the Saints propose as most efficacious is always to walk in God's presence. Seneca himself says that, "When we desire to be virtuous and to do all things well, we ought to imagine ourselves in the presence of some person of great merit and quality and accustom ourselves to say and do all things as we should do or say them were we actually in his presence." And if this may be sufficient to oblige us to perform our duty exactly, of what efficacy will it be to place ourselves always in God's presence and to think every moment that He sees us, especially since this is not a mere imagination, but a real truth, as the Scripture teaches us in divers places: "The eyes of the Lord are brighter than the sun, beholding round about all the ways of men and the bottom of the deep, and looking into the hearts of men, into the most hidden parts." (*Ecclus.* 23:28).

In another place, we shall treat expressly of the presence of God, where we shall show how profitable a thing it is and how much recommended by the Saints to place ourselves always in God's presence. What we ought to infer from this subject at present is to consider how much it will help us to perform our ordinary actions well. And though it is of so great importance, as we shall prove in its proper place, yet in our continually reflecting on it, we ought not to make the presence of God our principal object, but we ought to look on it as only a very proper means or help to perform our actions well. But should it happen that the attention we pay to the presence of God causes us to perform our actions negligently, and thereby makes us commit several faults, this would not be a good or true devotion, but an illusion. Some even add that the true presence of God, which we ought always to have before our eyes and which the Scripture and the Saints recommend to us, is to take great care in consequence that we do all our actions so that they may be fit to appear in His divine presence. In a word, we ought to perform them as if we performed them in His holy sight. St. John seems to remind us of this in the *Apocalypse* when, speaking of the four beasts he saw before the throne of God, he says, "That round about and within they are full of eyes" (*Apoc.* 4:8), to signify that those who would perfectly serve God and be worthy of His presence ought to be very careful to do nothing whereby they may render themselves unworthy to appear before Him. You ought to be full of eyes, within and without, in order to take care of all your actions, of your steps, your looks, your words; of what you hear, of what you think; of what you desire and what you love; to the end that, in all your thoughts, words and actions, there may be nothing disagreeable in the sight of God, in whose presence you are.

---

## 55

## THE SERVICE OF GOD

*"Thou shalt call Me, and I will answer thee."*
—Job 14:15

A POWERFUL means which the Saints recommend to us in order to serve God well is to do each action as if it were to be the last we are to perform in this life. St. Bernard, speaking of the manner in which a religious ought to comport himself, says that "In all his actions, he should often repeat to himself: Were you to die presently, would you do this?" And St. Basil gives us the same counsel when he says, "Have always your last hour before your eyes. When you rise in the morning, doubt whether you shall live till night; and when you go to bed at night, do not assure yourself that you shall live till next morning. And in this manner it will be easy for you to correct all your vices." If we could put ourselves into this disposition of mind and perform everything as if we were to die as soon as we had done it, we should perform our actions in a far different manner and with a far greater perfection than we do.

St. Francis of Borgia said that the best exercise for a religious would be to place himself twenty-four times a day in the situation of a dying man, and often to repeat to himself, "I must die this day." In this case, if he felt nothing to trouble him, his soul would doubtless be in a good state. Let everyone enter into himself, then, and examine himself frequently on this point, and if when you make this reflection you are not in the state you would wish to be in were you to die, endeavor to put yourself into it and prepare yourself well for this passage. Imagine that you ask from God some few days more to prepare yourself for it and that He grants them you, and endeavor to make good use of the respite He gives you by living during this time as if you were to die the moment after. Happy is he who is such during his life as he desires to be at the hour of his death!

"He who has promised pardon," says St. Gregory, "to those who repent, has not promised a next day for repentance to those who sin." We ordinarily say that there is nothing more certain than death, and nothing more uncertain than the hour in which it will happen. But the Saviour of the world says yet more than this: "Be ready," says He, "for at that hour you think not, the Son of man will come." (*Luke* 12:4). For though He speaks in this place of the day of General Judgment, yet this may be understood also of the hour of death, because then each one shall receive his Particular Judgment, and such sentence— as being once pronounced—will never be revoked, but confirmed on that Great Day. Jesus Christ does not content Himself with saying that the hour is uncertain, but He says that it will come at an hour when we shall least expect it, and perhaps when we are least of all prepared for it. St. Paul tells the Thessalonians that the day of the Lord "shall come like a thief in the night" (*1 Thess.* 5:2), and St. John, in the *Apocalypse,* speaking in God's name, says, "I will come to thee as a thief, and thou shalt not know at what hour." (*Apoc.* 3:3). A thief gives no notice when he will come, but awaits the hour when we are least upon our guard and when the world is buried in sleep, and this comparison made use of by the Son of God is an instruction to teach us how we ought to prepare ourselves, that death may not surprise us. "This know ye," says He, "that if the householder did know at what hour the thief would come, he would surely watch, and would not suffer his house to be broken open." (*Luke* 12:39). But because he cannot foresee the hour—whether it will be in the beginning, or towards the middle, or in the end of the night—he continually stands upon his guard. It is thus that we ought to be ready at all times and in all places whatsoever, since death will probably attack us when we least think of it.

The Saints hereupon observe that it is a very great mercy of God that the hour of death should be uncertain, to the end that we should always be prepared for it, for if we knew its time, this assurance would give us occasion to relax and to sin with greater confidence. If, uncertain as we are of the hour of death, we live notwithstanding so greatly negligent, what would we do if we were assured we should not die for some time! St. Bonaventure says that God has decided to leave us in this uncertainty that we might set no value on temporal things, that seeing at every hour, nay, at every moment, we may lose them, we might not in any way be attached to them, but aspire to those we shall always possess when we shall once have gained them. "Thou fool," says the Son of God to the rich, covetous man, "this night do they require thy soul of thee: and whose shall those things be which thou hast provided?" (*Luke* 12:20).

---

# 56

## MOTIVES FOR SERVING GOD

*"With a good will, serving as to the Lord."*
—Ephesians 6:7

THERE are several ways of seeking and serving God. To serve Him through fear of punishment is to seek Him and to do a good action because fear, though servile, ceases not to be good and to be a gift of God; and therefore the Royal Prophet begged it of God when he said, "Pierce Thou my flesh with Thy fear." (*Ps.* 118:120). But if we should truly say to ourselves and had the same sentiments in our hearts, "If there were no Hell and I were not afraid of being punished, I would offend God," then theologians hold that such an act as this would be a new sin, because this is actually to have our very will ill-disposed. However, to avail ourselves of the fear of punishment—with the apprehension of death and the fear of God's judgments—in order to excite ourselves the better to serve God and to abstain from offending Him cannot but be laudable, because it is upon this account that Holy Scripture frequently recommends this very thing to us and holds out such terrible menaces.

It is moreover because we seek God, if we serve Him for the reward that we hope for in glory, and it is also because we seek Him after a more perfect manner than from fear, because there is more perfection in doing our actions with a view to recompense than through fear. Moses acted after this manner, as St. Paul teaches us, when he says "Moses . . . rather choosing to be afflicted with the people of God, than to have the pleasure of sin for a time, esteeming the reproach of Christ greater riches than the treasures of the Egyptians, he looked unto the reward." (*Heb.* 11:25, 26). It is also upon the same account and with the same intention that the Psalmist said, "I have inclined my heart to do Thy justifications for ever, for the reward" I have hoped for. (*Ps.* 118:112).

The two motives of fear and hope, therefore, are good, and we may avail ourselves of them in order to excite ourselves to do good and avoid evil. But St. Ignatius will have us go still further and desires that we should elevate our hearts yet more and entertain still higher thoughts: "I will show you a more excellent way." (*1 Cor.* 12:31). He is not content that we should seek and serve God in an ordinary manner, but he teaches us a more perfect way: he will have us seek Him and serve Him purely for Himself, on account of His infinite goodness and because He is God, and in this is comprised all we can imagine to be excellent, great and sublime.

There is a great difference between the service of a slave or of a hireling and that of a son. The slave serves his master only through fear of punishment; the hireling through hope of recompense, and if he be careful to serve well, it is because he believes that by this means he shall be more amply rewarded. But the son acts after a different manner: it is out of pure love that he serves his father, and when he takes great care to do nothing that may displease him, it is not that he fears any punishment nor that he hopes for any reward, but it is because love naturally gives him this tenderness of affection and attention. And thus though his father be poor and able to leave him nothing, yet he serves and honors him nevertheless, because the relationship of father obliges him to do so; and if his father only be pleased, he believes himself rewarded for all his pains and services. We ought to serve God after the same manner, not as slaves, through fear of punishment, nor as hirelings, who regard nothing but gain, but as the true children of God, since He has done us the favor to raise us to that dignity. "Behold what manner of charity the Father hath bestowed upon us," says St. John, "that we should be the sons of God." (*1 John* 3:1). Since therefore we are truly such and since it is not without reason that we call God our Father and Jesus Christ our Brother, let us love and serve Him as it becomes true children; let us honor and respect Him as our Father, and as a Father completely worthy of and deserving our obedience and respect. Let it be only for His love that we act; let it be purely to please Him and because He deserves it by being what He is and because His infinite goodness deserves still a thousand times more than we can do, though we had a thousand hearts and a thousand lives to devote to His love and service.

---

# 57

## SALVATION THROUGH THE MERITS OF JESUS CHRIST

*"Christ suffered for us, . . . bearing our sins in His own body upon the tree."* —1 Peter 2:21-24

THE first object of our hopes is attaining eternal blessedness, that is, the blessedness of God: the "fruition of God," as St. Thomas teaches. And all the *means* which are necessary for obtaining this salvation, which consists in the enjoyment of God—such as the pardon of our sins, final perseverance in divine grace and a good death—we must hope for, not from our own strength, nor our good resolutions, but solely from the merits and grace of Jesus Christ. That our confidence, therefore, may be firm, let us believe with infallible certainty that we must look for the accomplishment of all these means of salvation only from the merits of Jesus Christ.

And first, in speaking of the pardon of sins, we must remember that, for this very end, our Redeemer came upon earth, that He might pardon sinners: "The Son of man came to save that which was lost." Therefore the Baptist, when he showed to the Jews that their Messias was already born, said, "Behold the Lamb of God, behold him who taketh away the sin of the world." (*John* 1:29). As it was foretold by Isaias, "As a sheep before her shearers, He shall be dumb." (*Is.* 53:7). He was first foreshadowed in the paschal lamb ordered by Moses to be sacrificed just before the exodus from Egypt, and then by the sacrifice of a lamb to God under the Old Law every morning and by other evening sacrifices. All these lambs, however, could not take away a single sin; they served only to represent the sacrifice of the Divine Lamb, Jesus Christ, who with His Blood would wash our souls and thus free them both from the stain of sin and from the eternal punishment of sin, for this is implied by the words *"take away,"* taking upon Himself the duty of satisfying the divine justice for us by His death, according to what Isaias wrote: "The Lord hath laid upon Him the iniquity of us all." Wherefore, St. Cyril writes, "One is slain for all, and the whole human race is restored to God the Father." By dying, Jesus desired to regain for God all mankind who were lost. Oh how great is the debt we owe to Jesus Christ! If a criminal condemned to death were already standing at the gibbet with the rope around his neck and a friend were to come and take the rope and bind it round himself and die in place of the guilty man, how great would be his obligation to love such a friend! This is what Jesus Christ has done; He has been willing to die on the Cross to deliver us from eternal death.

St. Peter says that Jesus "bore our sins in His Body on the tree, that, being dead to sin, we might live to justice; by whose stripes we were healed." (*1 Ptr.* 2:24). "What can be more wonderful," cries St. Bonaventure, "than that wounds should heal and death give life?" St. Paul says that God "has graced us in His beloved Son, in whom we have redemption through His Blood, the remission of sins, according to the riches of His grace, which have superabounded in us." (*Eph.* 1:7). And this resulted from the covenant made by Jesus Christ with His divine Father, that He would pardon us our offenses and receive us into His favor for the sake of the Passion and death of His Son.

And in this sense, the Apostle called Jesus Christ the Mediator of the New Testament. (*Heb.* 9:15). In the Holy Scriptures the word "Testament" has two senses: that of a "covenant," or an agreement between two parties who formerly disagreed; and that of a "promise," or disposition by will, by which the testator leaves an inheritance to his heirs, which testament is not valid until the testator's death. We have formerly spoken of the Testament as a "promise"; we now speak of it as a "covenant," in the sense in which the Apostle uses it when he calls Jesus Christ the Mediator of the New Testament. Man, by reason of his sin, was a debtor to the divine justice and an enemy of God; the Son of God came on earth and took man's flesh, and thus being God and man, He became a mediator between God and man, acting on behalf of both. And in order that He might bring about peace between them and obtain for man the divine grace, He offered Himself to pay with His blood and His death the debt due by man. This was the reconciliation prefigured in the Old Testament by all the sacrifices of animals and by the symbols ordained by God, such as the tabernacle, the altar, the veil, the candlestick, the censer and the ark of the Covenant (wherein were contained the rod of Aaron and the Tables of the Law). All these things were signs and figures of the promised Redemption, and because this Redemption was to be accomplished by the Blood of Jesus Christ, therefore God appointed that all the sacrifices should be offered with the pouring forth of the blood of animals (which was a figure of the Blood of the Lamb of God), while all the instruments above named were sprinkled with their blood. (*Heb.* 9).

# 58

# REMISSION THROUGH THE BLOOD OF CHRIST

*"This is My blood of the new covenant, which shall be poured forth for many for the remission of sins."*
—Matthew 26:28

S T. PAUL says in the Epistle to the Hebrews that the first testament, that is, the first alliance, covenant or mediation, which was accomplished by the Old Law and which prefigured the mediation of Jesus Christ under the New Law, was celebrated with the blood of goats and calves, and that with this blood were sprinkled the book, the people, the tabernacle and all the sacred vessels: "When the commandment of the law of Moses was read to all the people, the priest taking the blood of calves and goats, with water and with scarlet wool" (the scarlet wool signified Jesus Christ, for as wool is by nature white and becomes red by being dyed, thus Jesus, who was white by nature and innoccent, appeared on the Cross all red with Blood, being condemned as a malefactor, and thus fulfilled in Himself the words of the spouse in the Canticles, "My beloved is white and ruddy" [*Cant.* 5:6], "and with hyssop" (a lowly herb, which expressed the humility of Jesus Christ) sprinkled both the book and all the people, saying, "This is the blood of the covenant, which God has commanded; and in like manner he sprinkled the tabernacle and all the vessels of ministration with blood. For all things are purged with blood according to the law, and without shedding of blood there is no remission." The Apostle repeats the word "blood" several times, in order to fix in the hearts of the Jews, and of all men, that without the Blood of Jesus Christ, we have no hope of pardon for our sins. As then in the Old Law, by the blood of the victims the outward defilement of sin was taken away and the temporal punishment due to them was remitted, so in the New Law, the Blood of Jesus Christ washes away the inward stain of sin, according to St. John's words, "He loved us, and washed us with His own blood." (*Apoc.* 1:5).

St. Paul thus explains the whole truth in the same chapter of the Epistle to the Hebrews. "Christ being come a high priest of the good things to come, by a greater and more perfect tabernacle not made with hand, that is, not of this creation, neither by the blood of goats, or of calves, but by His own Blood, entered once into the holies, having obtained eternal redemption." (*Heb.* 9:11-12). The high priest entered by the tabernacle into the holy of holies, and by sprinkling the blood of animals, purged sinners from their outward defilement and from temporal punishment; for in order to gain the pardon of their sins, and for their liberation from eternal punishment, contrition, plus faith and hope in the coming Messias, who was about to die to obtain pardon for them, were absolutely necessary for the Jews. Jesus Christ, on the other hand, by means of His own Body (which was the greater and more perfect tabernacle spoken of by the Apostle) which was sacrificed on the Cross, entered into the holy of holies of Heaven, which was closed to us, and opened it to us by means of this Redemption. Therefore, St. Paul, in order to encourage us to hope for the pardon of all our sins by trusting in the Blood of Jesus Christ, goes on to say, "If the blood of goats and of oxen, and the ashes of a heifer, being sprinkled" on the unclean, "sanctifies such as are defiled, cleansing of the flesh, how much more shall the Blood of Christ, who, by the Holy Spirit, offered Himself without stain to God, cleanse our conscience from dead works to serve the living God." (*Heb.* 9:13-14). This he says because Jesus offered Himself to God without shadow of sin, for otherwise He would not have been a worthy mediator, fit to reconcile God with sinful man, nor would His Blood have had virtue to purge our consciences from dead works—that is, from sins, from works without merit, and works deserving of eternal punishment—to serve the living God. God pardons us for no other purpose than that for the rest of our lives we should devote ourselves wholly to loving and serving Him. And, finally, the Apostle concludes, "Therefore He is the Mediator of the new testament." (*Heb.* 9:15). Because our Redeemer, through the boundless love He bore us, was willing, by the price of His Blood, to deliver us from eternal death, therefore He obtained for us pardon, grace and eternal blessedness from God, if we are faithful to love Him until death. This was the mediation or covenant accomplished between Jesus Christ and God, by the terms of which, pardon and salvation are promised us.

This promise of pardon for our sins by the Blood of Jesus Christ was confirmed to us by Jesus Himself the day before His death, when leaving to us the Sacrament of the Eucharist, He said, "This is my blood of the new testament, which shall be shed for many unto the remission of sins." (*Matt.* 26:28). Therefore, He desired that this Sacrifice should be renewed every day at every Mass that is celebrated, in order that His Blood might continually plead in our favor. And therefore He is called a priest after the order of Melchisedech: "Thou art a priest for ever, according to the order of Melchisedech." (*Heb.* 5:6). Aaron offered sacrifices of animals, but Melchisedech offered bread and wine, which was a figure of the Sacrifice of the Altar, in which our Saviour, under the species of bread and wine, offered at His Last Supper His Body and Blood to God, as He was about to sacrifice it on the following day in His Passion, and which He now constantly offers by the hands of His priests, renewing by them the Sacrifice of the Cross. Therefore David called Jesus Christ an eternal Priest, as St. Paul explains it, saying, "That he continueth for ever, hath an everlasting priesthood." (*Heb.* 7:24). The ancient priests came to an end by their death, but Jesus, being eternal, has an eternal priesthood. But how does He exercise His priesthood in Heaven? The Apostle explains this, adding, "Whereby He is able also to save for ever them that come to God by Him, always living to intercede for us." (*Heb.* 7:25). The great Sacrifice of the Cross, re-enacted still in that of the Altar, has power forever to save those who, by means of Jesus Christ (being rightly prepared by faith and good works), approach to God; and this Sacrifice, as St.

Ambrose and St. Augustine write, Jesus, as man, continues to offer to the Father for our benefit, performing there, as He did on earth, the office of Our Advocate and Mediator—and also of our Priest—which is to intercede for us.

---

## 59

## THE LOVE OF OUR NEIGHBOR

*"If God hath so loved us, we ought also to love one another."* —1 John 4:1

WE might here ask why the conclusion the Apostle draws from the love that God has for us is that we ought to love our neighbor, since it would seem a more just and natural one to infer that we are obliged to love God because He has in so extraordinary a manner loved us? To this many answers may be given. The first is that the Apostle speaks in this manner to let us see the excellency of the love of our neighbor, and what a great value God sets on it. It is for this reason that, as St. Matthew relates, a doctor of the law asking Our Lord, which was the great commandment of the law, our Saviour answered, "Thou shalt love the Lord thy God with thy whole heart, with thy whole soul, and with thy whole mind. This is the greatest and the first commandment. And the second is like to this: Thou shalt love thy neighbour as thyself." (*Matt.* 22:37-39). They asked Him only about the first commandment; why, therefore, does He speak of the second? It is to show the excellency of the love of our neighbor, and in what esteem God holds it.

Secondly, the love of God and the love of our neighbor are like two rings joined together and put upon a finger, one of which rings cannot be taken off without the other, but both must be pulled off together. The love of God and the love of our neighbor are inseparable. The one can never subsist without the other, so that it is but one love of pure charity which makes us love God, and our neighbor for the love of God. We can therefore neither love God without loving our neighbor, nor love our neighbor with the love of pure charity without loving God Himself, because the motive we have to love our neighbor again is God. Wherefore the same Apostle, wishing to show us that we cannot love God without loving our neighbor, presently adds: "If we love one another, God abideth in us, and His charity is perfected in us." (*1 John* 4:12). And afterwards, to show us also that the love of our neighbor is included in the love of God: "This commandment we have from God, that he who loveth God love also his brother." (*1 John* 4:21).

The third answer is that St. John speaks in this epistle, not of a barren, but of a fruitful love—of a love accompanied with benefits and good works. "Let us not love," says he, "in word nor in tongue, but in deed and in truth." (*1 John* 3:18). And in order to inform us that it is for the good of our brethren that God desires we should perform these good works, he draws no other conclusion from his proposition than the love of our neighbor. It happens very often that a creditor who is absent writes thus to his debtor: "You will do me a favor by paying to such a one what you owe me, and what you shall give him I shall consider as received by myself." It is after this manner that St. John, speaking in God's behalf, to whom we owe so much, says to us, "If God has loved us in so extraordinary a manner, we ought also to love one another." The love which each of us owes Him is a debt He has transferred to our neighbor, and the charity you exercise towards your brother, you exercise towards God, who receives it as if it were done to Himself. It is this which Jesus Christ declares in these words: "Amen, I say to you, that as long as you did it to the least of these brethren, you did it to Me." And without doubt, this ought to be a powerful motive to excite us to love our brethren and to do them all the good we can, because though it seems to us that we do it to those to whom we owe nothing, yet if we look upon God and reflect upon the infinite obligations we are under to Him and consider that He has transferred all His right to them, we shall find that we are indebted to them for all we have. Father Avila, therefore, speaking on this subject says when the carnal man that is within you shall ask of you, "What great obligations have I to such a one to move me so far as to do him any favor?" And, "How can I be able to love him since he has so much injured me?" Answer him, that perhaps you should give ear to what he says, if your neighbor were the only motive, object or cause of this love. But it is Jesus Christ Himself who is the cause and object thereof, and it is He Himself who receives the good you do to your neighbor and who looks upon the pardon you bestow as if it were a favor and a pardon you bestowed upon Himself. And thus, whosoever your neighbor is and whatsoever injury he may have done you, yet there is nothing that ought to cool your charity towards him or hinder its effects, since it is not him, but Jesus Christ you ought to consider in all your thoughts and actions. Wherefore, it is a most just consequence that St. John draws, who, after he had proved the great love that God has for us, infers the obligation we therefore have to love our neighbor. We ought to observe further that to move us the more, he takes notice of the mystery of the incarnation of the Son of God, in the same proposition from which he draws this conclusion. For, setting before our eyes "that God has sent His only-begotten Son into the world" (*1 John* 4:9), he gives us occasion to consider that God has allied Himself to men and consequently would have us think that, since they are allied to God and brothers of Jesus Christ, we ought to love them as such.

---

# 60

## CHARITY IN CONVERSATION

*"The tongue of the wise is health."* —Proverbs 12:18

ONE of the things most conducive to the preservation and increase of fraternal charity is sweetness in our conversation. "A sweet word multiplieth friends and appeaseth enemies" (*Ecclus.* 6:5), says the wise man, and on the contrary, "A harsh word stirreth up fury" (*Proverbs* 15:1), and occasions quarrels and dissensions. For all of us being men, words of this sort hurt our feelings, and when the mind is once incensed, we look not upon our brother as we did before, but presently find something blamable in his conduct and often do not stop at blaming him in our hearts only, but go further and speak ill of him. It is therefore of great importance that our discourse be always so seasoned with sweetness that thereby we may gain the goodwill of our brethren, according to that saying of Scripture, "A man wise in words shall make himself beloved." (*Ecclus.* 20:13). To attain this end we must take care not to deceive ourselves by imagining that our brethren, because they are men of information and virtue, will not notice or be scandalized at a sharp word we may say to them. The question is not what they are, but what you ought to be and how you ought to conduct yourself towards them. If you say they will not be angry at so trifling a thing, "the more trifling it is," answers St. Bernard, "the easier it is for you to abstain from it." St. Chrysostom goes further and says that the smallness of the matter is what aggravates the fault, because the more easy the victory, the more culpable are you for not having obtained it. Because your brother has a great deal of moderation, ought you to have none at all? It is very true that we ought to have a good opinion of our brethren and not believe they are so alive to resentment as to be angry at any small matter, but still we are bound to converse with them and to deal with them with as much circumspection as if we knew they were sensible of the least thing. We ought to be as tender toward them as if they were more brittle than glass; in a word, be their temper and feelings what they may, we must scrupulously abstain from giving any cause whatsoever of offense. We should apply ourselves to this, as well on our own as on our brother's account, because the wisdom of our neighbor excuses not our indiscretion and because all are not (at least not always) disposed to take things in the best way and to overlook such offenses.

Now it only remains to observe that it is very easy to judge what words may or may not offend our brother. Every man can do this by following the rule which the Holy Ghost gives us by the mouth of the wise man: "Judge of thy neighbour by thyself." (*Ecclus.* 31:18). Let every one consult himself and see whether he be content that others should speak coldly of him, that they should answer him sharply and command him in a haughty and imperious manner; and if he finds this will hurt his own feelings, let him abstain from anything similar, because his neighbor is a man like himself and may have the same sentiments and feelings as he himself has. Humility also is a very proper means to make us never speak except as we ought to do, for if we be humble and esteem ourselves the least of all, we need no other precaution. This virtue alone is sufficient to teach us how to behave toward everyone, so that we shall never speak a hasty word at which anyone may be offended, but rather shall speak to everyone with respect and sweetness.

———————

# 61

## THE EXCELLENCE OF PRAYER

*"Let my prayer be directed as incense in Thy sight."*
—Psalm 140:2

ST. JOHN in the book of the Apocalypse expresses admirably the excellence and merit of prayer. He says in the eighth chapter "that there came an angel, and stood before the altar, having a golden censer, and there was given to him much incense, that he should offer the prayers of all saints upon the golden altar, which is before the throne of God; and the smoke of the incense of the prayers of the saints ascended up before God from the hand of the angel."(*Apoc.* 8:3,4). St. Chrysostom, speaking of this passage, tells us that "one proof of the merit of prayer is that in the Holy Scripture it alone is compared to incense, which is a composition of many admirable perfumes. For as the smell of well-composed incense is very delicious, so prayer also, when well made, is very acceptable to God and gives great joy to the Angels and inhabitants of the heavenly Jerusalem." Wherefore, St. John, speaking of the twenty-four elders who worship perpetually before the throne of God, relates "that they had golden vials, full of odours, which are the prayers of the saints" (*Apoc.* 5:8), "so that," says St. Austin, "what can be more excellent than prayer? What is there more profitable in this life? What more sweet to the mind? And what in our whole religion more sublime?" St. Gregory of Nicea is of the same opinion and says that "of all things which we esteem in this life, none ought to be preferred before prayer."

St. Bernard, the better to make us understand the merit of it, says that "though it is certain the Angels (albeit invisibly) are often really present with God's servants, to defend them from the deceits and ambushes of the devil and more and more to raise their thoughts and desires to God, yet nevertheless they more particularly favor us with this presence when we are employed in prayer." He proves this proposition by several passages of Scripture, as in these: "I will sing praise to thee in the sight of the angels" (*Ps.* 137:2); "When thou didst pray with tears, I offered thy prayer to the Lord." (*Tob.* 12:12). We see by this last passage that prayers scarcely go out of the mouth of him that prays, but presently the Angels who are by us receive them from us and present them to God. St. Hilary also assures us that "the Angels preside at the prayers of the faithful and continually offer them to God," so that when we are in prayer, we are surrounded by Angels, and indeed we perform their function, practicing now what we must perform with them for all eternity. And therefore they already look upon us as their companions, and beholding us beforehand as in Heaven, filling up the places of their fallen companions, they are with us more particularly during our devotions than at other times.

St. Chrysostom, speaking of the excellence of prayer, says: "Consider to what a degree of happiness you are raised by prayer and how great prerogatives are attributed to it. You thereby speak to God Himself; you entertain yourself and converse with Jesus Christ; you therein desire what pleases you, and you ask whatsoever you desire." There is no tongue able to express of how great a value this communication is which man has with God, and what profit it brings along with it. We see in the world that those who ordinarily keep company with wise and prudent persons reform and improve their minds and judgments by their conversation with them. If therefore they become virtuous by frequenting the company of virtuous persons, what advantage may we not believe we gain by a frequent communication with God? "Come ye to Him," says the Royal Prophet, "and be enlightened." (*Ps.* 33:7). With what light, with what knowledge, must we not be filled by such means! What good, what happiness must we not assuredly gain by this kind of converse! Wherefore, St. Chrysostom assures us that nothing can so much contribute to our progress in virtue as frequent prayer and conversation with God, for by this means the heart of man comes to be filled with and to relish the most noble thoughts; it is enabled to raise itself above all earthly things, and in short, to become spiritual and holy, and in a manner transforming itself into God.

———————

# 62

## ON THE MYSTERIES OF THE GOSPEL

*"Thy law is my meditation."* —Psalm 118:174

IT is of very great importance to fathom things well and not to pass over them lightly in the meditations we make upon the mysteries of the Gospel, for it will be of far greater profit to us to examine only one mystery deliberately than to touch on many superficially. St. Ignatius in his "Spiritual Exercises" makes such account of this that at the end of each exercise he wishes to repeat the meditation twice or thrice over, *"because, he that seeketh findeth, and to him that knocketh it shall be opened." (Matt. 7:8).* Perseverance overcomes all difficulties and attains its end. It was necessary that Moses should strike twice upon the rock to make water issue forth. (*Num.* 20:11). And even Jesus Christ Himself did not immediately cure the blind man mentioned in the Gospel. He first anointed his eyes with spittle and asked him whether he saw anything, and the man, who as yet could not see any objects distinctly, answered Him, "I see men, as trees, walking." (*Mark* 8:24). Then our Saviour touched his eyes a second time with His hand, and perfected their cure. This then is what ordinarily happens in prayer, for by means of going over the same matter several times and persevering in it, we discover those things which at first we did not perceive. It is much after the same manner that we enter into a dark room. At first we see nothing, but if we remain for some time in it, we begin grad-

we begin gradually to distinguish the objects.

Let us now come to the means which may help us to make long and salutary reflections upon these mysteries. When God is pleased to impart His light to a soul and to open its eyes, it will find so many things to consider and such a variety of things to dwell on that it may say with the Psalmist, "Open Thou my eyes, and I will consider the wondrous things of Thy law." (*Ps.* 118:18). And I will rejoice at Thy words as one that hath found great spoil." (*Ps.* 118:162). St. Austin and St. Francis passed whole days and nights in repeating these words: "Who art Thou, O Lord, and who am I? Oh that I could know Thee! Oh that I could know myself! Thou art my God and all things to me." This manner of prayer is conformable to that which the prophet Isaias says the blessed make in Heaven, when ravished with the contemplation of the Divine Majesty, they incessantly sing, "Holy, holy, holy." The *Apocalypse* says the same of those holy and mysterious creatures which were before God's throne: "They rested not day and night, saying, 'Holy, holy, holy, Lord God Almighty, who was, and who is, and who is to come.'" (*Apoc.* 4:8).

But, to attain to this level of understanding, it is necessary that we on our part accustom ourselves to reflect seriously upon those mysteries and that we exercise ourselves in penetrating into all their particulars. Gerson says the best means to succeed in this prayer *is to practice it;* it is not a thing which is gained by the force or acuteness of arguing, nor is it learned by hearing it spoken of, nor by reading many treatises; but, to acquire a knowledge of it, we must set our hand to work and practice it a long time. When a mother wishes to teach her boy to walk, she holds not long discourses with him to show him what he must do, but by practicing with him, she makes him form his steps, and thus in a very short time teaches him to walk alone. So it is in the science of prayer, for though it be true that it is a supernatural gift and consequently not to be obtained by us if it come not from the liberal hand of God, "because the Lord giveth wisdom, and out of His mouth cometh prudence and knowledge" (*Prov.* 2:6), yet it is very certain that God wishes that we practice it as diligently, as if it were to be obtained by our own industry. He is the eternal Wisdom, "who reaches from end to end mightily, and ordereth all things sweetly." (*Wisd.* 8:1). He acts in the order of grace as He does in that of nature, and as He would have all human arts and sciences acquired by practice, so He would have us acquire the divine science of prayer in the same manner.

It will greatly help us also to persevere a long time in the exercise of prayer if we have an ardent love of God and a great affection for spiritual things. "How have I loved Thy law, O Lord; it is my meditation all the day." (*Ps.* 118:97). "I meditated," says he in another place, "upon Thy commandments, which I loved." (*Ps.* 118:47). Everyone willingly thinks of what he loves and of what is most to his taste, and therefore the Holy Scripture gives us this invitation, "Taste and see how sweet our Lord is." (*Ps.* 33:9). We must taste God before we see Him; that is to say, we must love Him to be able to think upon Him. And the more we think upon Him the more we shall love Him, for love, according to St. Thomas, augments itself by contemplation, and as it is the beginning, so it is also the end. Hence it is that when we love God, we are easily induced to think upon Him and contemplate Him, and the more we contemplate and think upon Him, the more we love Him because that which is good excites us to love it and the more we behold it the more we love it—as also the more we love it, the more joy and pleasure we feel in beholding and thinking of it.

*Absolutely Remember This*

## 63

### SPIRITUAL READING

*"I will consider the wondrous things of Thy law."*
—Psalm 118:18

SPIRITUAL reading is a great help to prayer, and it is on this account that St. Paul, writing to Timothy, recommended to him "to attend to reading." (*1 Tim.* 4:13). St. Athanasius esteems it so necessary for one who would walk in the path of God that in an exhortation he made to religious he says, "You will see no one truly intent on God's service who is not also given to reading. We can neither practice nor leave it off without receiving profit or prejudice." St. Jerome also testified to the esteem he had for it when, writing to Eustochium, he said, "Let sleep surprise you with a book in your hand, and let the Holy Scripture receive your reclining head." In short, all Saints in general recommend unto us spiritual reading, and experience, moreover, shows us clearly the profit of it because history records innumerable wonderful conversions which God has wrought by this means.

St. Ambrose, exhorting us to apply ourselves as much as we can to spiritual reading, says: "Wherefore do you not employ the time you have to spare in spiritual reading? Wherefore do you not return to take a view of Jesus Christ? Why do you not speak to Him? And why do you not hearken to what He says to you? For we speak to Him while we are in prayer, and we hear Him speak while we read the Holy Scripture." Let this, therefore, be the first means we adopt to profit by spiritual reading: let us believe that it is God who speaks to us and that it is He who dictates to us what we there read. "Read the Holy Scripture in such a manner as always to bear in mind that all the words that are therein are the words of God, who would have us not only know His law, but also fulfill it."

What the Saint says elsewhere furnishes us with another very profitable means, and many pious reflections. "The Holy Scriptures," says he, "are like so many letters sent to us from our own country; let us therefore read them with the same eagerness that a man would read the letters he receives from his native country from which he has been a long time absent and from which he is far away. Let us read them to see what news we receive from Heaven, which is our true country, to see what they tell us

*Absolutely Remember This*

of our Father's brethren and friends that are there, to see what they say of that place to which we so earnestly desire to go."

St. Gregory, writing on the same subject, says that Holy Scripture is like a looking-glass, which we ought to set before the eyes of our soul, to behold our interior, in which it is very easy to perceive what of good or bad there is within us and how near we are to perfection, or how far off. For sometimes it sets before us the admirable exploits of the Saints, to excite us to imitate them, that the sight of their victories and triumphs may augment our courage in temptations and sufferings; sometimes it speaks also of their falls, that we may know what we ought to avoid. It sets before us the example of Job, whose virtue increased amid temptations, as foam does amid the waves and billows of the sea; it also represents to us David, who fell at the first attack. The constancy of the one helps to strengthen us in the greatest trials, and the frailty of the other teaches us always to have a humble fear, even in prosperity and amid the consolation that grace brings along with it, and never to presume upon ourselves or our own strength, but to conduct ourselves always with all imaginable precaution. St. Austin speaks in like manner: "You will make a good use of Holy Scripture if you use it as a looking-glass, that your soul, beholding herself therein, may correct what is bad, and perfect what is good in her." And what they say of Holy Scripture may also be applied to all kinds of spiritual reading.

St. Bernard also instructs us how we may profit

by spiritual reading: "He who sets himself to read," says he, "does not so much seek to learn as to taste the things of God." For the bare knowledge of the understanding is dry and barren if it warms not the will and excites not that fervor which renders the reading profitable and fruitful." He teaches us also that "we must take care to keep in our minds all day long some passage that we have that day read, that we may afterwards digest it the better, by calling to mind and often re-examining it. And this [reflection] must be something also that agrees with the good purposes and resolutions you have made before and that may be proper to strengthen them and hinder your mind from distracting or dissipating itself upon other thoughts." For as we do not eat only to spend the time that is taken up in it, but that the food we take may sustain and nourish us all the day after, so we must not apply ourselves to spiritual reading, which is the spiritual food of our souls, only to employ the time allotted for it, but we must perform it so as to make our profit by it the whole day. For this purpose it will be very advantageous to us if we lift up our hearts to God before we begin to read and beg His grace that our reading may become fruitful, that it may penetrate our heart and take such root in it and so fortify it, that it may render us more fervent in virtue, that it may show the deceits of the world and make us more firm and constant in what regards our spiritual advancement. St. Gregory never applied himself to his spiritual reading without first preparing for it by prayer and reciting this verse of the Psalmist: "Depart from me, ye wicked, and I will search the commandments of my God." (*Ps.* 118:115).

------

## 64

## CHRISTIAN SIMPLICITY

*"In simplicity of heart we have had our conversation in Thy works."* —2 Corinthians 1:12

S IMPLICITY is nothing else than an act of pure and simple charity, which has only one purpose, namely, that of pleasing God. And our soul is simple when we have no other pretensions in whatever we do.

The well-known story of Martha and Mary, who exercised hospitality towards Our Lord, is very remarkable on this point. Although the object of Martha was praiseworthy in wishing to treat Our Lord well, she was nevertheless reproved by our Divine Master because, beyond the good purpose she had in view, in her haste she mixed up other purposes with it, and thus she lost her singleness of purpose, for which reason she was reproved: "Martha, Martha, thou art careful, and art troubled about many things; but one thing is necessary. Mary hath chosen the best part, which shall not be taken away from her." (*Luke* 10:41-42).

Christian simplicity, then, is an act of simple charity, which makes us have no other view in all our actions than the sole desire of pleasing God. This is the part which Mary took, and it is the one thing necessary. It is a virtue which is inseparable from charity, which looks straight to God and which cannot suffer any interference from the consideration of creatures: God alone finds place in it.

This virtue is purely Christian. The pagans, even those who have spoken the best concerning other virtues, had no knowledge of it, any more than they had of humility. They have written well concerning magnificence, liberality, constancy—but nothing about simplicity and humility. It was Our Lord Himself, coming down from Heaven, who gave the knowledge of these virtues to man; otherwise they would have remained unknown. "Be as wise as serpents," said He to His Apostles, but do not stop there: moreover, be "as simple as doves." Let us learn of the dove to love God in simplicity of heart, having only one object or end, which is to please Him by the means corresponding to our vocation.

Thus, simplicity banishes from the soul the care and anxiety with which many uselessly seek out a multiplicity of means to enable them to love God, as they say; and they fancy that if they do not do all that the Saints have done, they cannot arrive at that end. Poor people, who torment themselves to discover the art of loving God! Do they not know that there is no other way but simply to love Him? They think there is some stratagem or other for gaining this love, while the greatest stratagem in the matter is to proceed with all simplicity.

But this simplicity ought to have no other motive for being excited to seek for the love of God but the objective itself; otherwise it would not be perfectly simple, for simplicity cannot allow itself to look toward anything else, howsoever perfect, save the pure love of God, which is its only object.

This virtue does not allow us to worry ourselves with what people will say or think of us because its only thought is to please God and not creatures, except so far as the love of God requires it. After the soul embued with simplicity has done an action which it thinks it ought to do, it thinks no more about it; and if the idea occurs what people will say or think of it, such a soul at once rejects the thought, because it cannot allow any interference with its object, which is to keep itself attentive to God in order to increase the love of Him in itself. The consideration of creatures in nowise moves it, because it refers everything to its Creator.

The soul possessed of simplicity practices this virtue even in conversation and recreation, as in every other action, although in these areas there ought to be a holy liberty to entertain oneself with such subjects as serve to promote the spirit of joy and recreation. We must be frank in conversation, but we must not for that reason be inconsiderate, inasmuch as simplicity always follows the rule of the love of God. But if we happened to say any little thing that seemed not to be so well received as we could wish, we ought not on that account to amuse ourselves with making reflections and examens on all our words. Oh no! For it is self-love that causes us to make all these reflections, but holy simplicity does not run after its words and its actions, but leaves the event of them to Divine Providence, to which it supremely attaches itself without turning to the right hand or the left, but following its path simply. And if simplicity meets with an occasion for practicing any virtue, it diligently avails itself of the opportunity, as of a means proper to enable it to arrive at its own perfection, which is the love of God, but it does not agitate itself to seek for the opportunity; neither does it despise it; simplicity keeps itself peaceful and tranquil in the confidence that it has that God knows its desire, which is to please Him, and that suffices for it.

Then all unusual events and every type of accident which occur will be received sweetly and gently. For whoever has placed himself in the hands of God and who "reposes in His bosom" like the Apostle John, whoever has abandoned himself to His love and has given himself up to His good pleasure— then no one and nothing can shake or trouble him. Despite whatever he meets with—without concerning himself by philosophizing on the causes, reasons and motives which lead up to the events—he utters from his heart that holy acquiescence of the Saviour, "Yea, Father, for so it hath seemed good in Thy sight."

Then we shall be all filled with sweetness towards our brethren because we shall see those souls in the bosom of the Saviour. Alas, he who looks at his neighbor, except there, runs the chance of not loving him, either purely or constantly or agreeably; but seeing others as abiding in Christ's love, how can we not love them; who would not support them, who would then object to his imperfections, who would then find him ill-favored? That neighbor of ours is in the bosom of the Saviour as one well-beloved, and so lovely is he that the Heavenly Lover died for love of him.

Then also the natural love stemming from relationship, propriety, convenience, corresponding dispositions, sympathies, graces, will be purified and reduced to the obedience of the all-pure love of the divine good-pleasure. And certainly the great good and the great happiness of the souls who aspire to perfection would be to have no desire of being loved by creatures except with that love of charity which makes us regard our neighbor with affection, and each in his rank, according to the desire of Our Lord.

---

## 65

## THE PRESENCE OF GOD

*"Seek ye the Lord, and be strengthened, seek His face evermore."* —Psalm 104:4

ST. AUGUSTINE says that the face and presence of God are one and the same thing, so that to seek continually God's face is to walk always in His presence, by turning all the desires and motions of our heart towards Him. St. Bonaventure affirms "that to employ ourselves continually in the exercise of the presence of God is to begin in this life to enjoy the happiness of the blessed in the next." For though on earth we cannot clearly see Him as He is in Himself and as the Blessed do in Heaven, yet we may at least imitate them, as much as our weakness will permit, by placing ourselves continually in His presence by acts of love and adoration. For His goodness was not satisfied with having created us to enjoy Him eternally in Heaven, but He would have us enjoy a part of this beatitude even while we are upon earth, by always walking in His presence and continually adoring and beholding Him through the clouds and obscurity of Faith—which make us at present "see Him through a glass darkly," instead of seeing Him as we shall hereafter, "face to face." (*1 Cor.* 13:12).

The Saints and Patriarchs of the Old Testament took particular care to walk always in God's presence. The Royal Prophet was not contented with praising Him only seven times a day, but as he says, "I set the Lord always in my sight, for He is at my right hand, that I be not moved." (*Ps.* 15:8). It was in short, so familiar and customary a practice with them to place themselves in God's presence that they commonly had no other way of expressing themselves than to say, "The Lord, in whose sight I stand." (*3 Kings* 17:1). And without doubt their great attention to this devotion proceeded from the perfect knowledge they had of the great advantage of walking in God's presence and of thinking that He continually beholds them. This awareness alone is sufficient to make us very particular in all our actions, for what servant is there so insolent as to despise his master's orders in his very presence? But God is *our* Master; He continually beholds us; He is our Judge; He is all-powerful; He can make the earth open and cause Hell to swallow us up, as He has several times done to those who displeased Him or provoked Him to anger. Who, therefore, dare be so bold as to provoke Him? "When I attentively consider, O Lord," says St. Austin, "that Thou hast Thine eyes continually fixed upon me, and that night and day Thou keepest a continual watch over me with so great care as if neither in Heaven nor in earth Thou hadst any other creature to govern besides myself—when I think that Thou dost behold all my actions, and penetrate my most hidden and secret thoughts, and that all my desires are exposed to Thy view, I feel myself filled with confusion." Without doubt they impose upon themselves a strict obligation to live well who consider that all they do is done in the presence of a Judge who sees all and from whom nothing can be concealed. If the presence of a grave person is sufficient to keep us doing our duty, what effect ought not the presence of the infinite majesty of God produce in us?

The presence of God is that sovereign and universal remedy which St. Basil prescribes for overcoming all the temptations of the devil and all the repugnances of nature—so that if you desire a short and easy means to gain perfection, and such a one as contains within itself the force and efficacy of all the others, make use of this which God Himself gave to Abraham: "Walk before Me, and be perfect." (*Gen.* 17:1). Upon this we must take notice, that though the text says "be perfect," yet here, as in many other places of Scripture, the future is expressed by the imperative, thereby to let us see the infallibility of success using this method of perfection. Success in this is therefore a thing so certain that you will become perfect by setting God before your eyes, that from the very moment you apply yourself with all attention to His presence, you may account that you are perfect. For, as the stars borrow all their luster and virtue from the sun, so the just, who are stars in God's Church, derive from His presence and from their continual elevation of heart to Him all that light with which they inwardly burn before Him and outwardly before men—and also all the power they possess in promoting the general good of the whole world. Nothing can better express the need we always have of God's presence than this simile. See how the moon depends upon the sun; see how necessary it is for her to keep her face always toward it. Her light varies as her position with respect to the sun varies; she acts not upon sublunary bodies, but according to the light communicated to her by the sun, so that this action increases or diminishes accordingly as her borrowed light increases or diminishes. And as soon as anything interposes between the sun and the moon, the moon presently loses its light and force. The same thing happens between the soul and God, who is its sun, and it is for this reason that the Saints so earnestly exhort us to have the presence of God constantly before our eyes.

---

## 66

## GOD'S PROVIDENCE OVER US AND
## OUR CONFIDENCE IN HIM

*"My people shall sit in the beauty of peace, and in the
tabernacles of confidence, and in wealthy rest."*
—Isaias 32:18

ONE of the greatest benefits enjoyed by the faithful is a confidence in the providence of God
and the assurance they have that nothing can befall
them which is not an effect of His own decree and
a present bestowed by His own hand. Wherefore, the
Royal Prophet said: "Lord, Thou hast crowned us
with a shield of Thy good will." (*Ps.* 5:13). And it is
certain that we are so surrounded and protected on
all sides with the love which God bears us that nothing can approach or molest us which has not first
passed this guard. Hence, there is nothing that can
put us in fear, since it is clear He lets nothing happen but what contributes to our greater good and
profit. "He hath hidden me in His tabernacle," says
the same prophet; "in the days of evil, He hath protected me in the secret place of His tabernacle." (*Ps.*
26:5). Yet He does more; He hides us under His
wings. And the care He still takes of us makes Him
go so far as to hide us in the very apple of His eye.
This accords well with what is said elsewhere by the
same prophet, who begs of God "to protect him as
the apple of His eye" (*Ps.* 16:8), and with what Our
Lord Himself says by the prophet Zacharias, where
He assures us, "he who touches us, touches the

apple of His eye." (*Zach.* 2:8). Can anyone conceive a thing more precious than this protection so signal and tender?

What a singular comfort should we receive in all our adversities, and what strong confidence and ease should we have in the midst of our greatest afflictions and pressing calamities, were we but thoroughly convinced of this truth! If a son saw his father invested with great titles, abounding in wealth and one of the chief favorites of his king, what assurance would he not have that the credit and power of his father would never be wanting to him in his most important affairs? With how much greater reason, then, ought we to have this assurance, when we consider that we have Him for our father who is absolute Lord of Heaven and earth, and that nothing can happen to us without His order and permission? And with how much more reason ought we to have a thorough confidence in the special providence of Him who is by a thousand degrees more our Father than all earthly fathers, who, in comparison to Him, deserve not even the name of father? For there is no tenderness nor affection that can come near to that which God bears toward us. It infinitely exceeds all that nature imprints in the hearts of fathers, so that we may rest satisfied, that whatever such a Father ordains, He ordains it for our greater advancement and good. The love He bears us in His only Son will never permit Him to be backward in procuring the good of those for whose sake He gave up this Son to the sufferings and death of the Cross. "He that spared not even

His own Son, but delivered Him up for us all, hath He not also with Him freely given us all things?" (*Rom.* 8:32). And He who has so freely given us all that He had most precious and dear, will He not also give us whatever else we stand in need of?

From the filial confidence which the just repose in God arises that peace of mind and that happy tranquillity described by Isaias when he says: "My people shall sit in the beauty of peace, and in the tabernacles of confidence, and in wealthy rest." (*Is.* 32:18). The prophet joins peace and confidence together. Because, in reality, peace of mind is but a necessary effect of confidence, and he who trusts in God fears nothing, nor troubles himself at whatever occurs, since he knows God is his protector. But the confidence we speak of affords us not merely tranquillity; it also replenishes us with the joy of the faithful. "The God of hope," says the Apostle, "fill you with all joy, and peace in believing; that you may abound in hope, and in the power of the Holy Ghost." (*Rom.* 15:13). The firm belief we have that God knows what is for our good better than ourselves is the reason that we are not only exempt from all those troubles and anxieties incident to those who view things with the eyes of flesh and blood, but even in the most unexpected accidents we enjoy an entire content and satisfaction. And the more perfect this confidence is, the greater also will be the joy and tranquillity, because the more we love God and confide in Him, the more assured shall we be that all which comes from Him will turn to our advantage, it being impossible we can expect anything else from the goodness and tenderness of affection He always has for us.

———————————

## 67

## CONFORMITY TO THE WILL OF GOD IN DEATH

*"If our earthly house be dissolved, we have a building of God, a house not made with hands, eternal in the heavens."* —2 Corinthians 6:1

OUR conformity to the will of God ought to extend itself as well to what relates to dying as to living. For although, generally speaking, this is one of the most difficult points, inasmuch as nothing is more terrible than death, nevertheless, this difficulty is greatly diminished for the good Christian because he has already advanced halfway, or rather surmounted almost all the obstacles. First, one of the motives which makes worldly persons have such a horror of death and tremble at its approach is that death deprives them of their riches, their honors, their pleasures, their amusements and all the comforts they enjoyed in this life. But the Christian is already disengaged from the things of this life. He feels no difficulty in parting with them at his death because he has already parted with them voluntarily during his life, by the way he lives. But people of the world, forsaking these things only through constraint and necessity, forsake them consequently with great difficulty and reluctance and sometimes even without any merit; since we may justly say they do not so much forsake these things as these things forsake them. Persons of the world, as St. Chrysostom well remarks, being attached to their wealth, to their pleasures and to the conveniences of life, find death very dreadful. "O death, how bitter is the remembrance of thee to a man that hath peace in his possessions!" (*Ecclus.* 51:1). If while they contemplate it at a distance it is so terrible, what will it be when they behold it present at hand? And if the very thought of it be so frightful, what will it prove when they come to experience it? It is not so with true Christians, who instead of finding afflictions and miseries in death, feel comfort and content. They look upon it as the term of all their sufferings and as a passage by which they are to go to receive the recompense of all they hitherto forsook for the love of God.

We must take notice here of one thing very suitable to our present purpose: It is that one of the chief signs of a good conscience and of our having made our peace with God is to be entirely conformed to His will in all things touching the hour of our death and to expect it "as they who expect their master's return from the marriage." (*Luke* 12:36). On the contrary, it is a bad sign not to possess the submission we here speak of and to feel pain at the idea of death. A sheep is led to the slaughter without any resistance, and therefore the Holy Scripture, speaking of the death of our Saviour Jesus Christ, says that He was "led as a sheep to the slaughter." (*Is.* 53:7). But the sow makes a most hideous noise when it is to be killed and struggles with all its force against the approach of death. The same difference is found between the just, who are signified by the sheep, and the wicked, who are signified by the swine. A criminal condemned to die, and who knows he is only to leave the prison to be brought to execution, trembles every time he hears the prison door opened, but he who is declared innocent feels joy and comfort when he hears the same door opened, because it is to restore him to his liberty. In like manner a bad Christian, when he is brought to his agony and feels in his body the approaching pangs of death, is troubled and afflicted and even sometimes falls into despair because, having a conscience burdened and guilty, he fancies each moment he is to be precipitated into eternal flames; whereas, he who has his conscience clear, and sees his end approach, finds in himself a joy and delight, as being persuaded that the time of his deliverance is arrived and his eternal repose is at hand. Let us act, therefore, as becomes true Christians, and we shall not only feel no repugnance in conforming ourselves to God's holy will as to the hour of our death, but on the contrary, shall rejoice when it is at hand. We shall even prevent it by our wishes and say with the Psalmist, "O Lord, bring my soul out of prison, that I may praise Thy name." (*Ps.* 141:8).

St. Gregory, upon these words of Job, "Thou shalt not be afraid of the beasts of the earth" (*Job* 5:22), says, "The security of a soul at the moment of death is the beginning of a just man's recompense. He begins then to enjoy that spiritual peace and tranquillity which he is soon hereafter to enjoy for eternity, and he then feels, as it were, a foretaste of his felicity." "It is a very laudable practice," says St. John Climachus, "to expect death continually, but it belongs only to the just to long for it every moment." And St. Ambrose greatly commends such as are possessed of this holy disposition. It is the same state of soul the ancient patriarchs were in "when they declared themselves to be pilgrims and strangers upon earth." For, as the Apostle says, "they that say these things do signify that they seek a country." (*Heb.* 11:13, 14).

---

## 68

## CONFORMITY TO THE WILL OF GOD AS TO NATURAL GIFTS AND TALENTS

*"Having different gifts, according to the grace that is given us."* —Romans 12:6

WE must all be content with the talents we have received from God without envying others who are possessed of superior abilities. All persons stand in need of this instruction. For though some seem to surpass in certain things, they have as yet their own particular defects, which counterbalance their advantages and which render necessary even to them the conformity we here speak of. It is our duty, then, to use precaution in this particular problem area, and the more so since the devil attacks many persons on this point. Let us say you are in the course of your studies, and others signalize themselves at the public exhibitions more than you do; therefore, you are inclined presently to conceive a secret sort of envy of them. This envy, it is true, may not influence you so far as to afflict you at your neighbor's good, yet you will feel ashamed and chagrined on seeing that others have the precedence. Hence will arise dejection and discontent, which may at last work so far upon you as to tempt you to quit your studies—as in reality this temptation has made some do who had not laid strong enough the foundations of humility.

For it is through absence of humility that we do not content ourselves with those qualities and talents we have; it is for this reason we cannot bear that anyone should consider us as possessed of less ability and capacity than our companions. What banished our first parents from Paradise and robbed them of the great advantages they enjoyed was that they wished to be more than God had made them and sought after more than God had bestowed upon them. "You shall be," said the serpent, "as gods, knowing good and evil." (*Gen.* 3:5). This was the bait and allurement the devil made use of to delude them and to work their destruction, and we have inherited this their desire of becoming gods, that is, their folly, or rather their madness, in striving to be greater than we really are. Against our first parents this diabolical enemy of ours was so successful by this argument that he makes use of the same even to this day, persuading and pushing us on to desire to be more and greater than what God would have us be and not to rest satisfied with the talents He has given us or the condition He has placed us in. "It is for this reason," says St. Austin, that "the Royal Prophet asks of God that He would give him a heart wholly disinterested and faithfully inclined to all that shall please the Divine will, a heart entirely devoid of self-satisfaction and self-interest."

But though we had no other motive for contenting ourselves with those talents which God has conferred upon us and the state and condition in which He has placed us but purely that of the Divine will, this motive alone might suffice to oblige us to a perfect conformity to the orders of His providence. "All these things," says St. Paul, "one and the same Spirit worketh, dividing to every one according as He will." (*1 Cor.* 12:2). How profound are the judgments of God! How incomprehensible they are! What man is there who can penetrate into the secret designs of God? All things, O Lord, come from Thee, and we ought to praise Thee in all. Thou knowest what is most proper and expedient for each one of us and why Thou conferrest more upon one than upon another, and it is not for us to search into the reason. For who knows what would have become of us had we received more knowledge and capacity?

If with the little capacity and knowledge you have and your humble science (and perhaps less than humble), you are so presumptuous as to compare and even prefer yourself to others and to look upon it as an injury done you not to be selected for the most honorable functions, what would you do if in reality you were master of those rare qualities and those extraordinary talents and endowments? Wings are not granted to the ant, as the saying goes, but for her ruin; and perhaps had great talents been conferred upon you, it would have been for your ruin. If we seriously reflect upon these things and not look upon them through a disordered imagination, we shall find sufficient reason to thank God during all our lifetime for having placed us in this state of subjection and humility and given us so scanty a portion of talents. We may say with the pious à Kempis, "Lord, I look upon it as a most signal favor and happiness not to have received a great many things which might have gained the applause and esteem of men." The Saints knew very well the danger which accompanies these great gifts and advantages, and so they not only abstained from desiring them, but they even dreaded them, knowing that those who are possessed of them are so much exposed to the danger of vainglory. And thus the Saints became more pleasing to God, who prefers humility of heart to sublimity of genius. Were we but well convinced that all things, except the accomplishment of God's holy will, are but pure vanity, and could we persuade ourselves to place all our satisfaction and contentment in that, we should find nothing else worth our desiring or seeking after. God knows well how to mark out to all the part most proper for them and distributes His talents "to every one according to his proper ability." (*Matt.* 30:15). Our chief business is to do the part assigned us and to give a good account of the talent we are entrusted with, for so we shall please God more and receive from Him a greater recompense.

---

## 69

## CONFORMITY AND UNION WITH THE WILL OF GOD

*"The will of the Lord be done."* —Acts 21:14

THAT we may better understand what that perfection is which is included in the exercise of conformity to the will of God and that we may clearly show how far we may advance by this means, let us briefly consider the exercise acknowledged by the Saints and masters of the spiritual life to be the most sublime of all. This exercise is that of the love of God, for since one of the principal effects of love is, according to St. Denis, to endeavor that those who love have but one will in all things, it follows in consequence that the more we love God, the more we shall conform ourselves to His divine will. And again, the more strict this conformity is, the more perfect also is our love. The better to explain this point, it is requisite that we elevate ourselves in thought to Heaven and there behold the continual occupation of the Blessed, which is to love God, to conform themselves entirely to His holy will and to have no other will but His; and the nearer we approach this ideal, the greater will our perfection be in this exercise. St.

John says that the sight of God makes the Blessed like to Him: "When He shall appear, we shall be like to Him, because we shall see Him as He is." (*1 John* 3:2). And this is true because at the same instant that they see God, they are so transformed into Him that their will becomes one and the same with His. Let us then see what is His will and what He most of all loves, that by so knowing what is the will and the love of the Blessed in Heaven, we may also know at the same time what will and love we ought to have in ourselves.

The will and supreme love in God is the will of His own glory and the love of His own being sovereignly perfect and sovereignly amiable. The will and love of the Blessed is the same thing with the will and love of God, so that their love is a continual act by which they are moved incessantly to will with all their power that God may be what He is, that He be equally good, equally perfect, equally happy, equally worthy of honor and praise as He is in Himself. And as they see in Him all they can wish may be, they thence feel an inconceivable joy on seeing that He whom they love is so complete in perfection and so filled with all good.

What we see sometimes happen in this life may give us some faint idea or representation of that supreme and all-divine joy, which the Blessed receive in Heaven. Consider how sensible the joy of a son is, who, loving his father with all affection and tenderness, sees him rich, wise, powerful, honored and esteemed by the whole world, and particularly favored by his prince. Doubtless there are children so nobly born as not to feel any joy comparable to that of seeing their parents so highly esteemed and in so sublime a post and degree of dignity. If then in the world, where sentiments of love are so weak and where all happiness is so contemptible, this joy, notwithstanding, arrives at such greatness, what must that of the Blessed be in beholding their Sovereign Master—their Creator and their heavenly Father, who is infinitely good, infinitely holy, infinitely perfect and infinitely powerful and into whom they are wholly transformed by love in beholding all things created receiving their being and perfection from His holy will only, and that not so much as one leaf falls from a tree without His permission? It is of this joy that the Apostle speaks when he says, "Eye hath not seen, nor ear heard, neither hath it entered into the heart of man, what things God has prepared for them that love Him." (*1 Cor.* 2:9). This is that "river of water of life" which St. John saw "proceeding from the throne of God and of the Lamb" (*Apoc.* 22:1), that river whose stream "makes the city of God joyful" (*Ps.* 45:5), that river in which the Blessed continually quench their thirst and inebriate themselves with divine love, blessing God eternally and singing, "Alleluia: for the Lord our God the Omnipotent hath reigned; let us be glad and rejoice, and give glory to Him." (*Apoc.* 19:6, 7). They rejoice at the glory and greatness of God; they make themselves happy incessantly, and animating one another, as it were, they say, "Benediction, and glory, and wisdom, and thanksgiving, honour, and power, and strength to our God for ever and ever. Amen." (*Apoc.* 7:12).

See here—to speak according to the narrow extent of human capacity—what is the continual exercise and love of the Blessed in Heaven and how great their conformity and union to the Divine Will. And see, consequently, what we are to endeavor to imitate, as far as in our power, in order that this may be "done on earth as it is in Heaven." When God ordered Moses to make Him a tabernacle, He said, "Look and make it according to the pattern that was shown thee in the mount." (*Ex.* 25:40). It is thus that, in imitation of what is performed upon this high mountain of glory, we are to exercise ourselves always in loving and willing what the Blessed love and will in Heaven and what God Himself loves and wills, that is to say, the grandeur of His glory and the immensity of His being, sovereignly perfect and sovereignly happy.

---

# 70

## THE EXCELLENCE OF HUMILITY

*"Learn of Me, because I am meek and humble of heart."* —Matthew 11:29

ST. AUSTIN says on this passage, that "the whole life of our Saviour upon earth was a continual lesson in morality but that in a special manner He proposed His humility for our imitation." To comprehend well the excellence of this virtue and the need we have of it, we are to consider that the Son of God descended from Heaven to teach it to us, not only by His words, but more especially by His actions and that His whole life was but a long example and living model of humility. To prove this, St. Basil makes a study of the life of our Saviour, and having examined it from His birth to His death, shows that all His actions particularly teach us the virtue of humility. He is circumcised as a sinner; He flies into Egypt, as too weak and unable to resist violence to His person; He is baptized with sinners and publicans, as one of them. When the people wish to honor and make Him king, He hides Himself; when they wish to cover Him with reproaches, He shows Himself. Men praise Him, and even the devils themselves do so by the mouths of the possessed, and He commands them to be silent. Men load Him with outrage and injury, and He answers not a word. After all this, to recommend humility to us, as it were, by His last will and testament at the close of life, He stoops so low as to wash His disciples' feet, and at last He crowns so many examples by the most shameful death of the Cross. "He wished to annihilate Himself," says St. Bernard, "to show first by His example what He was afterwards to teach by His words." But why, O Lord, does majesty so exalted stoop so low? It is, "that none should henceforth presume to magnify himself upon earth." At all times previous to Him there existed an extravagance in man's nature to yield to vanity; but now, as St. Bernard adds, "it would be an insufferable impudence for a worm to swell with pride when the majesty of the eternal God has humbled and annihilated Himself." The Son of

God, equal to His Father, takes the form of a servant; He wishes to be humbled and despised; and shall we, who are but dust and ashes, seek to be honored and respected?

It is with reason that the Saviour of the World says that He is master of this virtue and that it is of Him we ought to learn it. For not Socrates, nor Plato, nor Aristotle, nor any other philosopher ever knew how to teach it. When they valued themselves for other virtues, as fortitude, temperance and justice, they were so far from being humble that they aimed only at reputation and vainglory. It is true that Diogenes, and some others who made open profession of holding in contempt whatever the world valued, seemed indeed to despise the world and themselves too, but in that very thing they only sought vainglory in a way different from others, as they have been all accused of since, and as Plato reproached Diogenes in his own days. Plato, it seems, had invited him with some other philosophers to dinner and ordered the dining room to be hung with rich tapestry. Diogenes entered in his filth and dirt; he pulled down a piece of the hangings and trampled it under foot. Plato asked him what he was doing? "I am trampling," said he, "on the pride of Plato." "You are, indeed," answered Plato, "but in doing so, you are showing your own pride, though in another way." But so far were the philosophers from knowing what was meant by the contempt of one's self, in which Christian humility consists, so far were they from knowing what true humility is, that they were ignorant of its very name. It is a virtue peculiar to Christians, which was never taught before Jesus Christ preached it.

St. Austin remarks that, in the very first words of His Sermon on the Mount, our Saviour recommended humility. For by the words, "Blessed are the poor in spirit" (*Matt.* 5:3) are understood the humble, as not only St. Austin, but St. Jerome, St. Gregory and several others teach. He begins, continues and ends His sermon on the subject of humility, and it is this virtue especially that He will have us learn of Him. "He says not," continues St. Austin, "learn of Me to make Heaven and earth, to create all visible things, to work miracles, to raise the dead, but learn of Me to be meek and humble, for solid humility," as the Saint adds, "is much more powerful and safe than empty grandeur." It is better to be humble and serve God with fear than to work miracles. The first is an even and sure way; the other a very difficult and dangerous one.

To speak more particularly: the necessity of the virtue of humility is so great that without it we cannot hope to advance one step in the way of perfection. "Humility," says St. Austin, "must precede, accompany and follow all the good we do; for from the very moment that pride enters, it snatches all merit from us." Nay, it is for that very reason that pride and vainglory are the more to be feared, for other vices spring from bad actions, but pride springs from good ones, "so that we are to be more on our guard against pride in our good actions, lest by too great a desire of praise we come to lose the fruit of all we have done that was praiseworthy." It is easy for us to keep ourselves from other vices; they have certain marks which reveal them; they are accompanied by other sins; but pride takes its place in the midst of good works and continually endeavors to destroy them. Yes, let a Christian be steering a happy course on the sea of the world and thinking of nothing but Heaven, where from the beginning he intended to land, yet if there come a sudden puff of pride, a desire to please men, a self-complacency, this will send him to the bottom in the midst of his voyage. St. Gregory and St. Bernard say that "he who without humility treasures up other virtues does nothing more than throw dust before the wind"— the first puff blows all away.

---

# 71

## HUMILITY—THE FOUNDATION OF ALL OTHER VIRTUES

*"It is better to be humble with the meek than to divide spoils with the great."* —Proverbs 16:19

S T. CYPRIAN says that "humility is the foundation of sanctity"; St. Jerome, that it is "the first Christian virtue"; St. Bernard calls it "the foundation and preservation of the virtues." St. Gregory at one time calls it "the mistress and mother," at another, "the spring and root of all other virtues." This metaphor of the root agrees exactly with its nature and explains very aptly its properties and conditions; for first, in the words of St. Gregory, just as a flower draws all its freshness and beauty from the root and quickly fades as soon as it is plucked, even so, if any virtue whatever be but separated from the root of humility, it presently withers and is quite lost. Again, as the root lies deep under ground and is trodden under foot and has ordinarily neither beauty nor smell, yet it is nevertheless the principle both of the plant's life and nourishment, so also, humility makes the man who is humble love to lie hid, as it were, under ground, and to be trod upon and despised. It shuns noise and splendor and seeks only the obscurity of retirement; nevertheless, it is this which preserves in itself all the other virtues and makes them daily grow more and more. Lastly, as a tree must take deep root in order to bear well and live long, and the deeper the root the longer the tree lives and the more fruit it bears—according to the words of Isaias, "It shall take root downwards, and bear fruit upwards" (*4 Kgs.* 19:30)—so too, in order that other virtues should thrive and fructify in our hearts, it is necessary that humility be deeply rooted there. And the deeper the root is, the more will these virtues increase, and the stronger will they grow. I shall conclude then with asserting, as I did in the beginning, that humility, according to the doctrine of all the holy Fathers, is the source, foundation and root of all virtues, just as "pride is the beginning of all sin" (*Ecclus.* 10:15), according to the words of the Wise Man.

But some perhaps may say, "How can humility be the foundation of all other virtues and of the whole spiritual edifice since it is certain that faith is the foundation thereof and that, according to the words of the Apostle, "none can lay any other foundation but that which is laid, which is Jesus Christ"? (*1 Cor.* 3:11). St. Thomas answers this objection very well. "Two things," he says, "are requisite to lay the foundation of a house well: first, the ground must be dug, everything light and sandy must be thrown out and persons must continue to dig till the ground is felt to be firm enough to build upon. In the second place, after having cleared away the sand and gone deep, they must lay the first stone, which together with the other stones laid in the same line, makes the principal foundation of the building. Here," continues the Saint, "we have a representation of what humility and faith do in the spiritual building. Humility opens the ground, digs the foundation and throws out all the sand—that is to say, the weakness of human strength. For you must not build upon your own strength, which is but quicksand and which you must remove by having a diffidence toward yourself and by digging always till you find sure and solid ground [on which] to lay the first stone, and that stone is Jesus Christ, who is the chief foundation of all the building. But as, in order to lay this foundation well, we must first of all dig with humility, so for this reason, humility is called the foundation of the edifice. Now if humility opens the ground well, if it penetrates into the knowledge of our nothingness, if it throws out all the quicksand that is in us—that is, all the confidence we have in ourselves—if it does this, in order to lay there the foundation stone, Jesus Christ, the building reared upon it shall never be shaken, neither shall the wind nor the rain ever be able to overthrow it. But if we build without humility, all the edifice will quickly fall to the ground, because it was built on sand."

All virtues which are not founded upon humility are not real virtues; they are virtues in appearance only. St. Austin, speaking of those virtues of the ancient Romans and philosophers, asserts that they were not real virtues, not only because they were not animated by charity, which gives spirit and life to all other virtues, but because they had not the foundation of humility. For in fortitude, justice, temperance and all their acts of virtue, these persons sought only worldly esteem and reputation, so that their virtues were rather the ghosts or phantoms of virtues, rather than real ones. He adds that as they were virtues only in appearance, so God rewarded them with the good things of this world only, which also are only apparent goods. If, therefore, you desire that real virtues should raise up a spiritual edifice in your souls, endeavor first of all to lay a solid foundation of humility. "You aspire," says St. Austin, "to great things, begin with little ones; You desire to erect a very high building; think first of the foundation of humility. The foundations are always sunk proportionately to the intended weight of the building, and the higher one intends it, the deeper must the foundation be laid." The height must answer to the depth, so that you can only raise the edifice of evangelical perfection which you intend to build pro-portionately to the depth of humility you give to the foundations. It is related of St. Thomas Aquinas that, speaking of humility, he was accustomed to say that a man who loves to be honored, who shuns contempt

contempt and who bears it with chagrin, however many good works he may do, is yet far from perfection, because all his virtue has no foundation.

————————

## 72

## HUMILITY—THE FOUNDATION OF ALL VIRTUES

*"The prayer of the humble hath pleased Thee, O Lord."* —Judith 9:16

LET US consider the principal virtues, in order to show more plainly the truth of the maxim of the Saints, that humility is the foundation of all other graces and therefore how necessary this foundation is for us.

First of all, Faith stands in need of humility. I speak not of infants—who receive Faith in baptism without exercising any act of faith—but I speak of those who have the use of reason. Faith requires a humble and submissive spirit, according to St. Paul, "bringing into captivity every understanding to the obedience of Christ." (*2 Cor.* 10:5). On the contrary, the spirit of pride hinders the receiving of Faith, according to the words of our Saviour: "How can you believe, who receive glory one from another, and the glory which is from God alone you do not seek?" (*John* 5:44). Now, as humility is necessary for the receiving of Faith, it is equally so for the preserving of it, for all holy writers hold that heresies spring from the pride we manifest in preferring our own light to the decisions of the whole Church. It is this the Apostle alludes to when he says, "Know also this, that in the last days shall come dangerous times; men shall be lovers of themselves, covetous, haughty, proud." (2 *Tim.* 3:1,2). And St. Austin observes on this passage that the Apostle attributes the cause of all heresies and errors particularly to pride and arrogance.

Hope likewise is supported by humility, because he who is humble knows his misery and weakness; he is sensible that of himself he can do nothing and so flies with greater ardor to God and fixes all his hope in Him.

Charity also, which consists in loving God, is very much increased by means of humility, for one of a humble spirit, seeing that he receives whatever he has from the hand of God and that he is very far from meriting it, feels himself excited to love his benefactor more and more. "What is man," says Job, "that Thou shouldst magnify him? Or why dost Thou set Thy heart upon him?" (*Job* 7:17). "Shall I, O Lord, remain thus rebellious to Thee, and Thou so good to me? Shall I go on still offending Thee, while Thou continuest to heap Thy favors upon me?" This is one of the chief considerations which the Saints have made use of to inflame themselves with the love of God. The more they reflected upon their own unworthiness, the more they thought themselves obliged to love Him who had condescended to cast His eyes upon their meanness. "My soul doth magnify the Lord," says the holy Virgin, "because He hath regarded the low estate of His handmaid." (*Luke* 1:46).

As to the charity which we exercise towards our neighbor, it is easily seen how necessary humility is for this, because one of the things which usually makes us so cold to our brethren is some judgment we form to their disadvantage, some impression made on us by their faults. A humble man is far from all this; he looks upon his own errors, not on those of others; and while he imagines everyone else perfect and himself alone imperfect, he thinks himself unworthy to live among his brethren and is, in consequence, full of love, esteem and veneration for them. Moreover, the humble man is not angry at others being preferred to him; he is willing that they should be esteemed and himself despised. He is content that they should get the highest and himself the lowest place. There is no envy among the humble because envy springs from pride, so that wherever humility reigns, you will not find envy, dispute, quarrel or anything to cool fraternal charity.

Patience—a virtue so necessary for a Christian—arises likewise from humility because he who is humble knows his own faults and is sensible at the same time that he deserves all manner of chastisement. He therefore meets with no mortifications which he looks not upon as less than what he has deserved and instead of complaining of them, he says with the prophet Micheas, "I will bear the wrath of the Lord, because I have sinned against Him." (*Mich.* 7:9). A proud man complains of everything and suspects without reason that he is wronged and not treated according to his merit. On the contrary, whatever injury is done to the humble man, he heeds it not nor takes it for an injury; nay, so far is he from imagining that an injury can be done to him in anything that he still reckons all as kindness; and however he is treated, he is always satisfied because he believes that he is treated better than he deserves. In short, humility is a great preparation for patience, and hence, after the Wise Man had admonished him who will engage in the service of God to prepare himself for a great many mortifications and to arm himself with patience, the means he proposes for that end is to humble himself. "Humble thy heart," says he, "and endure; wait upon God with patience." (*Ecclus.* 2:2). But what arms does he give him to ward off trouble, or to make him at least bear it courageously? "In thy humility, keep patience" (*Ecclus.* 2:4); that is to say, be humble, and then you will be patient.

Peace also—the blessing so much desired by all the world—springs from humility, and Jesus Christ Himself teaches us this truth when He says, "Learn of Me, because I am meek and humble of heart; and you shall find rest to your souls." (*Matt.* 11:29). Be humble, and you will be at rest both with yourselves and your brethren. "Among the proud there are always contentions," says Solomon (*Prov.* 13:10), but in the same measure are the humble free from them. Between such there is but one contest: it is to decide who shall be lowest and pay the greatest deference to his companion. The strife between St. Paul the Hermit and St. Anthony of the Desert as to who should break and divide the bread which the raven had brought them was of this nature. Paul would have Anthony do it as being a stranger, and Anthony would have Paul do it as being the elder, each of them seeking reasons to yield and give place to the other. It is good to have such contests, and as they spring from true humility, they are so far from troubling or destroying fraternal charity that they nourish and confirm it.

Lastly, if we consider prayer—which is the foundation of a spiritual life—it is certain that it is of no effect without humility; whereas, *with* humility, it pierces the heavens, according to the words of the Wise Man: "The prayer of him that humbleth himself shall pierce the clouds; and till it come nigh, he will not be comforted; and he will not depart till the Most High behold." (*Ecclus.* 35:21). And the Royal Prophet says that "God hath regard to the prayer of the humble, and hath not despised their petition." (*Ps.* 101:18). Fear not, therefore, that the humble will be turned away: he will obtain what he asks. Consider too how agreeable the prayer of the publican was to God: he dared not lift up his eyes to Heaven, nor approach the altar, but, "standing afar off," he struck his breast, saying, "O God, be merciful to me a sinner." (*Luke* 18:13). And Jesus Christ declared that he went down to his house justified rather than the proud Pharisee. We might thus run over all the other virtues and show that they all depend upon humility, so that if you seek a ready way to acquire them and a short lesson for attaining perfection, you have it in two words: *Be humble!*

## 73

# THE EXCELLENCE OF OBEDIENCE

*"An obedient man shall speak of victory."*
—Proverbs 21:28

"**D**OTH the Lord desire holocausts and victims, and not rather that the voice of the Lord should be obeyed? For obedience is better than sacrifices, and to hearken rather than to offer the fat of rams." (*1 Kings* 15:22). These were the words of Samuel to Saul when he had reserved the best and fairest flocks of the Amalekites for sacrifice, contrary to the express command of God, which was totally to destroy them and all that belonged to them. The holy Fathers take occasion from this and several other passages of Holy Scripture, which declare the excellence and merit of obedience, to bestow the highest praise on this virtue. St. Austin asks why God forbade Adam to eat of the tree of the knowledge of good and evil, and one of the reasons he gives is that it was "to teach man how great a good obedience is in itself and how great an evil disobedience is." Disobedience, and a breach of God's prohibition, was the cause of all the evil. And for this reason, St. Austin says that nothing shows the inherent evil of disobedience more than the punishment inflicted upon Adam for eating the forbidden fruit, which, independent of the prohibition, was, liberally speaking, a harmless and innocent act in itself.

Let those who dispense with obedience in small

matters learn from this to see their error and to correct it. For the sin does not arise from the nature of the thing, but from the disobedience, which is always evil, whether the thing be of great or small importance. This holy father, after passing a high encomium on this virtue, concludes by saying that one of the reasons which moved the Son of God to take human nature upon Himself was to teach us obedience by His own example. "Man," he says, "was disobedient even to death, that is, death was the deserved punishment of his disobedience. And the Son of God made Himself man that He might be obedient even to death. Adam's disobedience shut Heaven's gates against us; Christ's obedience threw them open." "For as by the disobedience of one man many were made sinners, so also, by the obedience of one, many shall be made just." (*Rom.* 5:19). Nor can there be a greater proof of the merit and excellence of this virtue than the glorious reward which God has given to the sacred humility of His Son Jesus Christ, "who was obedient unto death, even to the death of the cross; for which cause God also hath exalted Him, and given Him a name which is above all names, that in the name of Jesus every knee should bow." (*Philip.* 2:8ff).

Obedience is the essential virtue of a Christian. It is this that pleases God more than all the sacrifices we can make to Him; it is this that comprises humility, chastity and all other virtues. For admit that you are truly obedient, you cannot fail of being chaste, humble, modest, patient, mortified, and, in a word, master of all virtues. Virtuous habits are attained by a frequent exercise of their particular acts, and it is in this way that God is pleased to bestow them upon us. Now, obedience procures for us this frequent exercise, for all that our superior or our spiritual director commands is an exercise of some virtue. Take obedience for your guide and embrace all the occasions which it presents to you and you need do no more. Sometimes you will meet with occasions to exercise patience, sometimes humility, sometimes mortification and at other times temperance and chastity, and thus as you improve in obedience, you will advance in all other virtues. St. Austin calls obedience "the greatest of virtues and likewise the mother and source of all virtues." "This is the only virtue," says St. Gregory, "that plants other virtues in our mind and preserves them after they are once planted." St. Gregory and St. Bernard, in their explanation of these words of the Proverbs, "An obedient man shall speak of victory" (*Prov.* 21:28), say that an obedient man shall get not only one, but even many victories and with them make himself master of all virtues.

---

# 74

## SERVING GOD WITH JOY

*"The voice of rejoicing and of salvation is in the tabernacles of the just."* —Psalm 117:15

"REJOICE in the Lord always," says the Apostle, "and again I say, rejoice." (*Phil.* 4:4). The Psalmist also recommends the same to us very often:

"Be glad in the Lord," he says; "rejoice ye just, and glory all ye right of heart." (*Ps.* 31:11). "Sing joyfully to God, all the earth; serve the Lord with gladness." (*Ps.* 99:1). "Let the heart of them rejoice that seek the Lord." (*Ps.* 104:3). When the Angel Raphael saluted Tobias, he said nothing to him but this, "Joy be to thee always." (*Tob.* 5:2). St. Francis was accustomed to say that the devil and wicked men only ought to be sad, and that those who are truly religious men ought always to rejoice. And how is it possible we should be sad—we whom God has chosen from among so many, to place us in His own house and family?

That the advantages of serving God with joy may excite us the more, let us consider some of the reasons that ought to make us joyful. The first is that God desires to be served in this manner for as St. Paul says, God loves him who gives with cheerfulness. The Wise Man also teaches the same thing in these words: "In every gift show a cheerful countenance." (*Ecclus.* 35:2). As in the world masters wish to be served by their domestics with joy and cannot endure that they should serve them with sadness, even so, God, who is our supreme Lord and Master, desires to be served with joy and affection and is displeased with those that serve Him with chagrin and sadness.

The second reason is that, when we serve God with joy, we promote His honor and glory because we show that we do it with affection and that all we do is nothing compared to what we would wish to do. "All that I do for Thee, O Lord," said St. Bernard, "seems scarce to take up an hour's time, or if it takes up more, love hinders me from perceiving it." It is not so with those that serve God with sadness. One would say that they think they do very much because they groan under the burden and would seem, as it were, oppressed by the heaviness of the yoke. Now this greatly offends God and is a very bad sign, and it was on this account that St. Francis was always displeased when he saw any of his religious sad, because sadness is a sign of a will much indisposed and of a burdensome body.

The third reason is that God is not only more honored in this way, but that our neighbor also is more edified and the esteem of virtue more increased, for those who serve God with joy prove to worldlings that on the road of virtue there are not so many obstacles and difficulties as is imagined, and as that, men naturally love joy, they willingly travel the road in which they expect to find it.

The fourth reason for which we ought to serve God with joy is that our good actions gain by this means a greater merit in His sight and become more holy and perfect, for it is a maxim in philosophy that "joy perfects a work and sadness corrupts it." And do we not daily see that there is a great difference between him that does a work with cheerfulness and another that performs it unwillingly and with regret? It seems that the one does it slightly and superficially and only to be able to say that he has done it, but the other applies himself to do well what he does and to acquit himself of his duty in the best manner he is able. "Joy and contentment," says St. Chrysostom, "give strength and courage to perform good works," and therefore the Royal Prophet said to God, "I have run the way of Thy commandments when Thou didst enlarge my heart." (*Ps.* 118:32). But it is joy which enlarges the heart, and it is joy also that hinders the just from feeling pain in anything they do: "They run and are not weary, they walk and do not faint." (*Is.* 40:31). Sadness, on the contrary, shuts up the heart and takes from it not only the desire, but even the power of acting, and causes that which before was easy to become hard and insupportable.

The fifth reason why Christians should serve God with joy is that, when one begins in this manner to serve Him, there is good reason to hope that he will persevere. When we see a man that is laden walk heavily and uneasily and as if out of breath and stopping almost at every step to rest himself or replace and refit his burden anew, we at once conclude that he is a man who is quite spent and able to do no more. On the contrary, when we see another who steadily carries his burden and sings all the way as he goes, we conclude he will carry it on and that he will not fail on the way. It is the same with the Christian: those who have sorrow imprinted on their foreheads while they perform the duties of their profession and seem to groan under their burden give no flattering hopes of perseverance, for to ply continually at the oar as a slave is a task difficult to perform for any length of time. But those who bear the yoke of the Lord with joy and perform with cheerfulness even the meanest duties and the most laborious exercises give great hopes of remaining always faithful and constant in their course.

———————

## 75

## ENCOURAGEMENT UNDER TRIALS

*"Thy word hath enlivened me."* —Psalm 118:50

"GOD is faithful," says the Apostle, "who will not suffer you to be tempted above that which you are able, but will make also with the temptation an issue, that you may be able to bear it." (*1 Cor.* 10:13). This ought to be a great comfort to us in temptation. We already know on the one hand that the devil has no power but what God gives him and can tempt us no further than God permits, and on the other, that God will not permit the devil to tempt us above our strength. Who is there to whom this assurance ought not to give comfort and courage?

Upon these words of Sacred Scripture, "Jesus having entered into the boat, His disciples followed Him, and behold a great tempest arose in the sea, so that the boat was covered with waves; but He was asleep" (*Matt.* 8:23), St. Ambrose, says that the elect of Our Lord and those who accompany Him are tempted just like others; nay, regarding temptation, it even sometimes happens that God "pretends to sleep," thus industriously hiding the love He bears His children, that He may require them to have recourse more to Him. But He sleeps not, nor does He at all forget them. It seems to a sick person that the night is longer than ordinary and that the day is very long in coming, notwithstanding that it comes at the ordinary time. So in like manner, though God seems to you who are sick to stay away longer than He should do, yet it is not so. He knows at what time precisely He ought to come, and He will not fail to do so. "If it [the vision] make any delay, wait for it; for it shall surely come, and it shall not be slack." (*Hab.* 2:3).

Regarding this method of acting, St. Austin explains our Saviour's conduct when the sisters of Lazarus sent Him word that their brother was sick. "This sickness," He said, "is not unto death, but for the glory of God, that the Son of God may be glorified by it." (*John* 11:4). After this He waited two days longer, to make the miracle He planned to perform all the greater. It is thus, adds the Saint, that God sometimes treats His servants: He leaves them for some time in temptations and sufferings and seems as if He has forgotten them, but it is in order to procure greater advantages for them. God allowed Joseph to remain long in prison, but He afterwards drew him out of it with greater glory to make him governor of all Egypt. Therefore, if He leaves you for a long time in temptation and suffering, it is to draw you out of them in a way more advantageous to His own glory and your salvation. St. Chrysostom makes the same remark upon these words of the Psalmist: "Thou that liftest me up from the gates of death." (*Ps.* 9:15). Observe, he says, that the prophet does not say, "Thou who dost deliver me," but, "Thou that dost lift me up from," because God is not contented with delivering His servants from temptations, but He makes temptations serve to their greater elevation and glory. Therefore, though you feel yourself overwhelmed and imagine yourself to be already within the gates of death, yet you ought to believe firmly that God will draw you forth from there. "The Lord killeth and maketh alive; He bringeth down to hell, and bringeth back again." (*1 Kings* 2:6). "Though He should kill me," says Job, "I will trust in Him." (*Job* 13:15).

St. Cyprian, desiring to inspire us with the same confidence, makes use of the words of God in the prophet Isaias: "Fear not, for I have redeemed thee, and called thee by thy name: thou art Mine. When thou shalt pass through the waters, I will be with thee, and the rivers shall not cover thee: when thou shalt walk in the fire, thou shalt not be burnt, and the flames shall not burn thee; for I am the Lord thy God, the Holy One of Israel, thy Saviour." (*Is.* 43:1, 2, 3). Those words also, of the same prophet, are well fitted to strengthen us in the same holy confidence: "As one whom the mother caresses, so will I comfort you." (*Is.* 66:13). Imagine with what marks of love a mother receives her infant when, being frightened at anything, it casts itself into her arms. How she embraces it, how she presses it to her breast, how she kisses and tenderly caresses it, but the tenderness of God for those who have recourse to Him in temptations and dangers is without comparison far greater. It was this that gave so much comfort to the Psalmist when he cried out to God, "Be Thou mindful of Thy word to Thy servant, in which Thou hast given me hope. This hath comforted me in my humiliation; because Thy word hath enlivened me." (*Ps.* 118:49-50). Let us animate ourselves with the same hope, and let us make it the subject of our comfort because, as the Apostle says, "It is impossible that God should lie" (*Heb.* 6:18) or violate His word.

---

# 76

## DISTRUST OF OURSELVES UNDER TEMPTATION

*"The Lord is the protector of all that trust in Him."*
—Psalm 17:31

ONE of the best means of overcoming temptations is to distrust ourselves and to place all our confidence in God, for as the Scripture notices in several places, it is this which chiefly moves Him to assist us in our temptations and sufferings. "Because he hoped in Me, I will deliver him." (*Ps.* 90:14). The prophet alleges no other reason to God than this, to oblige Him to have mercy on him, "Have mercy on me, O God, have mercy on me; for my soul trusteth in Thee, in the shadow of Thy wings will I hope." (*Ps.* 56:1). It was the same reason that Azarias made use of in the fiery furnace when he begged of God to accept the sacrifice of his life, saying, "For there is no confusion to them that trust in Thee." (*Dan.* 3:40). The Wise Man, in like manner, assures us that "No one has hoped in the Lord, and has been confounded." (*Ecclus.* 2:2).

But let us now see why this entire distrust of ourselves and confidence in God is a means so well fitted to merit His help in our necessities. We have already touched on the reason in several places, and God Himself has given it to us when He said by the mouth of David, "Because he hoped in Me, I will deliver him; I will protect him, because he hath known My name." (*Ps.* 90:14). This is to say, according to St. Bernard, "I will protect him, and I will deliver him, on condition that, acknowledging his deliverance to come from Me, he attributes it not to himself, but gives all the glory of it to My name." The reason, therefore, why God so particularly protects those who hope in Him is that they attribute nothing to themselves, but give all the glory of it to Him so that, as they are regardless of their own honor and attentive only to that of God, He takes their cause in hand and makes it His own business, as a thing that regards His own honor and glory. He acts not so towards those who confide in their own light and rely upon their own strength, but since they attribute all to themselves and thus usurp a glory which belongs to God alone, He leaves them to their blindness and weakness and permits them not to succeed in anything. For according to the Prophet, "He shall not delight in the strength of the horse; nor take pleasure in the legs of a man. The Lord taketh pleasure in them that fear Him, and in them that hope in His mercy." (*Ps.* 146:10).

St. Austin says that God sometimes defers the help of His grace and permits that for a long time there

should remain in us an inclination to certain vices
without our being able to attain an entire victory
over them. "And this not to destroy, but to humble
us, that we may more esteem His grace and fear
also that if we should find a facility in all things,
we should believe that to belong to us which is His:
an error very dangerous to religion and contrary
to piety." Without doubt, if things became so very
easy, we should set less value on them and believe
we were indebted to none but ourselves for them.
St. Gregory, explaining these words of Job, "Behold
there is no help for me in myself" (*Job* 6:13), says,
"It often happens that some virtue which we possess becomes an instrument of our destruction and
that we should have been better off without it,
because it fills us with pride by inspiring a vain confidence in ourselves. And by means of this pride,
it kills the soul; while it seems to give it new
strength, it throws it down a precipice, after it has
separated it by presumption from that confidence
it ought to have had in God." This abuse of God's
graces often causes Him to refuse them to us, permitting in a thousand occasions, that we should
know by experience how little ability we have of
ourselves to do anything that is good and allowing
us to remain a long time in this state, to teach us
humility and that we should not to confide in nor
attribute anything to ourselves, but to render the
glory of all to God alone. When we shall be in such
a holy disposition of mind as this, then we may
assure ourselves of His divine assistance and sing
with the mother of Samuel, "The bow of the mighty

is overcome, and the weak are girt with strength."
(*1 Kings* 2:4).

---

## 77

### THE FRUIT OF TEMPTATION

*"Blessed is the man that endureth temptation, for when
he hath been proved, he shall receive the crown of
life." —*James 1:12

"THE Lord your God trieth you, that it may
appear whether you love Him with all your
heart, and with all your soul, or no." (*Deut.* 13:3).
Upon these words of Sacred Scripture, St. Austin asks
how they can be reconciled with the words of St.
James, who says that "God tempts no man"? (*James*
1:13). Answering his own objection, he says that there
are two ways of tempting, one of which tends to
deceive souls and make them fall into sin. Now God
does not make use of this, but the devil, whose business it is to tempt after this manner, according to
those words of the Apostle, "Lest he that tempteth
should have tempted you." (*1 Thess.* 3:3). The other
way of tempting goes no further than to try our
hearts, and in this sense it is that Scripture says here
that God tempts, and in another place that "God
tempted Abraham." (*Gen.* 22:1). God is pleased to try
us, to make us sensible of our own strength and to
show us how we should love and fear Him. And
therefore, as soon as Abraham had lifted up his hand

to sacrifice his son, "Now I know," said Our Lord to him, "that thou fearest God" (*Gen.* 22:12), that is, as St. Austin expresses it, "I have made thee know" that thou lovest Him. Thus, there are two sorts of temptations: the one which God Himself sends us, and the other which happens to us by His permission.

St. Gregory says that God, by a secret and adorable providence, is pleased that the elect should be tempted and afflicted here on earth, because this world is only a place of pilgrimage, or rather of banishment, where we must be continually traveling till we arrive at our heavenly country. And whereas travelers, on meeting with some agreeable meadow or grove, turn sometimes off the high road, God, who would not have anything put us off our path nor have us fix our minds upon earth or mistake the place of our exile for that of our True Country, permits this life to be full of labor and affliction, that the consideration of what we suffer here may make us more ardently sigh after the life to come. St. Austin similarly says that temptations and afflictions serve to show us the misery of this life and "to make us desire with greater ardor and seek more carefully the other," where we are to enjoy true happiness for all eternity. In another place he says that "afflictions hinder the traveler who is going to his own country from looking upon his inn as the place of his abode and from staying there too long." And St. Gregory says that the "afflictions which oppress us here below force us to have recourse to God and make us have no inclination for anything but Him."

St. Bernard, explaining the words of St. James,

already quoted above, says, "It is necessary that temptations should happen, for who shall be crowned but him that shall lawfully have fought, and how shall a man fight if there be none to attack him?" Scripture and holy writers show us that many advantages are attached to sufferings and adversities, and the same are also attached to temptations, among which advantages one of the chief is that proposed to us in the words of St. James. God sends us temptations, that our merits may be the greater and our reward the more eminent. "For through many tribulations we must enter into the kingdom of God." (*Acts* 14:21). Here we must hew and polish the stones that are to build the temple of the heavenly Jerusalem, for not one stroke of the hammer shall be given in that holy city. Now, the more considerable the place is where the stones are to be put, the more strokes of the hammer and chisel are requisite to polish them. Those, for example, that are to make up the front of the gate of a building must be more polished than the others, that so they may make the entrance of the building more beautiful. Nor is it for this only that Jesus Christ, having made Himself for us the Gate of Heaven, was pleased to be afflicted with so many sufferings and reproaches, but it is also, that being to pass through a door where sufferings and reproaches, if we may say so, had given so many strokes of the hammer and chisel to Him, we ought to be ashamed at not having received some ourselves, to make us more fit for this heavenly building.

The necessity of being proved by temptations is also shown to us by these words of the Angel to

Tobias, "Because thou wert acceptable to God, it was necessary that temptation should prove thee." (*Tob.* 12:13). And the Wise Man says of Abraham, "that in temptation he was found faithful." (*Ecclus.* 44:21). And because he was found steadfast in temptation, God lays before him the reward of his virtue and swears to him, "that He would multiply his seed as the stars of heaven, and as the sand by the seashore." (*Gen.* 22:17).

Temptation brings another advantage with it, which is that it makes us know ourselves. Many times we know not ourselves, but temptation shows us what we are, as Kempis well says: "Temptations are very profitable, though uneasy and troublesome to man, because in them he is humbled, purified and taught." This knowledge of ourselves is the foundation stone of the whole spiritual building, without which nothing can be built that will last long. And by means of it the soul leans its whole weight upon God, through whom it can do all things, and becomes capable of raising itself to the height of Christian perfection. "Were it not for temptation," says St. Gregory, "we should have too good an opinion of our own courage and strength, but when temptation comes, when we see ourselves just falling, and as it were within an inch of shipwreck, then do we sincerely acknowledge our weakness and conceive true thoughts of humility and lowliness." So the Apostle, speaking of himself, says, "Lest the greatness of the revelations should puff me up, there was given me a sting in my flesh, an angel of Satan, to buffet me." (*2 Cor.* 12:7).

Hence follows another advantage, which is that the knowledge of our weakness makes us know the need we have of God's assistance, of having recourse to Him in prayer and of cleaving fast to Him only. St. Bernard says that when God seems sometimes to withdraw Himself from us, it is that we should, then, as it were, call Him back again with more earnestness and endeavor more carefully to keep Him when we have Him. Thus it was that, being with His two disciples who were going to Emmaus, "He made as though He would go farther," that they should the more press Him to stay with them and say, as they did, "Stay with us, for it is towards evening, and the day is now far spent." (*Luke* 24:29).

Thus it is that, seeing the need we have of God's assistance, we esteem it the more. It is also this which made St. Gregory say that it is for our advantage that God sometimes withdraws His hand from us because, if He should never leave us, we might esteem His protection the less and think it not so necessary as it is. Whereas, when He leaves us but for a time and afterwards stretches out His hand to us, and that at the very moment we are ready to fall, we know much better the value of His favors. When we reflect, with the Psalmist that without Him we had been lost—"Unless the Lord had been my helper, my soul had almost dwelt in hell" (*Ps.* 93:17)—we have then a more lively sense of His favors and enter into deeper reflections on His mercy and bounty. As soon as we have recourse to God in temptation, we receive succor from Him; we find how faithful He is to assist us in time of necessity, and that proof makes us, by looking then more particularly upon Him as our Father and Defender, to be the more inflamed with love of Him and to sing His praises, as the children of Israel did when they saw their enemies that pursued them perish in the Red Sea.

---

# 78

## TEMPTATION

*"Son, when thou comest to the service of God, stand in justice and in fear, and prepare thy soul for temptation."* —Ecclesiasticus 2:1

S T. JEROME, upon these words, "There is a time of war and a time of peace" (*Ecclus.* 3:8), says, that as long as we are in this life, it is a time of war; and when we shall come to the other world, it will be a time of peace, for which reason the name of Jerusalem, that is to say, "the vision of peace," is given to this heavenly country to which we aspire. "Let nobody, therefore," adds he, "think himself at present secure in this time of war, in which we are continually to fight, that at length we may rest in peace, such a peace as nothing shall be able to interrupt." St. Austin, upon these words of the Apostle, "I do not the good that I would do" (*Rom.* 7:15), says that the life of a just man is not a triumph, but a combat, and therefore at present we hear the cries of war, such as are expressed by the words which the Apostle makes use of when he complains of the repugnance of nature to what is good, and of its inclination to evil. But songs of triumph will be heard when our mortal body shall be clothed with immortality, and then we shall cry out with the Apostle, "Death is swallowed up in victory! O grave, where is thy victory? O death, where is thy sting?" (*1 Cor.* 15:54).

But let us examine the cause of this continual war. The Apostle St. James shows us: "From whence," he says, "are wars and contentions among you? Come they not from your concupiscences, which war in your members?" (*James* 4:1). The source of all this is within ourselves, and this source is the repugnance we have to what is good, which has remained in our flesh since the entrance of sin. The earth of our flesh was no less cursed than earth itself, and therefore it produces so many thorns and thistles, which prick and torment us. The Saints compare us to that ship in the Gospel which was no sooner launched into the sea than a tempest rose and covered it with waves. For our soul is in our body, as a ship that leaks on all sides and which the winds of a thousand different passions expose every moment to shipwreck.

The cause, then, of the continual temptations which torment us is our corrupt nature—"For the corruptible body is a load upon the soul" (*Wis.* 9:15)—which is that incentive to sin we carry about us, that inclination to evil with which we are born. Our greatest enemy is within us and wages continual war against us. We are therefore not to wonder at our being tempted. For since we are children of

Adam and "have been conceived in iniquity" (*Ps.* 1:7), how can we be exempted from temptations, or how can we hinder our evil inclinations from making war continually against us? And therefore St. Jerome observes that, in the prayer which our Saviour taught us, He does not bid us beg of God to have no temptations, for that is impossible, but only that He would not allow us to fall or sink under them. So also He taught His disciples, when He said to them, "Watch ye, and pray, that ye enter not into temptation." (*Matt.* 26:41).

Many erroneously imagine that, as soon as they are attacked by any violent temptation, all is lost and that God has forsaken them. But they are much mistaken, for all men are subject to temptations, and they who aim at perfection are more subject than others. All who will advance in virtue shall be exposed to temptations. As for others, they often know not even what it is to be tempted; they are not sensible of the rebellion and struggle of the flesh against the spirit. Nor need the devil lose time in tempting them, since of themselves and without resistance, they yield to him. We do not go to hunt after tame animals, but after the stag and other wild beasts noted for their swiftness. It is after those whose feet God has made as swift as harts' feet and those who live upon the mountains that the devil hunts. Such as are like tame animals he has no need to run after; they are already his own. "He minds not," says St. Gregory, "to disturb those of whom he enjoys a quiet possession." Thus, we ought not only not to wonder at our having temptations, but should look upon them as a good sign, according to the words of

St. John Climachus, who says, "that the most infallible mark of having overcome the devil is that he
assaults you violently." For he attacks you only because
you struggled with him and shook off his yoke.

---

# 79

## MORTIFICATION

*"I will be to them as one that taketh off the yoke."*
—Osee 11:4

I SHALL now speak of those means that may help
us to render this necessary practice of mortification not only easy, but pleasant. The first means
is the grace of God, with which all things become
easy. St. Paul supplies us both with an example and
a proof of this truth. The sting of the flesh, the
angel of Satan, tormented him. Thrice he begged
of God to be delivered from it, and God made this
answer to him: "My grace is sufficient for thee." (*2
Cor.* 12:9). Again, he says, "I can do all things in
Him who strengtheneth me." (*Phil.* 4:13). Yet, as he
says elsewhere, "Not I, but the grace of God with
me." (*1 Cor.* 15:10). We must not believe that God
leaves us to our own strength in time of mortification and suffering. No! He bears the greater part of
the burden Himself, and for this reason the law is
called a yoke, which is to be borne by two. For Jesus
Christ joins Himself to us, to help us to support it,
and with His assistance, who can be discouraged?

Therefore, let nothing in the law appear to you too hard, since you will have nothing but the easiest part of it to bear. It is for this reason also that He calls it a yoke and a burden when He says, "My yoke is sweet, and My burden light." (*Matt.* 11:30). For though, as regards our nature and weakness, it be ever so hard a yoke, and ever so heavy a burden, yet the grace of God renders it easy and light, because our Lord Himself helps us to bear it.

St. Bernard, in His first sermon on the dedication of a church, says that, as in the consecration the walls are anointed with holy oil, so our Saviour does the same in religious souls, sweetening by the spiritual unction of His grace all their crosses, penances and mortifications. Worldlings are afraid of a religious life because they see its crosses, but perceive not the unction with which they are anointed and made easy. "But you," says the Saint, speaking to his religious, "know by experience that our cross is truly full of unction, whereby it is not only light, but all the bitterness and hardship we find in our state is, by the grace of God, rendered sweet and pleasant." St. Austin admits that before he knew the power of grace, he could never comprehend what chastity was nor believe that anyone was able to practice it. But the grace of God renders all things so easy that, if we possess it, we may say with St. John that "His commandments are not heavy" (*1 Jn.* 5:3), because the abundance of grace He bestows upon us renders them most sweet and easy.

The second means which makes the practice of mortification easy is the love of God. Love, more than anything else, sweetens pain of every kind. "He who loves," says St. Austin, "thinks that nothing is hard, and yet the least labor is insupportable to those who love not. Love alone is ashamed to find difficulty in anything." It is thus that those who love hunting make no account of the fatigue they endure, but rather look upon it as a pleasure. Is it not love that makes the mother find no difficulty in nursing her infant? Is it not love that keeps the wife day and night at her sick husband's bedside? Is it not love that causes all sorts of creatures to take so much care in nourishing their young that they even abstain from eating and expose themselves to dangers for their sakes? Was it not love that made Jacob think his many years' service for Rachel short and sweet? "They seemed but a few days, because of the greatness of his love." (*Gen.* 29:20). No sooner does love appear than all pain vanishes and all sweetness accompanies our labor. A holy woman said that from her first being touched with the love of God, she knew not what it was to suffer, either exteriorly or interiorly, neither from the world, the flesh or the devil because pure love knows not what pain or torment is. Love, therefore, not only raises the price of all our actions and renders them more perfect, but it gives us courage to support all kinds of mortification and makes us feel great ease and sweetness, even in the hardest things. It was thus that St. Chrysostom explains these words of the Apostle, "Love is the fulfilling of the law." (*Rom.* 13:10). For he not only says (as the Saint notices) that the law and all the commandments are included in love, but that it is love which renders the observance of both most easy.

Let us therefore love much, and nothing will be able to stop us in the way of perfection. Then we shall be able to say with the Apostle: "Who then shall separate us from the love of Christ? Shall tribulation, or distress, or famine, or nakedness, or danger, or persecution, or the sword? For I am sure that neither death, nor life, nor angels, nor principalities, nor powers, nor height, nor depth, nor any other creature, shall be able to separate us from the love of God, which is in Christ Jesus our Lord." (*Rom.* 8:35, 38).

---

## 80

## TRUST IN DIVINE PROVIDENCE

*"Cast thy care upon the Lord, and He will sustain thee."* —Psalm 54:23

WE learn from Holy Scripture that one of the most powerful means by which we may engage the loving heart of Jesus to bestow upon us His choicest blessings and to inflame us with the fire of His holy love is to show Him that we place unlimited confidence in His mercy and goodness and that we abandon ourselves entirely into the hands of His Providence. There is no maxim which our blessed Saviour has more strongly recommended to His disciples by His doctrine, as well as by His example, than that of throwing themselves with perfect confidence and without any reserve into the hands of

*Absolutely Remember This*

their heavenly Father. In the discourse which He made to them in order to strengthen them against the various trials to which they would be exposed, we find Him speaking thus: "I say unto you, My friends, be not afraid of them who kill the body, and after that have no more they can do. But I will show you whom you shall fear: fear ye Him who, after He hath killed, hath power to cast you into Hell. Yea, I say unto you, fear Him. Are not five sparrows sold for two farthings, and not one of them is forgotten before God? Yea, the very hairs of your head are all numbered. Fear not, therefore." And then He goes on to show, by a variety of similitudes, that we ought not to be solicitous about the things of life, but that we should trust implicitly the goodness and care of our Heavenly Father. (*Luke* 12).

How complete is this instruction of our Divine Master upon the manner in which the true lover of God ought to abandon himself into the merciful hands of Divine Providence! Here he will learn, in the first place, that the foundation of his full and unbounded confidence is Jesus Christ Himself, for He says, from the very commencement of this discourse, that those to whom He addresses these words are His friends. And by friends He would not be understood to mean only those who are already perfect, but all Christians. He calls those friends whom He has treated as such, those to whom He has manifested His Gospel. If, then, a man believe in Jesus Christ, his belief is of itself a foundation for unbounded confidence in his Heavenly Father.

He will learn, in the second place, that inasmuch

as it is reasonable to abandon ourselves into the hands of Divine Providence, so it is foolish to place our confidence in ourselves, because man is extremely feeble and cannot effect the least change in the course which God has marked out for everything in the universe, because his prosperity—nay, his very existence—are absolutely in the hands of God; and because it is impossible for him to extricate himself from His power—whatever he may do and whithersoever he may fly, even though he could ascend into Heaven or descend into the depths below.

He will learn, in the third place, that although he is forbidden to be anxious about human affairs and is bound to overcome all inordinate attachment to earthly goods, he is not forbidden to ask for what is necessary from his Heavenly Father, provided he ask for it as subservient to His kingdom and His justice, and only after them. And thus the daily bread which we petition for may, with very good reason, be called supersubstantial, as being a means of obtaining spiritual blessings. "Ask, and it shall be given you," says our Divine Master in another place; "seek, and you shall find; knock, and it shall be opened to you. For every one that asketh, receiveth; and he that seeketh, findeth; and to him that knocketh, it shall be opened." (*Matt.* 7:7). These words will teach the true lover of God to ask his Heavenly Father for all things with great simplicity and confidence, to lay open to Him all the desires of his heart, provided that he do this with the sole desire of that being always accomplished which is most pleasing to God. And thus he will always derive great advantage from his prayer, for God will hear him and correct at the same time his ignorance and his error if he petition for things useless or pernicious, granting him as many real benefits as he has made useless or pernicious requests, thus bestowing upon him more than he asked. For He is a good Father who knows only how to give good things to His children and never what is harmful.

He will learn, in the fourth place, that he is not forbidden to perform those actions which are, naturally speaking, requisite for satisfying the wants of life; it is solicitude and anxiety in the performance of them which is forbidden, because they disquiet the Christian and thus rob him of all that peace of heart and tranquillity which ever attend on those who trust and rest in God. As regards the time present, he can discover the Divine will and enjoy with thanksgiving and in simplicity the goods which he possesses; but an anxious care about the future is contrary to the abandonment of ourselves to Divine Providence, because as regards the future, the Divine will is not yet made manifest and we ought to love nothing but the Divine will. He may, therefore, enjoy his present goods with moderation and innocence because they are given by God, but he must not disquiet himself about the future because the Lord has not yet disposed of them. Thus, loving God's will, he will rejoice in the privation as much as in the acquisition of earthly goods, if God should so ordain to give them. For this reason Jesus Christ says again, "Seek ye, therefore, first the kingdom of God and His justice, and all these things shall be added unto you. Be not, therefore, solicitous for tomorrow; for the morrow will be solicitous for itself. Sufficient for the day is the evil thereof." (*Matt.* 6:33, 34).

Again, since the perfection of a Christian life consists in the firm resolution of seeking in all our actions only what is most agreeable to God and most conformable to His will, the true lover of God will make no change in his state of life from a motive of his own satisfaction—though in itself lawful—but from a motive of duty, or of being more pleasing in the sight of God.

From this maxim springs the steadiness of the perfect Christian. The Christian, in whatever condition he is placed by Providence, though his rank be low, contemptible and devoid of all that men chiefly seek, remains contented and happy and indulges no thought of change, unless he knows such change to be according to the will of God. While it is the peculiar character of worldlings never to be satisfied with their state of life, the Christian, on the other hand, seeks to be satisfied with whatever post is appointed him by Providence, having no solicitude but that of fulfilling the duties attached to his state: to him all things in the world are alike, provided he be pleasing to his God, whom he finds in every condition of life to which he is called by Him.

## 81

## ON MEEKNESS

*"Blessed are the meek, for they shall possess the land."* —Matthew 5:4

JESUS CHRIST does not desire, as the great St. Augustine remarks, that we should learn of Him to perform miracles, to enlighten the blind, to heal the lame, to restore health to the sick, to raise the dead to life, but that we should "learn of Him to be meek and humble of heart" (*Matt.* 11:29), without severity, without anger, without bitterness, full of sweetness and meekness. And the reproofs He gave to His disciples, James and John, are intimations of the spirit which He came to impart to us. When, transported by an indiscreet zeal, they desired that He would call fire from Heaven to consume the Samaritans who had cast Him out of their country, our loving Redeemer said to them: "The Son of man came not to destroy souls, but to save. You know not what spirit you are of." (*Luke* 9:56). Know that, instead of crying out for vengeance against sinners, I have the tenderest compassion for them and the greatest desire to call them to repentance and salvation. Run through in mind, O loving soul, the whole life of Jesus Christ, and you will be struck with astonishment at the spectacle of His meekness and gentleness in all circumstances. As the innocent lamb is dumb before his shearer and silent under the instrument which robs him and as he allows himself to be despoiled of his wool without uttering a complaint, so did Jesus Christ yield His shoulders to the scourge, bow His head to the thorns, give His hands and His feet to those who transfixed them with nails—so did He permit Himself to be stretched on the Cross, without a sigh and without speaking one word of complaint. And who shall describe the gentleness with which He treated sinners? When He desired to convert the Samaritan woman, He first asked her to give Him to drink with the greatest sweetness and then added with benignity, "Oh, if thou knewest who it was who asks thee to give Him to drink!" And then He revealed to her that He was the Messiahs. Even the perfidious Judas He admitted to eat at His own table; He washed his feet with His own hands; He warned him of the treachery he was about to commit. He gave him the affectionate appellation of friend, while he was consummating his execrable crime. And how did Jesus behave towards St. Peter, after he had thrice denied Him? He did not remind him harshly of his sin, nor did He conceal Himself from His erring but penitent disciple. He cast on him only one look, and that was enough to pierce him to the heart and cause him to weep bitterly during the rest of his life for the offense he had committed against his Lord.

Let us then be meek and humble of heart, for it is particularly by meekness and humility that we have to resemble Our Lord Jesus Christ. The holy and illustrious Joseph, who had been sold by his brothers into Egypt, when he dismissed them to return to their paternal home with the corn they had purchased, gave them this injunction, "Be not angry in the way." (*Gen.* 45:24). This earth is only a road to a blessed country; let us not, therefore, be angry on the way. Let us never give place to wrath nor open our hearts to passion, for if once we allow it to enter, it may not be in our power to dislodge it, or even to control it. All those Saints who have attained to the highest degrees of prayer have also possessed the greatest meekness and sweetness of heart. Moses was the meekest man that dwelt upon the earth, and therefore was admitted to so great a familiarity with God as no other prophet had ever attained. (*Numb.* 12:8). The prophet David was remarkable for his meekness, and to him were granted special revelations and union with God. And the same may be said of all the Saints of the New Law, that they who had the most intimate union with God were always those whose hearts were most calm and peaceful, most free from the agitations and disturbance of passion.

Those who have any charge over others must not omit their duty of correcting those under their charge when it is necessary, but they must do it with gentleness and mildness. When they are obliged to say any truth which will be hard to bear, they should take care to correct its bitterness by the sweetness of charity; otherwise, they will convert into poison what was intended to heal and invigorate. "It is necessary to sprinkle the wine of our zeal," says St. Francis de Sales, "with the sweet balm of meekness, for the human mind is so constructed that severity sometimes hardens it, when mildness would have softened it in an instant." Oh what astonishing victories have been achieved over the most obdurate hearts by the kindness and sweetness of the Saints! St. Francis de Sales, by his benign gentleness, obtained an influence over all who came into his presence and succeeded in gaining to God the most obstinate culprits. St. Vincent de Paul, by the same means, weaned to himself the hearts of the most desperate sinners, and he says, "Affability, love and humility have a wonderful effect in gaining the hearts of men and in inducing them to adopt what is most repugnant to their nature." We ought to reprove with firmness when the fault is a serious one, and especially if it is repeated after the culprit has been informed of its sinfulness, but we must be most careful to reprove without passion or anger, for correction administered in a passionate and angry manner is more calculated to produce evil than good. When the person who is deserving of reproof is angry, it is better to defer it and wait till his passion is cooled, or you will only add fire to fire. "He who desires the salvation of souls should deal with them as God and the holy Angels behave towards us, by holy suggestions, inspirations and prayers. He should knock at the door of their hearts like the Spouse and try gently to open it, and if he succeed in gaining admittance, let him enter with joy, but let him bear to be refused with patience. It is thus that the Lord works in us: although He is the Master of all hearts, He suffers our resistance to His light and bears with our opposition to His inspirations. And even when He is obliged to withdraw from us because we are obstinate in resisting His will, He still continues to send us inspirations and invitations. Our Guardian Angels imitate exactly this conduct of our God, for they advise, direct and assist as much as possible all those whom God has committed to their care. And when they perceive that they are obstinate and perverse, they do not desert them nor permit themselves to feel angry or so grieved as to lose their own blessedness. What better examples could we desire for our imitation?"

---

## 82

## THE NECESSITY OF PRAYER

*"Ask, and it shall be given to you; seek, and you shall find; knock, and it shall be opened to you."*
—Matthew 6:7

A MAN cannot take the smallest step in the way of divine love unless he is supported by divine grace. We are able of ourselves to enter into the way of perdition and stain ourselves with vice because we are naturally inclined to this and only require to be left a prey to our passions. But which of us is capable of doing one single act or of conceiving a thought which may assist him to attain eternal life? "Without Me," said Jesus Christ, "you can do nothing." (*John* 15:5). "Not that we are sufficient to think anything of ourselves as of ourselves, but our sufficiency is from God." Now, as it is of faith that we cannot make a single step in the way of Divine love without being supported by grace, so, according to

*Absolutely Remember 7th*

His ordinary rules, God does not grant this support except to those who ask for it.

But prayer is not only necessary for the attainment of divine graces, but is a most sure and efficacious means to procure them. Christ has promised this: "Therefore I say unto you, all things whatsoever you ask when you pray, believe that you shall receive, and they shall come unto you." (*Mark* 11:26). And in St. John, "Amen I say to you: If you ask the Father anything in My name, He will give it you." (*John* 16:23). "Prayer," writes Theodoret, "is but one thing, but it has power to procure all things." "It ascends to the throne of God," says St. Augustine, "and draws down upon us a shower of Divine mercy." A man of prayer is capable of all things and may say with the Apostle, "I can do all things through the help of Him who strengthens me." (*Phil.* 4:13).

However great our misery or however fierce the assaults of our passions, if we remain firm in the exercise of prayer, we shall triumph over every obstacle and shall infallibly advance in the way of divine love. "The soul," says St. Teresa, "which perseveres in the exercise of prayer amidst all the attacks, temptations and falls by which the devil opposes her progress may be certain that, sooner or later, the Lord will deliver her from danger and lead her safely to the gate of salvation. But woe to him who is not a man of prayer. He will go on getting colder and colder in his piety, till he falls headlong into the abyss of sin." St. Teresa relates of herself that, having neglected prayer for some time, she began to fall into certain light faults, which continued to increase every day and gain power over her heart. And she adds that God afterwards revealed to her that if she had continued in that state, she would finally have lost her soul and sunk into eternal perdition. Prayer is the blessed furnace in which the fire of Divine love is kindled and preserved, and he who does not make use of it frequently becomes tepid and cold. And in this state it is not difficult for the devil to introduce himself into his heart and so lead him to sin. For this reason he leaves no means untried to detach the soul from prayer. He knows how strong a weapon prayer is to ward off his attacks, and therefore he makes use of all his arts to ravish it out of their hands.

In order for us to advance in divine love, it is most important to exercise ourselves in mental prayer, because by it our whole mind becomes irradiated with heavenly light and the fire of Divine love is kindled in our heart. "In my meditation," said David, "a fire shall flame out." (*Ps.* 38:4). Mental prayer regulates the affections of our souls and guides our actions to God; without it, our hearts are chained down to the earth and our actions, guided by worldly affections, all lead to our ruin.

The four last things—death, Judgment, Heaven and Hell—are most useful subjects for meditation. But for him who loves Jesus Christ and desires to advance in this love it is a most useful practice to meditate on His Passion and death. St. Francis de Sales says, "that Mount Calvary is the mount for lovers, and all the lovers of Jesus Christ find their delight in this mountain, whence they breathe no air but that of divine love."

In order to preserve within us at all times the spirit of prayer and to keep our souls habitually in the presence of God, a man should make frequent use of devout aspirations and interior recollections of mind, by which means, St. Francis de Sales remarks, that the work of our perfection is commenced, carried forward and completed. Aspirations are certain dartings of the spirit towards God, and the more ardent they are, the better. Interior recollections are glances of the soul at God, which, where they are most simple, are most valuable. It is hardly possible to understand the wonderful power which these kinds of prayers possess to help us in the performance of our duties, to support us under temptation, to raise us when we have fallen and to unite us closely to God. And as we can make them at all times, in all places and with the greatest facility, they ought to be as common to us as breathing. St. Catherine of Siena, being prevented from prayer by being employed in all the domestic offices of the family, formed a cell in her own heart into which she constantly retired amid her most fatiguing occupations, to contemplate God and to hold familiar discourse with Him. She thus maintained a firm and constant union with her Divine Master, and she used to say that our hearts are the true kingdom of God where He fixes His seat. Oh what great advance have those souls made in divine love who have formed for themselves such cells and frequently retired into them to adore God and converse with Him affectionately and lovingly! "Those," says St. Teresa, "who can enclose within the little paradise of the soul Him who created Heaven and earth may well believe that they are on a good road and that they shall not fail to arrive at length at the fountain of life, because they will make a great progress in a short time."

Blessed are they to whom God has communicated His Holy Spirit and bound them with the sweet bands of His love! "Blessed be God, who has not turned away my prayer nor hid His mercy from me!"

---

## 83

### PATIENCE IN TEMPTATION

*"Our adversary, the devil, as a roaring lion, goeth about seeking whom he may devour."* —1 Peter 5:8

DO we enjoy the inestimable blessing of being in the state of grace? Have we succeeded in casting out from our hearts the enemy of our souls? Then let us be prepared to encounter a fierce combat, for when the spirit of darkness is forced to leave a man free, he is angry and takes in his company seven other spirits worse than the first and assaults him with greater fury, endeavoring to regain possession of him. The wicked one takes very little care to attack those unhappy ones whom he holds in his chains, but when he meets with a soul which has escaped from his power, he tries all his artifices to regain possession of him. To these fierce attacks of the infernal enemy the world unites itself, striving, by its false maxims and wicked examples, to draw the just man into sin. Lastly, added to the attacks of the devil and of the world, we must endure the allurements of the flesh and the furious warfare which the sensual appetite wages against the spirit. All this shows that the true lover of God, whatever may be his condition of life, to whatever degree of virtue he may have attained, must hold himself always ready to fight, until the time comes that he shall be delivered from this corruptible body and shall have entered into the joy of the Lord.

But it may be asked, "Why does the Lord permit His beloved children to be molested by temptations? Why does He allow them to be placed in danger of losing His grace, of forfeiting His love, of soiling their souls with heinous crimes, of ruining themselves for all eternity? For what reason are His beloved children left exposed to the frightful attacks of their fiercest enemies?"

The first reason why the Lord allows us to be assailed by temptations is to establish in us a deep foundation of humility, upon which the edifice of the spiritual life is to be raised. What opinion should we have of ourselves if we were never tempted? Should we not think of ourselves as if we were some great ones? But when some unexpected trial arrives, some fierce temptation occurs to us, our pride is brought low. When all is peaceful, we believe that we have attained to a high degree of virtue, that we are immovable in the service of God and not very far from being fit to associate with the Seraphim, but when the tempest arrives, we enter into ourselves, acknowledge our wretchedness, detest our past presumption, raise our eyes to God and say from our heart, with the Apostle, "Lord, save us; we perish." How highly did the Apostle St. Peter value himself before he was exposed to the trial of temptation! He believed himself unconquerable. What answer did he make when Christ predicted the infidelity he was about to be guilty of? He had not the smallest doubt of himself and exclaimed with boldness: "Though all should deny Thee, yet will I remain faithful." But it was not long before he had cause to repent of his presumption, when at the speech of a simple maid-servant, he fell a victim to his own weakness, which he confessed and lamented with bitter tears all his life. "Peter, who before his temptation presumed on his own strength, discovered his weakness," says St. Augustine, "when temptation arrived."

Another reason for which the Lord permits the attacks of temptation is to detach us from the world and make us fix our desires on Heaven. Oh how easy it is for the just soul to allow her affections to rest on this wretched world and to think but little of her true country, of the joys of Heaven! And the Lord, to guard her against this danger and make her sigh after Heaven, allows her to be beset with temptations, that wearied by them, she may desire, like St. Paul, to escape from the bonds of the flesh, to live with Christ in Heaven, that she may sigh to escape from the field of battle, through fear of being conquered by the enemy, that she may long after the safe harbor, where all fear of shipwreck shall disappear.

God permits temptations to assail us to increase our merit in this life and our glory in the next.

"Blessed," says the Apostle St. James, "is the man that endureth temptation: for when he hath been proved, he shall receive the crown of life, which God has promised to them that love Him." (*James* 1:12). Ah, my God, who will be so insensible to his own interests as not to combat his temptations, when he knows that for each act of victory which we gain over them we shall receive a corresponding degree of grace here upon earth and of glory hereafter! And who will be so blind as not to envy the happy lot of the just souls who acquire as many crowns in Heaven as they gain victories over their spiritual enemies on earth! We know that even a single degree of glory is sufficient to make our soul perfectly and eternally happy. Who then, shall describe the sublime throne to which those souls will be raised, who, by fighting valiantly against temptations, gain new victories every day—nay, every hour—over their spiritual enemies?

If you would know how to prepare yourself so to fight against temptations that they may not get possession of your heart, listen to the advice that St. Jerome gave to Eustochia: "Never allow a bad thought to remain in your mind; cast out the enemy while he is still young because if he gains strength, he will overpower you. Eradicate the weeds of temptation as soon as they appear, and do not let their roots strike deep into your heart, for they will ruin it." Be prompt, then, in rejecting temptations; never let them increase through your inattention, for there is great danger lest you should consent to them. What would you do if a spark fell on your clothes? You would not examine it curiously, but would instantly throw it off on the ground. Be, then, equally quick in ridding yourself of evil thoughts; they are sparks which, if allowed to rest in your mind, will set fire to your soul.

That you may obtain the strength necessary to fight courageously against temptations, have instant recourse to God in prayer, and with a few but earnest words entreat Him to come to your help. As soon as you feel yourself attacked by temptation, raise your mind, heart and voice to God and say to Him in perfect confidence, "Aid me, O Lord; help me, that I may not offend Thee."

---

# 84

## THE SEVEN WORDS OF OUR LORD UPON THE CROSS

---

### THE FIRST WORD

*"Father, forgive them, for they know not
what they do."* —Luke 23:34

O LOVING tenderness of Jesus towards men! St. Augustine says that at the same time that the Saviour was injured by His enemies, He besought pardon for them, for He thought not so much of the injuries He received from them and the death they inflicted upon Him as upon the love which brought Him to die for them. But some may say, "Why did

Jesus pray to the Father to pardon them when He Himself could have forgiven their injuries?" St. Bernard replies that He prayed to the Father, not because He could not Himself forgive them, but that He might teach us to pray for them that persecute us. In another place, the Holy Abbot also says, "O wonderful thing! He cries, 'Forgive'; they cry, 'Crucify.'" Arnold of Carnota remarks that while Jesus was laboring to save the Jews, they were laboring to destroy themselves, but the love of the Son had more power with God than the blindness of this ungrateful people. St. Cyprian writes: "Even he who sheds the Blood of Christ is made to live by the Blood of Christ." Jesus Christ, in dying, had so great a desire to save all men that He made even those enemies who shed His Blood with torments to be partakers of that very Blood. "Look," says St. Augustine, "at thy God upon His Cross; see how He prays for them that crucify Him; and then you deny pardon to thy brother who has offended thee!"

St. Leo writes that it was through this prayer of Christ that so many thousands of Jews were converted at the preaching of St. Peter, as we read in the Acts of the Apostles; while St. Girolama says that God did not will that the prayer of Jesus Christ should continue without effect, and therefore at that very time He caused many of the Jews to embrace the Faith. But why were they not all converted? I reply that the prayer of Jesus Christ was conditional and that they who were converted were not of the number of those of whom it was said that they had resisted the Holy Ghost.

Further, in this prayer Jesus Christ included *all* sinners, so that we all may say to God: "O eternal Father, hear the prayer of Thy beloved Son, who prayed to Thee to pardon us. We deserve not this pardon, but Jesus Christ has merited it, who by His death has more than abundantly satisfied for our sins. No, my God, I would not be obstinate like the Jews; I repent, O my Father, with all my heart, for having offended Thee, and through the merits of Jesus Christ I ask for pardon. And Thou, O my Jesus, Thou dost know that I am poor and sick, and lost through my sins, but Thou hast come from Heaven on purpose to heal the sick, and to save the lost, when they repent of having offended Thee. Of Thee St. Matthew writes, 'The Son of man is come to save that which was lost.' (*Matt.* 18:11)."

---

# 85

## THE SECOND WORD

*"Amen, I say to thee, this day thou shalt be with Me in Paradise."* —Luke 23:43

ST. LUKE writes that of the two thieves who were crucified with Jesus Christ, one continued obstinate, the other was converted, and seeing his miserable companion blaspheming Jesus Christ and saying, "If Thou art the Christ, save Thyself and us," he turned and reproved him, saying that they were deservedly punished, but that Jesus was innocent. Then he turned to Jesus Himself and said, "Lord, remember me when thou comest into Thy kingdom," by which words he recognized Jesus Christ as his true Lord and the King of Heaven. Jesus then promised him Paradise on that very day: "Amen, I say to thee, this day thou shalt be with Me in Paradise." A learned author writes that, in conformity with this promise, the Lord, on that very day, immediately after His death, showed Himself openly and rendered the repentant thief blessed, though He did not confer on him all the delight of Heaven before He Himself entered there.

Arnold, in his treatise on the seven words, remarks upon all the virtues which the Good Thief exercised at the time of his death: "He believed, he repented, he confessed, he preached, he loved, he trusted, he prayed." He exercised faith when he said, "When Thou comest into Thy kingdom," believing that Jesus Christ after His death would enter into His glorious kingdom. He believed, says St. Gregory, that He whom he saw dying was about to reign. He exercised penitence, together with the confession of his sins, saying, "We indeed justly, for we receive the due reward of our deeds." St. Augustine observes that before his confession he had not the boldness to hope for pardon; he did not dare to say, "Remember me," until, by the confession of his guilt, he had thrown off the burden of his sins. On this St. Athanasius exclaims, "O blessed thief, thou hast stolen a kingdom by that confession!" This holy penitent also exercised other noble virtues; he preached, declaring the innocence of Jesus Christ, "This man hath done no evil." He exercised love toward God, receiving death with resignation, as the punishment due to his sins, saying, "We receive the due reward of our deeds."

In this circumstance let us also remark upon the goodness of God, who always gives us more than we ask for, as St. Ambrose says, "The Lord always grants more than we ask; the thief prayed that Jesus would remember him, and Jesus said, 'Today thou shalt be with Me in Paradise.'" And thus it was that the cross of the wicked thief, being endured with impatience, became to him a precipice leading to Hell, while the cross endured with patience by the good thief became to him a ladder to Paradise. Happy wert thou, O Holy Thief, who didst unite thy death with the death of thy Saviour. O my Jesus, from henceforth I sacrifice to Thee my life, and I seek for grace to enable me at the hour of my death to unite the sacrifice of my life with that which Thou didst offer to God upon the Cross, and through which I hope to die in Thy grace and, loving Thee with pure love stripped of every earthly affection, to attain to love Thee with all my powers throughout all eternity.

————————

## 86

## THE THIRD WORD

*"Woman, behold thy son. After that, He saith to the disciple, Behold thy mother."—John* 19:27

WE read in St. Mark, that on the Calvary there were present many women who watched Jesus on the Cross, but from afar off, among whom was Mary Magdalen. We believe also that among these holy women was the Divine Mother; while St. John says that the Blessed Virgin stood not afar off, but close to the Cross, together with Mary of Cleophas and Mary Magdalen. Euthimius attempts to reconcile this discrepancy and says that the Holy Virgin, seeing her Son drawing nearer to death, came from among the rest of the women close up to the Cross, overcoming her fear of the soldiers who surrounded it and enduring with patience all the insults and repulses which she had to suffer from these soldiers who watched the condemned, in order that she might draw near to her beloved Son. Thus also a learned author who wrote the life of Jesus Christ, says, "There were His friends, who watched Him from afar, but the Holy Virgin, the Magdalen and another Mary stood close to the Cross with John; wherefore, Jesus, seeing His mother and John, spoke to them the words above mentioned."

Mary and John, then, stood nearer to the Cross than the other women, so that they could more easily hear the words and mark the looks of Jesus Christ in so great a tumult. St. John writes, "When Jesus then saw His Mother and the disciple standing, whom He loved, He saith to His Mother: Woman, behold thy son." But if Mary and John were accompanied by other women, why is it said that Jesus beheld His Mother and the disciple, as if the other women had not been perceived by Him? St. John Chrysostom writes that love always makes us look more closely at the object of our love. And St. Ambrose in a similar way writes that it is natural that we should see those we love before any others.

Jesus said to her, "Woman, behold thy son" with His eyes pointing out St. John, who stood by His side. But why did He call her *woman* and not *mother?* He called her "woman," we may say, because, drawing then near to death, He spoke as if departing from her, as if He had said, "Woman, in a little while I shall be dead, and thou wilt have no Son upon earth; I leave thee, therefore, John, who will serve and love thee as a son." And from the moment of the Lord's death, as it is written, St. John received Mary into his own house and assisted and obeyed her throughout her life, as if she had been his own mother. Jesus Christ willed that this beloved disciple should be an eye-witness of His death, in order that he might more confidently bear witness to it in his gospel and might say, "He that saw it has borne witness," and in his Epistle, "What we have seen with our eyes, that we both testify and make known to you." And on this account, the Lord, at the time when the other Apostles abandoned Him, gave to St. John strength to be present until His death in the midst of so many enemies.

But let us return to the Holy Virgin and examine more deeply the reason why Jesus called Mary "woman" and not "mother." By this expression He desired to show that she was the great woman foretold in the Book of Genesis, who would crush the serpent's head: "I will put enmities between thee and the woman, and thy seed and her seed: she shall crush thy head, and thou shalt lie in wait for her heel." (*Gen.* 3:15). It is doubted by none that this woman was the Blessed Virgin Mary, who by means of her Son, would crush the head of Satan—or rather, that her Son, by means of her who would bear Him, would do this. Naturally was Mary the enemy of the serpent, because Lucifer was haughty, ungrateful and disobedient; whereas, she was humble, grateful and obedient. It is said, "She shall crush thy head," because Mary, by means of her Son, beat down the pride of Lucifer, who lay in wait for the heel of Jesus Christ, which means His holy humanity, which was the part of Him which was nearest to the earth, while the Saviour by His death had the glory of conquering him and of depriving him of that empire which, through sin, he had obtained over the human race.

God said to the serpent, "I will put enmities between thy seed and the woman." (*Gen.* 3:15). This shows that after the Fall of man through sin, notwithstanding all that would be done by the redemption of Jesus Christ, there would be two families and two posterities in the world—the seed of Satan, signifying the family of sinners, his children corrupted by him, and the seed of Mary, signifying the Holy Family, which includes all the just, with their head, Jesus Christ. Hence Mary was destined to be the mother both of the Head and of the members, namely, the Faithful. The Apostle writes: "Ye are all one in Christ Jesus; and if ye are Christ's, then ye are the seed of Abraham." Thus, Jesus Christ and the Faithful are one single body, because the Head cannot be divided from the members, and these members are all spiritual children of Mary, as they have the same spirit of her Son according to nature, who was Jesus Christ. Therefore, St. John was not called John, but the disciple beloved by the Lord, that we might understand that Mary is the Mother of every good Christian who is beloved by Jesus Christ and in whom Jesus Christ lives by His Spirit. This was expressed by Origen when he said, "Jesus said to Mary, 'Behold, thy son,' as if He had said, 'This is Jesus, whom thou hast borne, for he who is perfected lives no more himself, but Christ lives in him.'"

---

# 87

## THE FOURTH WORD

*"Eli, Eli, lamma sabacthani? that is, My God, My God, why hast Thou forsaken Me?"*—Matthew 27:46

ST. MATTHEW writes that Jesus uttered these words with a loud voice. Why did He thus utter them? Euthimius says that He thus cried out in order to show us His Divine power, inasmuch as, though He was on the point of expiring, He was able thus to cry aloud, a thing which is impossible to dying men, through their extreme exhaustion. Also, He thus cried out in order to show us the anguish in which He died. It might perhaps have been said that, as Jesus was both God and man, by the power of His divinity He had diminished the pains of His torments. In order to prevent this idea, He thought fit in these words to declare that His death was more bitter than that which any man had endured and that whereas the martyrs in their torments were comforted with Divine sweetness, He, the King of martyrs, chose to die deprived of every consolation, satisfying the utmost rigor of the Divine justice for all the sins of men. And therefore Silveira remarks that Jesus called His Father God and not Father, because He was then regarding Him as a judge, and not as a son regards his father.

St. Leo writes that this cry of the Lord was not a lamentation, but a doctrine, because He thus desired to teach us how great is the wickedness of sin, which as it were, compelled God to abandon His beloved Son without a comfort, because He had taken upon Him to make satisfaction for our sins. At the same time, Jesus was not abandoned by the Divinity, nor deprived of the glory which had been communicated to His blessed Soul from the first moment of His creation, but He was deprived of all that sensible relief by which God is wont to comfort His faithful servants in their sufferings, and He was left in darkness, fear and bitterness—pangs which were deserved by us. This deprivation of the sensible consciousness of the Divine Presence was also endured by Jesus in the Garden of Gethsemane, but that which He suffered on the Cross was greater and more bitter.

Further, this abandonment of Jesus Christ was the most dreadful suffering in all His Passion, for we know that after suffering so many bitter pangs without complaining, He lamented over this particular one; He cried with a loud voice and with many tears and prayers, as St. Paul tells us. Yet all these prayers and tears were poured forth in order to teach us how much He suffered to obtain the Divine mercy for us and to enable us at the same time to comprehend how dreadful a punishment it would be for a guilty soul to be driven from God and to be deprived forever of His love. St. Augustine also says that Jesus Christ was agitated at the sight of His death, but that He was so for the comfort of His servants in order that, if ever they should find themselves disturbed at their own death, they should not suppose themselves reprobates or abandon themselves to despair, because even He was disturbed at the sight of death.

Therefore, let us give thanks to the goodness of our Saviour for having been willing to take upon Himself the pains which were due to us and thus to deliver us from eternal death, and let us try from henceforth to be grateful to this our Deliverer, banishing from our hearts every affection which is not for Him. And when we find ourselves desolate in spirit and deprived of the sense of the Divine Presence, let us unite our desolation with that which Jesus Christ suffered in His death on the Cross.

# 88

## THE FIFTH WORD

*"I thirst."*—John 19:28

S T. JOHN writes, "Jesus then, knowing that all things were accomplished, that the Scripture might be fulfilled, said, I thirst." "Scripture" here refers to the words of David: "They gave me gall to eat, and in my thirst they gave me vinegar to drink." Severe was this bodily thirst which Jesus Christ endured on the Cross through His loss of blood, first in the Garden and afterwards in the hall of judgment at His scourging and crowning with thorns, and lastly, upon the Cross, where four streams of blood gushed forth from the wounds of His pierced hands and feet as from four fountains. But far more intense was His spiritual thirst, that is, His ardent desire to save all mankind and to suffer still more for us, as Blosius says, in order to show us His love.

"He thirsted after us," says St. Lawrence Justinian, "and desired to give Himself to us." "He thirsted after our thirst," says St. Gregory Nazianzen. In this His desire He subjected Himself with joy to hunger, to watching, to fatigue, to the burden and heat of the day. There was not a moment of His life which He did not devote to the welfare of man. "You know," says the Apostle, "the grace of our Lord Jesus Christ, that being rich, He became poor for your sakes, that through His poverty you might be rich." (*2 Cor.* 8:9).

Jesus once sat near a well, wearied from a long

journey, and said to the Samaritan woman who came
there to draw water, "Give me to drink," which is
as much as to say, *I thirst*. That His thirst on this
occasion was not the result of ordinary necessity, but
was of an infinitely higher kind, we may easily learn,
as His request served Him for an occasion to excite
the thirst of this woman for justice and truth. For
He said to her: "If thou didst know the gift of God,
and who He is who saith to thee 'give me to drink,'
thou wouldst, perhaps, ask Him to give thee living
water." But Our Lord did not everywhere find docile
hearts which received with joy His heavenly gifts, as
did this happy woman of Sichar, who immediately
became the apostle of her fellow citizens. Rather,
almost everywhere His untiring labors were met by
pride and wickedness. Nor was this role of teaching
and of working sufficient for Him; a higher one was
marked out for Him. He knew that for the perfect
fulfillment of His obedience, a painful sacrifice was
laid upon Him, a painful death, from which the
omnipotence of God would not deliver Him; He
knew that, as the source of a new life, He must sink
deeper and deeper into the misery of the human
race and that the work of redemption must be
effected by His sacrifice. And did He ever manifest
a dread of this bitter hour? The more ardent was
His desire for the redemption of the world, the
greater was His desire for this sacrifice, a desire
which He on every occasion displayed. And when
at length this hour with all its frightful sufferings had
come, when not only the pangs of corporeal death
pierced Him through and through, but when His

Soul also was seized with a feeling of abandonment, He well knew that He had emptied the bitter chalice, even to the dregs, that He had reached the extreme of suffering and that consequently all was consummated. Then He exclaimed, "I thirst." If we take this word as the expression of extreme *corporeal* want, the pain of thirst must be considered as the last and the greatest which He had to endure, for after long hours of bleeding, in a burning fever, covered with wounds, He languished, so that the prophetic words were fulfilled in Him: "My strength is dried up like to an earthen potsherd, and my tongue hath cleaved to my jaws." If we take this same word as the expression of the sufferings of His Soul, it manifests to us the desire of the human nature of Our Lord to be united with God, to experience that holy feeling which was taken from Him at the moment when He was forsaken. "As the hart thirsteth after the fountains of water, so doth my soul thirst after Thee, O God; when shall I come and appear before Thy face?" The wounded and bleeding hart hastens to the refreshing coolness of the spring; the soul of Jesus, in its struggle with death, sighed after the eternal fountain of light.

But as far as His entire life and sufferings upon earth were proper to His human nature and consecrated solely to our redemption, His parching thirst in this moment of the consummation of His sacrifice had a third signification—namely, that this His sacrifice might bring salvation to all. Well known is the noble conduct of Rudolph of Hapsburg, who, as he was leading his army under the oppressive heat of summer and the reapers from a field had presented him with a vessel of fresh water, refused the proffered gift and said, "Not I, but my companions thirst!" Thus Our Lord, who as the Apostle says, did not seek Himself, thirsted not for Himself, but for us. The eternal fountain seemed for a moment to have ceased to flow, that it might afterwards burst forth with renewed abundance to refresh the whole earth. "On that day," says the prophet (on the day when our redemption shall be consummated), "there shall be a fountain open to the house of David for the washing of the sinner." (*Zach.*13:1). "I will pour out waters upon the thirsty ground, and streams upon the dry land; I will pour out My spirit upon thy descendants, and My blessing upon thy stock." (*Is.* 13). Such is the promise of God to His Church, and it contains its own explanation, for by the figure of a fountain of living waters was signified grace, the imparting of Divine strength and grace by the Holy Ghost to all who should be redeemed. And as by the sending of the Holy Ghost, the Church was completed; and when that cry of the Apostles, "All you who thirst come to the waters, and you that have no money, make haste and buy without money and without price," sounded amongst the Gentiles, they hastened from all sides to draw from the fountain of the Redeemer. And who were those who followed this voice and came? Not those who were plunged in vice and in the idolatry of nature, immersed in the sleep of a sensual life; not the ambitious, whose actions and desires were only for this outward world; not those who, weakened by satiety, weary of life, had placed their miserable greatness in doubting everything and who had ceased in their search for truth; not those who were too deeply sunk in idolatry to feel the necessity of spiritual things. But those heard and came who knew the void of their own hearts, who did not conceal their inquietude, who saw themselves abandoned by the world, by their friends and by their imaginary deities and who had always aspired after something higher, that might satisfy their longing after truth and that might insure their peace.

As it happened in the first ages of the Church and in all places where the Gospel was preached, so it happens through all time. Many not only recognize the benefits of Christianity, but willingly follow the voice, run to the fountains of their Redeemer and rejoice in His doctrine and in His many graces. To the others, the complaint of Our Lord must apply, "My people have done two evils: they have forsaken Me, the fountain of living waters and have digged to themselves cisterns, broken cisterns that hold no water." (*Jer.* 2:13). He who rejects the means of holiness—which the Church alone offers to him—and forsakes the only path of life which Christ has marked out, if he wish to satisfy his thirst after truth and happiness, to alleviate the miseries of this earthly life and to draw something from the barren waste around him, must dig many cisterns; he must form to himself his religion, his ideas of God, of this world and of futurity, and must so regulate his earthly relations that he may by them attain to the highest degree of happiness, peace and repose. But these cisterns are not only not fountains of inexhaustible abundance, they are but artificial reservoirs, and they have, moreover, so soft a foundation that the water within them must become foul and finally sink into the earth. Man can no more redeem himself through his own inventions and devices than he can find true life, which comes from God alone. "We have all sinned," says the Apostle, "and need the glory of God," that is, His mercy, which commences its work on earth through Jesus Christ, and which shall be fully glorified in the renewed lives of the Saints, of whom the Prophet says, "They shall not hunger nor thirst, neither shall the heat of the sun strike them; for He that is merciful to them shall be their Shepherd, and at the fountains of water He shall give them drink." (*Is.* 49:10).

---

# 89

## THE SIXTH WORD

*"It is consummated."*—John 19:3

ST. JOHN writes, "Jesus, therefore, when He had taken the vinegar, said, It is consummated." At this moment Jesus, before breathing out His Soul, placed before His eyes all the sacrifices of the Old Law (which were all figures of the Sacrifice upon the Cross), all the prayers of the Patriarchs and all the prophecies which had been uttered respecting His life and His death, all the injuries and insults which it was predicted that He would suffer, and seeing that all was accomplished, He said, "It is consummated."

St. Paul encourages us to run generously and encounter with patience the struggle with our enemies, which awaits us in this life, in order to obtain salvation: "Let us run with patience to the fight purposed to us, looking to Jesus, the Author and Finisher of faith, who for the joy set before Him, endured the Cross." The Apostle thus exhorts us to resist temptations with patience unto the end, after the example of Jesus Christ, who would not come down from the Cross while life remained. On this point St. Augustine says: "What did He teach thee, who, when He hung upon the Cross, would not come down, but that thou shouldst be strong in thy God? Jesus thought fit to complete His sacrifice, even to death, in order to convince us that the reward of glory is not given by God except to those who persevere to the end, as He teaches us in St. Matthew, 'He that shall persevere unto the end, shall be saved.' Therefore, when, through inward passions or the temptations of the devil, or the persecutions of men, we feel ourselves disturbed and excited to lose our patience and to abandon ourselves to displeasing God, let us cast our eyes upon Jesus crucified, who poured forth all His Blood for our salvation, and let us reflect that we have not yet poured forth one drop of blood for love of Him: 'Ye have not yet resisted unto blood, striving against sin.'" (*Heb.* 12:4).

When, therefore, we are called to yield up any point of human esteem, to abstain from any resentful feeling, to deprive ourselves of any satisfaction, or of anything we are curious to see, or to do anything which is unpleasant to our tastes, let us be ashamed to deny this gift to Jesus Christ. He has treated us without holding anything back; He has given His own life and all His Blood. Let us, then, be ashamed to treat Him with any reserve. Let us oppose to our enemies all the resistance we are bound to make, and hope for victory from the merits of Jesus Christ alone, by means of which alone the Saints, and especially the holy martyrs, have overcome torments and death: "In all things we overcome, through Him who loved us." (*Rom.* 8:37). Therefore, when the devil paints to our thoughts any obstacles which, through our weakness, seem extremely difficult to overcome, let us turn our eyes to Jesus crucified, and wholly trusting in His help and merits, let us say with the Apostle, "I can do all things in Him that strengtheneth me." By myself I can do nothing, but by the help of Jesus I can do everything.

———————

## 90

## THE SEVENTH WORD

*"Jesus, crying with a loud voice, said, Father, into Thy hands I commend My spirit."*—Luke 23:46

EUTYCHIUS writes that Jesus uttered these words with a loud voice, to make all men understand that He was the true Son of God, calling God His Father. But St. John Chrysostom writes that He cried with a loud voice to teach us that He did not die of necessity, but of His own free will, uttering so strong a voice at the very moment when He was about to end His life. This was in conformity with what Jesus had said during His life, that He voluntarily sacrificed His life for His sheep and not through the will and malice of His enemies: "I lay down My life for My sheep. . . . No man taketh it from Me, but I lay it down of Myself." (*John* 10:15,18).

St. Athanasius adds that Jesus Christ, in thus recommending Himself to the Father, recommended at the same time all the Faithful who through Him would obtain salvation, since the head with the members form one single body. On this the Saint remarks that Jesus then intended to repeat the prayer He had before offered, "O holy Father, keep them in Thy name, that they may be one, as We also are." And then He added, "Father, I will that those whom Thou hast given Me should be where I am, and that they should be with Me." (*John* 17:24).

This made St. Paul say, "I know whom I have believed, and I am certain that He is able to keep that which I have committed unto Him until that day." (*2 Tim.* 1:12). Thus the Apostle wrote while he was in prison, suffering for Jesus Christ, into whose hands he committed the deposit of his sufferings and of all his hopes, knowing how grateful and faithful He is to those who suffer for His love. David placed all his hope in the future Redeemer when he said, "Into Thy hands, O Lord, I commend my spirit; Thou hast redeemed me, O Lord the God of truth." (*Ps.* 30:5). And how much more ought not we to trust in Jesus Christ, who has now completed our redemption? Let us then say with great courage, "Thou hast redeemed me, O Lord; into Thy hands I commend my spirit."

"Father, into Thy hands I commend my spirit." Great comfort do these words bring to the dying at the moment of death—against the temptations of Hell and against their fears on account of their sins. But O Jesus, my Redeemer, I would not wait for death to recommend my soul to Thee! I commend it to Thee now! Let me not to turn my back upon Thee again! I see that my past life has only served to dishonor Thee! Let me not continue to displease Thee during my days that yet remain. O Lamb of God, sacrificed upon the Cross, and dead for me as a victim of love and consumed by all griefs, grant by the merits of Thy death that I may love Thee with all my heart and be wholly Thine while life remains. And when I shall reach the end of my days, grant me to die glowing with love for Thee. Thou hast died through love of me; I would die for love of Thee. Thou hast given Thyself wholly to me; I give myself wholly to Thee: "Into Thy hands, O Lord, I commend my spirit! Thou hast redeemed me, O Lord God of truth!"

THE END

***If you have enjoyed this book, consider making your next selection from among the following . . .***

Miraculous Images of Our Lady. *Joan Carroll Cruz* . . . . . . . . .20.00
Brief Catechism for Adults. *Fr. Cogan* . . . . . . . . . . . . . . . . . . 9.00
Raised from the Dead. *Fr. Hebert* . . . . . . . . . . . . . . . . . . . . .16.50
Autobiography of St. Margaret Mary . . . . . . . . . . . . . . . . . . . . 4.00
Thoughts and Sayings of St. Margaret Mary . . . . . . . . . . . . . 5.00
The Voice of the Saints. *Comp. by Francis Johnston* . . . . . . . . 6.00
The 12 Steps to Holiness and Salvation. *St. Alphonsus* . . . . . . 7.50
The Rosary and the Crisis of Faith. *Cirrincione/Nelson* . . . . . . 1.25
Sin and Its Consequences. *Cardinal Manning* . . . . . . . . . . . . . 5.00
Fourfold Sovereignty of God. *Cardinal Manning* . . . . . . . . . . . 5.00
Dialogue of St. Catherine of Siena. *Transl. Thorold* . . . . . . . . 9.00
Catholic Answer to Jehovah's Witnesses. *D'Angelo* . . . . . . . . 8.00
Twelve Promises of the Sacred Heart. (100 cards) . . . . . . . . . . 5.00
Life of St. Aloysius Gonzaga. *Fr. Meschler* . . . . . . . . . . . . . .10.00
The Love of Mary. *D. Roberto* . . . . . . . . . . . . . . . . . . . . . . . . 8.00
Begone Satan. *Fr. Vogl* . . . . . . . . . . . . . . . . . . . . . . . . . . . . . 2.00
The Prophets and Our Times. *Fr. R. G. Culleton* . . . . . . . . . . .11.00
St. Therese, The Little Flower. *John Beevers* . . . . . . . . . . . . . 6.00
Mary, The Second Eve. *Cardinal Newman* . . . . . . . . . . . . . . . 2.50
Devotion to Infant Jesus of Prague. *Booklet* . . . . . . . . . . . . . . .75
The Wonder of Guadalupe. *Francis Johnston* . . . . . . . . . . . . . 7.50
Apologetics. *Msgr. Paul Glenn* . . . . . . . . . . . . . . . . . . . . . . . . 9.00
Baltimore Catechism No. 1 . . . . . . . . . . . . . . . . . . . . . . . . . . . 3.00
Baltimore Catechism No. 2 . . . . . . . . . . . . . . . . . . . . . . . . . . . 4.00
Baltimore Catechism No. 3 . . . . . . . . . . . . . . . . . . . . . . . . . . . 7.00
An Explanation of the Baltimore Catechism. *Kinkead* . . . . . . .13.00
Bible History. *Schuster* . . . . . . . . . . . . . . . . . . . . . . . . . . . . .10.00
Blessed Eucharist. *Fr. Mueller* . . . . . . . . . . . . . . . . . . . . . . . . 9.00
Catholic Catechism. *Fr. Faerber* . . . . . . . . . . . . . . . . . . . . . . . 5.00
The Devil. *Fr. Delaporte* . . . . . . . . . . . . . . . . . . . . . . . . . . . . 5.00
Dogmatic Theology for the Laity. *Fr. Premm* . . . . . . . . . . . . .18.00
Evidence of Satan in the Modern World. *Cristiani* . . . . . . . . . 8.50
Fifteen Promises of Mary. (100 cards) . . . . . . . . . . . . . . . . . . . 5.00
Life of Anne Catherine Emmerich. 2 vols. *Schmoeger* . . . . . .37.50
Life of the Blessed Virgin Mary. *Emmerich* . . . . . . . . . . . . . .15.00
Prayer to St. Michael. (100 leaflets) . . . . . . . . . . . . . . . . . . . . . 5.00
Prayerbook of Favorite Litanies. *Fr. Hebert* . . . . . . . . . . . . . .10.00
Preparation for Death. (Abridged). *St. Alphonsus* . . . . . . . . . . 7.50
Purgatory Explained. *Schouppe* . . . . . . . . . . . . . . . . . . . . . . .13.50
Purgatory Explained. (pocket, unabr.). *Schouppe* . . . . . . . . . . 7.50
Spiritual Conferences. *Tauler* . . . . . . . . . . . . . . . . . . . . . . . . .13.00
Trustful Surrender to Divine Providence. *Bl. Claude* . . . . . . . 4.50
Wife, Mother and Mystic. *Bessieres* . . . . . . . . . . . . . . . . . . . . 7.00
The Agony of Jesus. *Padre Pio* . . . . . . . . . . . . . . . . . . . . . . . . 1.50

Prices guaranteed through June 30, 1997.

Prices guaranteed through June 30, 1997.

Eucharistic Miracles. *Joan Carroll Cruz* .................15.00
The Curé D'Ars. *Abbé Francis Trochu* ...................20.00
Humility of Heart. *Fr. Cajetan da Bergamo* .............. 7.00
Love, Peace and Joy. (St. Gertrude). *Prévot* ............. 7.00
Pére Lamy. *Biver* ......................................10.00
Passion of Jesus & Its Hidden Meaning. *Groenings* ........12.50
Mother of God & Her Glorious Feasts. *Fr. O'Laverty* .......10.00
Song of Songs—A Mystical Exposition. *Fr. Arintero* ........18.00
Love and Service of God, Infinite Love. *de la Touche* ......10.00
Life & Work of Mother Louise Marg. *Fr. O'Connell* .......10.00
Martyrs of the Coliseum. *O'Reilly* .....................16.50
Rhine Flows into the Tiber. *Fr. Wiltgen* .................13.00
What Catholics Believe. *Fr. Lawrence Lovasik* ............ 4.00
Who Is Teresa Neumann? *Fr. Charles Carty* .............. 2.00
Summa of the Christian Life. 3 Vols. *Granada* .............36.00
St. Francis of Paola. *Simi and Segreti* .................. 7.00
The Rosary in Action. *John Johnson* ..................... 8.00
St. Dominic. *Sr. Mary Jean Dorcy* ...................... 8.00
Is It a Saint's Name? *Fr. William Dunne* ................. 1.50
St. Martin de Porres. *Giuliana Cavallini* .................11.00
Douay-Rheims New Testament. *Paperbound* .............13.00
St. Catherine of Siena. *Alice Curtayne* .................12.50
Blessed Virgin Mary. *Liguori* .......................... 4.50
Chats With Converts. *Fr. M. D. Forrest* ................. 9.00
The Stigmata and Modern Science. *Fr. Charles Carty* ....... 1.25
St. Gertrude the Great .................................. 1.25
Thirty Favorite Novenas ................................. .75
Brief Life of Christ. *Fr. Rumble* ....................... 2.00
Catechism of Mental Prayer. *Msgr. Simler* ............... 1.50
On Freemasonry. *Pope Leo XIII* ........................ 1.25
Thoughts of the Curé D'Ars. *St. John Vianney* ............. 1.50
Incredible Creed of Jehovah Witnesses. *Fr. Rumble* ........ 1.00
St. Pius V—His Life, Times, Miracles. *Anderson* .......... 4.00
St. Dominic's Family. *Sr. Mary Jean Dorcy* ..............24.00
St. Rose of Lima. *Sr. Alphonsus* .......................12.50
Latin Grammar. *Scanlon & Scanlon* .....................13.50
Second Latin. *Scanlon & Scanlon* .......................12.00
St. Joseph of Copertino. *Pastrovicchi* ................... 4.50
Three Ways of the Spiritual Life. *Garrigou-Lagrange* ....... 5.50
Mystical Evolution. 2 Vols. *Fr. Arintero, O.P.* .............30.00
My God, I Love Thee. (100 cards) ....................... 5.00
St. Catherine Labouré of the Mirac. Medal. *Fr. Dirvin* .......13.50
Manual of Practical Devotion to St. Joseph. *Patrignani* ......13.50
The Active Catholic. *Fr. Palau* ......................... 6.00

Prices guaranteed through June 30, 1997.

Ven. Jacinta Marto of Fatima. *Cirrincione* . . . . . . . . . . . . . . 1.50
Reign of Christ the King. *Davies* . . . . . . . . . . . . . . . . . . . . . 1.25
St. Teresa of Ávila. *William Thomas Walsh* . . . . . . . . . . . . . . .18.00
Isabella of Spain—The Last Crusader. *Wm. T. Walsh* . . . . . . .20.00
Characters of the Inquisition. *Wm. T. Walsh* . . . . . . . . . . . . . .12.50
Philip II. *William Thomas Walsh*. H.B. . . . . . . . . . . . . . . . . . . .37.50
Blood-Drenched Altars—Cath. Comment. Hist. Mexico . . . . . .18.00
Self-Abandonment to Divine Providence. *de Caussade* . . . . . . .18.00
Way of the Cross. *Liguorian* . . . . . . . . . . . . . . . . . . . . . . . . . . .75
Way of the Cross. *Franciscan* . . . . . . . . . . . . . . . . . . . . . . . . . . .75
Modern Saints—Their Lives & Faces, Bk. 1. *Ann Ball* . . . . . . .18.00
Modern Saints—Their Lives & Faces, Bk. 2. *Ann Ball* . . . . . . .20.00
Saint Michael and the Angels. *Approved Sources* . . . . . . . . . . . 7.00
Dolorous Passion of Our Lord. *Anne C. Emmerich* . . . . . . . . . .15.00
Our Lady of Fatima's Peace Plan from Heaven. *Booklet* . . . . . . .75
Divine Favors Granted to St. Joseph. *Pere Binet* . . . . . . . . . . . 5.00
St. Joseph Cafasso—Priest of the Gallows. *St. J. Bosco* . . . . . . 3.00
Catechism of the Council of Trent. *McHugh/Callan* . . . . . . . . .20.00
Padre Pio—The Stigmatist. *Fr. Charles Carty* . . . . . . . . . . . . .15.00
Why Squander Illness? *Frs. Rumble & Carty* . . . . . . . . . . . . . 2.00
Fatima—The Great Sign. *Francis Johnston* . . . . . . . . . . . . . . . 7.00
Heliotropium—Conformity of Human Will to Divine . . . . . . . .13.00
Charity for the Suffering Souls. *Fr. John Nageleisen* . . . . . . .16.50
Devotion to the Sacred Heart of Jesus. *Verheylezoon* . . . . . . .15.00
Sermons on Prayer. *St. Francis de Sales* . . . . . . . . . . . . . . . . . 4.00
Sermons on Our Lady. *St. Francis de Sales* . . . . . . . . . . . . . . .10.00
Sermons for Lent. *St. Francis de Sales* . . . . . . . . . . . . . . . . . . .12.00
Fundamentals of Catholic Dogma. *Ott* . . . . . . . . . . . . . . . . . . .20.00
Litany of the Blessed Virgin Mary. (100 cards) . . . . . . . . . . . . 5.00
Who Is Padre Pio? *Radio Replies Press* . . . . . . . . . . . . . . . . . 1.50
Child's Bible History. *Knecht* . . . . . . . . . . . . . . . . . . . . . . . . . 4.00
The Life of Christ. 4 Vols. H.B. *Anne C. Emmerich* . . . . . . . .60.00
St. Anthony—The Wonder Worker of Padua. *Stoddard* . . . . . . . 5.00
The Precious Blood. *Fr. Faber* . . . . . . . . . . . . . . . . . . . . . . . . .13.50
The Holy Shroud & Four Visions. *Fr. O'Connell* . . . . . . . . . . . 2.00
Clean Love in Courtship. *Fr. Lawrence Lovasik* . . . . . . . . . . . 2.50
The Secret of the Rosary. *St. Louis De Montfort* . . . . . . . . . . . 3.00
The History of Antichrist. *Rev. P. Huchede* . . . . . . . . . . . . . . . 3.00
Where We Got the Bible. *Fr. Henry Graham* . . . . . . . . . . . . . . 6.00
Hidden Treasure—Holy Mass. *St. Leonard* . . . . . . . . . . . . . . . 5.00
Imitation of the Sacred Heart of Jesus. *Fr. Arnoudt* . . . . . . . . .13.50
The Life & Glories of St. Joseph. *Edward Thompson* . . . . . . . .15.00

### *At your Bookdealer or direct from the Publisher.*

Prices guaranteed through June 30, 1997.

# NOTES

**NOTES**

# NOTES

**NOTES**